KU-752-763

This book is dedicated
to the memory of my parents

Eileen O'Shea
and
John Courtney

# Why adults learn

Towards a theory of participation in
adult education

**Sean Courtney**

NORTHUMBERLAND COL
LIBRARY &
LIBRARY
LRC
ARTS & TECHNOLOGY

**R**
ROUTLEDGE

London and New York

374.973          A9          175288

First published 1992 by Routledge
11 New Fetter Lane, London EC4P 4EE

Simultaneously published in the USA and Canada
by Routledge
a division of Routledge, Chapman and Hall, Inc.
29 West 35th Street, New York, NY 10001

© 1992 Sean Courtney

Typeset in Times by LaserScript Limited, Mitcham, Surrey
Printed and bound in Great Britain by
Biddles Ltd, Guildford and King's Lynn

All rights reserved. No part of this book may be reprinted or
reproduced or utilized in any form or by any electronic,
mechanical, or other means, now known or hereafter
invented, including photocopying and recording, or in any
information storage or retrieval system, without permission in
writing from the publishers.

*British Library Cataloguing in Publication Data*
Courtney, Sean
  Why adults learn: towards a theory of participation in adult education (Theory
and practice of adult education in North America)
  1. Mature students. Motivation
  I. Title  II. Series
  374.181

*Library of Congress Cataloging in Publication Data*
Courtney, Sean, 1948-
  Why adults learn: towards a theory of participation in adult education/Sean
Courtney
  p. cm. – (Routledge series on theory and practice of adult education in North
America)
  Includes bibliographical references (p. ) and index.
  1. Adult education – Social aspects – United States.
2. Community and school – United States. 3. Adult education – Psychological
aspects – United States. I. Title. II. Series: Theory and practice
of adult education in North America series.
LC5225.S64C68      1991
374'.973–dc20                                                    91-10116
                                                                      CIP

ISBN 0-415-02480-3

# Why adults learn

Against a background of profound worldwide social and economic change, the concept of lifelong learning has come increasingly into the public eye. As educators and policy-makers rethink the meaning of education, the purpose of schooling and the place of learning in our everyday lives, education institutions are opening up to those traditionally deprived of the opportunity. This book looks at the whole phenomenon of adult education by exploring the nature of the motivation that moves men and women to return to school or to seek involvement in organized learning activities. Sean Courtney challenges the psychological emphasis of most modern research on adult learning. He concentrates instead on the concept of social participation and its implications for a reinterpretation of adult learning as an aspect of a person's involvement with his or her community or society. Written for researchers and academics concerned with the general advancement of adult education knowledge and theory, it will also appeal to practitioners and all those involved with understanding and motivating adult learning.

**Sean Courtney** is Assistant Professor, specializing in the areas of adult and continuing education and human resource development, at the University of Nebraska-Lincoln.

ROUTLEDGE SERIES ON THE THEORY AND
PRACTICE OF ADULT EDUCATION IN NORTH
AMERICA
Edited by Peter Jarvis, University of Surrey

**Planning adult learning: issues, practices and directions**
Edited by W.M. Rivera

**Learning democracy**
Stephen Brookfield

**The Americanization syndrome: a quest for conformity**
Robert A. Carlson

**Towards a history of adult education in America: the search for a unifying principle**
Harold W. Stubblefield

**Training educators of adults: the theory and practice of graduate adult education**
Edited by Stephen Brookfield

**Adult education in a multicultural society**
Edited by Beverly Benner Cassara

**Early innovators in adult education**
Huey B. Long

**Self-direction in adult learning: perspectives on theory, research, and practice**
Ralph G. Brockett and Roger Hiemstra

# Contents

# Figures and tables

## Figures

## Tables

# Editor's note

The Routledge Series of books on the Theory and Practice of Adult Education in North America provides practitioners, scholars and students with a collection of studies by eminent scholars of all aspects of adult education throughout the whole continent. The series already includes books on planning, history and learning in the workplace. It is intended that others will be added to the list from all the sub-disciplines of adult education. They will cover both theoretical and practical considerations and each will constitute a major contribution to its own specific field of study. Some of these will be symposia while others will consist of single authored treatises.

This series of books has been well received throughout the adult education world and this current volume is another relevant and significant study. One of the most predominant features of adult education studies in North America has been examining participation in adult education and this book by Sean Courtney reviews the extensive literature on the subject, but also adds to that analysis in a variety of ways including the use of both psychological and sociological approaches and by moving the thinking beyond the current paradigm. This is important not only for reasons of theory but also for practice, and so the book should be of considerable interest to both practitioners and students of adult education.

Sean Courtney is currently Assistant Professor of Adult Education and Human Resource Development at the University of Nebraska–Lincoln. He has published widely in the field both in the United Kingdom and the United States of America.

Peter Jarvis
Series Editor

# Preface

For a number of reasons the subject of adults and their learning has become a modern focus of concern in the United States, as well as elsewhere in the industrialized world. For example, since the Second World War, the population of this country has been aging. In 1900, about 4 per cent were 65 and over. By 1975, this proportion had risen to 10 per cent and represented some 22 million persons. By the year 2000, if present trends continue, approximately 31 million people will be in that age category, constituting almost 12 per cent of the American population. This phenomenon, sometimes referred to as the 'graying' of the United States, has made medical care and the plight of the elderly major issues for political parties as well as agencies who deliver social services.

Less noticed, among the many dramatic statistics on this sector of the population and its general demography, is the fact that those over 50 currently enjoy better health and a higher level of educational attainment than their cohorts of any previous generation. They live longer, retire earlier and have more leisure time to enjoy. They have the background and, in many cases, the resources to return to the world of education, to take up school or college where they once left off, or simply to begin to explore the world of learning as they have never had the opportunity or leisure to do before.

Concern for older adults and their well-being is but one example of an ever-broadening concern with social change in the United States and how to deal with it. A report on the Lifelong Learning Act (sometimes referred to as the Mondale Act), which became law in 1976 but for which money was never appropriated, discusses other groups besides the aging who require special attention from law-makers and educators because of their size and special needs. These groups include women, workers and urban youth.

Women are turning up with increasing frequency in the workforce, are sharing in occupations traditionally reserved for men or are being compelled to earn a pay-check to produce or supplement the family income. Continuing education has figured strongly in this movement, which, since the 1950s, has taken on the force and ideology of a revolution. The United States is also entering what is being called a 'post- industrial' phase, whose symptoms include the disappearance of heavy manufacturing, the rise of the service sector and a tremendous emphasis, in theory at least, on information and language as key elements of the new workworld. Where once, we are told, brute strength and a native cunning might have been sufficient to secure a fortune, now it is education and an ability to deal with the world of 'high' literacy which stand between men and women and their shot at the American Dream.

It often appears that the kind of educational diet fed to young people will suffice for older clients, because the need is great and the 'pupils' are willing. But what of those whose rate of drop-out and record of poor discipline is giving compulsory schooling its greatest headache since it first began to be implemented at the close of the nineteenth century? What of the failure of traditional schooling to reach urban youth, those of black, white and Hispanic origin who often come from or head up one-parent families, are the victims of gangs and drugs, and who are most likely to lead a life umbilically linked to welfare? How are they to be reached by traditional educational means? And if not, what are their chances of success?

Profound social and economic changes, many predating the Second World War, have thus combined to bring to the front of stage the concept of 'lifelong learning.' Defined in many different ways, depending on context and author, at the very least it means the opening up of educational institutions to those traditionally deprived of the opportunity. Hence, the emphasis on women and workers as learners. But much more is at issue here than the extension of traditional schooling to non-traditional populations. The failure to staunch the flow of drop-outs and 'stay-outs' has required that educators and policy-makers rethink the meaning of education, the purpose of schooling and the place of learning in our everyday lives. Hence, the concept of lifelong learning has also implied a reinterpretation of the question of needs and who is being served by traditional institutions, the relationship between teacher and student, the nature of the curriculum and even the very ways in which knowledge itself is discovered, organized and taught.

For the foreseeable future, education will be tied closely to people's perceptions of social and occupational mobility. As long as these perceptions remain, then the United States will remain a country where demand churns up the tide of supply. Adult education has become a part of that vast ebb and flow wherein people's dreams are tested and reformed. To understand then the whole phenomenon of adult learning in the United

States it appears necessary to understand the nature of the motivation that moves men and women to return to school or otherwise embrace educational endeavors, often many years after they have left the classroom far behind. Such an understanding would be incomplete, however, without a similar effort to comprehend the context within which men's and women's motives play out their ritual tatoo. For adult learning is as much a phenomenon of a society and how it defines itself and its destiny as it is a function of individual men and women and their efforts to interpret that destiny in their own terms. Adult learning rests on individual interest and initiative. It also emerges from a particular kind of society at a particular moment in its history. These essentially are the themes of the present work.

This is primarily an attempt to bring to the attention of adult educators and reseachers alike the fruits of research on a subject that many would judge to be central to the adult education enterprise in this country: voluntary participation in organized learning activities by the adult population and the reasons for it. Participation is probably the most researched subject in the literature of adult education and has had a long pedigree, as Chapter 1 attempts to demonstrate. Indeed, surveys of adult learners within a broad empirical-positivist or policy-oriented framework are still, probably, the most frequent form that research in adult education takes, as Chapter 2 reveals.

However, theoretical attempts to explain participation have been much less plentiful, until recently. Moreover, that body of literature is at best fragmented and suffers from an ahistoricism which has condemned much that was of value to oblivion, leaving in its place isolated studies bereft of the big picture. The present work is an attempt at the big picture. Building a systematic picture of adult learning in the United States and the factors responsible for it has meant also restoring a balance which may once have existed but has now almost certainly been lost. By that I mean that most modern research on adult learning and its causes is by and large psychological in tone and tendency and fails to do justice to the environment or social context in which the activity under scrutiny takes place. Hence my interest in the concept of social participation and its implications for a reinterpretation of adult learning as an aspect of the person's totality of involvement with his or her community and society.

The strengths and weaknesses of the psychological paradigm are examined in Chapters 3 and 4. In the latter also the transition is made away from learning as intrinsically psychobiological in nature and towards a view of it as a species of socially significant and normative action. In Chapter 5 the implications of this view are developed through a study of the concept of social participation, especially as that relates to two of the more significant dimensions of that concept: membership in voluntary associations and the uses of leisure. Chapter 6 extends this interpretation by examining adult education in the context of society at large and its major functions, which include the survival of its culture and the promotion of order among its citizens, an order to which education contributes by aiding in the process of socialization. Finally, in Chapter 7, major themes are restated and the issue of participation and adult learning are briefly discussed within the context of American educational history at large.

## ACKNOWLEDGMENTS

Since this book has been a long time in the making there are many whom I would like to acknowledge for their help at different stages in the process. In Northern Ireland I found a necessary source of inspiration in the writings and friendship of Tom Lovett on behalf of 'radical' adult education and in the tireless self-sacrifice of Frank D'Arcy on behalf of adult students. Phyllis Cunningham and John Niemi were important mentors at Northern Illinois University when the work in Ireland evolved into a dissertation. To Phyllis, in particular, I owe a special debt of gratitude for her openness, unflinching integrity and infectious excitement about this strange hybrid we call adult education. My interest in and commitment to adult education, especially as expressed in this book, has been deepened and expanded by the friendship and colleagueship of peers, among them: Roger Boshier, Steve Brookfield, the late Dave Castellanos, Michael Collins, Sue Davenport, David Little, Fred Schied, Bob Smith, Harold Stubblefield, Charlene Sexton and John Dirkx. A special thanks to Harold Stubblefield for agreeing to read and comment on the final manuscript. Finally, I am indebted to my wife, Audrie Berman, whose six 'letters' of advice I have tried, not always successfully, to follow: 'BB BC BD' (Be brief, be clear and be done).

Sean Courtney
Nebraska

# 1 Explaining participation in American adult education

> Research on elementary and secondary education has largely ignored the topic [of participation] and in the higher education arena it has seldom been considered of major importance. Yet participation is central to theory and practice in adult education because the great majority of adults are voluntary learners.
>
> (Darkenwald and Merriam, 1982)

Between work and sleep, labor and love, men and women carve out for themselves moments of leisure – discretionary slots – in which they engage in a variety of activities of greater or lesser meaning, more or less fulfillment. They participate in politics, join and become active in clubs, knock a ball around a field, or simply sit in the pleasant tribal gloom of the movie-house, eager for an hour or two to escape the human condition. They spend a third of their day, free enterprise notwithstanding, expending energy in the service of others. They may spend a third sleeping. Into the remaining third they cram all the rest: love-making, eating, visiting friends, watching television, pounding on a hobby in the basement, walking for health, helping elect reactionary politicians, writing letters, and so on.

Among this motley collection falls an activity which seems at times to belong more to the realm of labor than of leisure, of work than of play. Often thought of as an activity in its own right, it may also appear as a perspective on some other activity, a ghost of purpose hovering about that which is being pursued for its own ends. For the most part, however, in an age with its penchant for the visible, it is something which has been detached from the flux and thrust into a realm of its own, with a sign hung over its head and a label on its chest. It is adult education. And it reflects the behavior of millions of men and women on the American continent busy in the business of life, now laboring, now loving, and, in between bites, now learning.

In 1989, approximately 25 million Americans will have taken part in some form of organized learning activity.[1] This constitutes about 14 per cent of the total adult population of the country. In 1984, the last year for which we have up-to-date figures, the figure was 23 million. By 1990, other things being equal, the percentage will increase slightly to 15 per cent. While these numbers suggest a leveling off in the total participant population since the beginning of the 1980s, they remain impressive by any measure. Moreover, this species of voluntary, social action appears to have dramatically increased in recent years. Between 1969 and 1984, the overall adult population, meaning those aged 17 and over, increased by about 27 per cent. The proportion of those participating in adult education, however, increased by 63 per cent, more than twice the rate for the adult population as a whole. That is indeed impressive. It means that for millions of American men and women, deliberate and planned learning is a significant factor in their lives.

And this may not be the whole story. Some independent surveys have put the real number of adult learners as high as 35 per cent (Carp, Petersen and Roelfs, 1974) or even 50 per cent (Aslanian and Brickell, 1980) of the adult population, while there are some researchers, following the line of inquiry initiated by Allen Tough, who have pegged the number even higher. For example, a national survey conducted by Patrick Penland in the mid-1970s estimated that

> about 80 per cent of the American population 18 years and older perceive themselves to be continuing learners, . . . [while] over 3/4 of the U.S. population . . . had planned one or more learning projects on their own in the year before . . . the data were collected. (Penland, 1979, p. 173)

Whether attending classes in schools and community colleges, sending away for correspondence packages, or doing on-the-job training, Americans are engaging in behaviors many of which are universal in nature; others are quintessentially their own. They are attempting to learn a language with headphones and a cassette, how to repair a car armed with 'power' tools and the latest five-hundred-page manual. A man about to retire is reading all he can on the subject 'Is there life after work?' A woman returns to college to earn a degree now that her children are all grown up and moved away. From birthing to 'deathing,' in the popular and scientific literature, this unending variety of classes, encounter groups, and self-directed, self-improvement projects constitutes the phenomenon of mass, adult education, perhaps one of the most popular forms of recreation on the North American continent. What was once the domain of the few today constitutes, or so it seems, a genuine 'Learning Society.'[2]

There can be no doubting a new awareness about the nature and pervasiveness of adult education in American society. While traditionally, education has been identified with schooling and with all that takes place roughly between the ages of 5 and 20, there is now a growing sense that schooling, even where successful, is but half of the total picture and that learning itself is a much more varied, boundary-crossing, unplanned, spontaneous, problem-specific, need-driven phenomenon than was formerly thought.[3]

The purpose of this book is to construct an explanation of why this is happening. Why do adults continue to learn after they have escaped the chalky ennui of the classroom? What motivates them to return? What are their goals and how do they achieve them? Why do some seem such eager learners while others, who are similar to them in many ways, seem not to care? What, more generally, accounts for the variety of educational opportunity in the United States? Why do adults learn?

## THE PROBLEM OF PARTICIPATION

For most of us, whether administrators of programs, teachers of adults, or program planners, these questions and the possible answers they generate seem relatively straightforward and uncomplicated. Survey research has provided the following list. There is the need to acquire basic information and apply it in one's daily life, the desire to advance professionally, or the need to increase efficiency at work. People learn for cultural enjoyment, to become more useful in the community, because friends or family urge one to get involved, out of boredom and the desire for the company of like-minded people, because they like a particular subject matter or enjoy a particular hobby, and so forth. To change, to gain confidence, to meet everyday challenges – these and many more litter the stage on which the question of motivation is raised.

In our everyday lives we witness the vitality of people in the pursuit of knowledge and greater skills. We encounter many who find it natural to continue the life of learning from school into adulthood. We encounter many others who were not motivated by school, but who decide to return to the scene of earlier disappointments only because they have been persuaded that without it, without a 'sheepskin,' survival in today's advanced 'post-industrial' age will be difficult. For we have been told by politicians and religious leaders that change is the order of the day and that further education is needed to cope with, understand and indeed embrace change. We have the witness of our own eyes and ears when we read of the inexorable demise of the great dinosaurs which once made America great: the steel foundries of US Steel and Republic lying dead along the shores of South Chicago and the Monongahela River in Ohio. Only retraining can help the unemployed of these companies to go forward into the next age. Even without the competition from Japan and South Korea, the accelerated march of technology is creating new jobs, at the same time rendering whole occupational categories obsolete. So the need is there, apparently, and the opportunities also, apparently, are there: plenty of community colleges, classes run by schools and universities, programs for retraining skilled manual workers at one end of the status continuum, and programs of continuing professional education to update current skills and knowledge at the other end.

Two assumptions underlie this somewhat idealized scenario. According to the first, those responsible for organizing educational opportunities for adults will assume that wherever educational needs exist they are being fulfilled or shortly will be. According to the second, there is a fairly direct line from the 'felt' need to its fulfillment, from the person's believing he or she ought to learn more to his or her actually engaging in various types of goal-related activities. Both assumptions may be wrong, and it is the way in which they may be wrong that gives this study its rationale.

## Adult education as a response to personal and social needs

Since researchers first began to survey the phenomenon of participation in adult education (PAE) back in the late 1920s (Marsh, 1926; Lorimer, 1931), they have been uncovering basically the same findings time and time again. Despite the apparent need, in the quick-silver environment of job change and obsolescence, for new skills and new knowledge and despite the apparent willingness of American postsecondary institutions to respond to this apparent demand, there are fewer participants than nonparticipants in organized learning programs, fewer learners, apparently, than non-learners. Moreover, those who do participate are in precise ways distinct from those who do not.

Organized adult education in the United States is essentially the social domain of white, middle-class American men and women who are relatively well-educated and young. What was true over twenty years ago when Johnstone and Rivera (1965) constructed their now famous and much-quoted profile of the 'average' participant, and what was certainly true before that time, remains the case today:

The participant is just as often a woman as a man, is typically under 40, has completed high school or better, enjoys an above-average income, works full-time and in a white-collar occupation, is white, Protestant, married and has children, lives in an urbanized area (more likely the suburbs than the city), and is found in all parts of the country, but more frequently on the West coast than would be expected by chance. (Johnstone and Rivera, 1965, p. 78)

Those who have not completed high school and those who occupy manual, blue-collar occupations are far less likely to be represented among the ranks of the educationally participating. It is a phenomenon whose socio-economic structure has hardly altered since the first systematic surveys documented the relationship in the late 1920s. It is a profile that was in place before Johnstone and Rivera and, with few exceptions, runs counter to the egalitarian, compensatory and social reformist ethos which has permeated the rhetoric if not the practice of American adult education since the early decades of this century.[4] Indeed, it may well be the case that as the gap between classes in the United States is perceived to widen, adult education may be contributing to the process by widening it further:

> One out of 25 adults who did not graduate from high school seeks further education, for those who graduated . . . the proportion is three out of 25; for those with some postsecondary education, the proportion rises to 5 out of 25; and for college graduates, it peaks at 8 out of 25. (Arbeiter, 1977, p. 4; quoting Kimmel, 1976)

The *Chronicle of Higher Education* (1/11/84), reporting on a survey of community colleges by the California Postsecondary Education Commission, noted that 'The typical student in the . . . community college system is a middle-class white woman seeking to update job skills or pursue personal interests, not a low-income student from a minority group', as was supposed to be the case.

Organized adult education, especially that which is sponsored by our schools, colleges and universities, does not appear to be reaching those sectors of the population that would appear to need it most. And the inequalities to be found at the primary and secondary school levels – inequalities which are perpetuated in higher education and which favor some ethnic groups and social classes over others – appear to be repeated and possibly exaggerated by the normal forms of adult and postsecondary education.

While there is then a perception shared by both the public and those who provide and teach educational programs that opportunities for learning in adulthood are open to all, reflecting a true market economy, the reality appears to be otherwise. Adult education is not the open supermarket into which all by virtue of their purchasing power can enter and buy at will. At times it appears more to resemble a club, of moderate to high exclusivity, whose entrance is on Main Street and thus visible to all, whose doors revolve for anyone to enter, but whose rules confront everyone once inside, beckoning some to advance further while rejecting many more as unworthy.

## Motivation-to-learn and involvement with formal education

In 1979, Anderson and Darkenwald, two researchers with the College Entrance Examination Board, published a report in which they analyzed survey data gathered by the National Center for Educational Statistics (Washington, DC), and published as part of its triennial series on PAE. The purpose of the College Board study was to tackle questions which had been raised and discussed before. What factors distinguished between those who became involved with adult education and those who did not? What factors were associated with persistence in and drop-out from programs of organized instruction for adults?

Their findings, with one exception, were not unexpected. As in previous studies of this kind, 'the most powerful predictor of participation in adult education is amount of formal schooling' (Anderson and Darkenwald, 1979, p. 3), meaning that those who become involved with formal learning as adults tend to have a much higher level of education than those who do not. Similarly, and in line with previous research, they found a high correlation between age and participation: the older the individual the less likely he or she is to engage in formal learning activities.

Together, both variables accounted for the greatest amounts of statistical variance. In other words, of all the potentially relevant variables, age and formal schooling together were the most likely causes of participation and persistence in adult education. It is the exceptional finding, however, which catches our attention:

> Despite a very large and representative sample (n=79,631) and data on a very large number of seemingly important variables, only 10 per cent of the variance associated with participation and persistence could be accounted for statistically. *In other words, 90 per cent of whatever it is that leads adults to participate in and drop out from adult education has not been identified by this or by other similar studies conducted in the past.* (Anderson and Darkenwald, 1979, p. 5, emphasis added)[5]

Translated, these findings seem to confirm what many researchers had long suspected. Demographic or sociological variables, while important in the overall picture, are not the real causes of PAE. They are a 'front' for something else; they 'mediate' the significant variables. In other words, when comparing two adults who may be similar in many other ways, researchers cannot say definitively just what it is that makes one more interested in education than another and, even when both have similar orientations to learning, what makes one person more likely to participate in organized learning activities than the other.

For those researchers who have cut their teeth on this problem the Anderson and Darkenwald conclusion was as inevitable as it was disappointing. In their eyes, it pointed to the extreme limitations of the 'descriptive' approach to the problem: the conducting of surveys on relevant populations without the benefit of theories or hypotheses. This, too, was the perspective taken by Anderson and Darkenwald. They concluded by calling for a more consistently theoretical approach to the problem, arguing that descriptive research like theirs had outlived its usefulness.

This criticism was not new. Nearly thirty years ago, it was remarked that '[in] spite of the growing body of empirical studies, the research reports present only a fragmentary and unintegrated picture of participation in adult education programs' (Knox and Videbeck, 1963, p. 102). The same view was uttered some fifteen years later: 'One feature common to most of the information being collected about the characteristics of adult participation is that it is almost exclusively descriptive' (Grotelueschen and Caulley, 1977, p. 22). While these authors praised the usefulness of the 'descriptive' study or survey, others were less kind: 'The absence of testable theory has crippled adult education participation and dropout research for decades' (Boshier, 1973, p. 255). Nor, it seemed, had the problem disappeared with the passing of time, the dramatic growth of graduate programs, and a concomitant growth in more theoretically oriented research, as evidenced, for example, by the various content analyses of the journal, *Adult Education*, now *Adult Education Quarterly*.[6]

One of the most underutilized vehicles for understanding various aspects of adult learning is theory. The notable lack of theory . . . has led to some harsh words by some of its best friends. Boshier . . . goes so far as to call adult education a 'conceptual desert,' and Mezirow . . . complains that the absence of theory is a 'pervasively debilitating influence' in adult education. Unfortunately they are correct in their judgement that theory is almost nonexistent. (Cross, 1981, p. 109)

The picture then presented here is of a field of research which has been 'long' on descriptive studies, surveys, and the like, and lamentably 'short' on the stuff of which knowledge is surely made: theory and critical analysis, experiments and the testing of hypotheses. The work of Roger Boshier over the last ten years, for example, and the recent writings of Patricia Cross all seem to point to a new departure in the field: the willingness of researchers to grapple with real theoretical questions and an eagerness to raise issues vital to practice.

It appears, then, that both of these assumptions, assumptions fundamental to the field of practice, are open to doubt. First, it is not at all clear that adult education is being provided for those who appear to need it most, nor that the institutions designed to provide it are fulfilling their proper mission, assuming that this mission ought to focus more on the fulfillment of individual rather than organizational or societal needs. Second, research has been slow to establish the link between motivation and PAE, while researchers generally have shied away from the kinds of studies that would make a theoretical case for this link.

In conclusion, it appears that as a form of moral or social intervention (Courtney, 1986), organized adult education in the United States is far from fulfilling the mission spelled out by those who 'launched' it in the early decades of this century,[7] while as an applied discipline, it is not at all clear what has been accomplished with respect to a phenomenon judged by some to be one of the major forces distinguishing adult education from other forms of education: voluntary participation in organized learning.

## RESEARCHING THE PROBLEM

Contrary to common beliefs expressed in the literature, research on the problem of PAE goes back a long way. The first systematic surveys, and the earliest studies of PAE on the American subcontinent, can be traced back to the 1920s, based on a report by Jacques Ozanne to the American Association for Adult Education. According to Ozanne (1934), the first 'thorough' survey of participants in adult education and their reasons for participation was conducted by Marsh in Buffalo, in 1926.[8] Following this came Lorimer's survey of Brooklyn, in 1929. A major study by the Cleveland Conference for Educational Cooperation followed in 1931. Buffalo was again the site of a major study in 1938: McGrath's comprehensive survey of over 9,000 men and women enrolled in non-traditional programs in that Depression-ridden city. By the early 1950s, research on PAE was plentiful. Brunner's (1959) *Overview of Adult Education Research* depicts a subject matter being systematically, if not imaginatively, pursued.

This research effort benefited from an enormous outpouring of work in the burgeoning field of scientific sociology, which had come to the American universities in the late 1800s. Lorimer, for example, was himself a sociologist, hired by the Brooklyn Conference on Adult Education to determine who provided educational opportunities for the residents of an area which was, at that time, the second largest urban unit in the United States. Like the sociologists of his day – Brunner, Lynd, and many others – he undertook an intensive community survey replete with statistical samples and questionnaires. It is also worthy of note, given their popularity among academic sociologists at this time, that the first of his nine chapters contains a series of Case Studies with such titles as 'Gus Politrides – Mass Culture in a Coffee Pot' and 'A Stenographer Cultivates the Muses.'

McGrath (1938) attempted to replicate and up-date Marsh's study in Buffalo, by using a questionnaire similar to his and sampling from the same set of institutions. In the case of Kaplan (1945), the Springfield (Mass.) public school system had set up a Bureau of Adult Education to expand provision and cooperate with other groups having similar goals. Thus, it was necessary that 'information be secured concerning the kind of people or the socio-economic characteristics of those who do and those who do not take advantage of educational and cultural offerings' (p. 7). Consequently, Kaplan undertook a 5 per cent sampling of the entire metropolitan area of Springfield in such a way as to permit comparative analysis of samples from different 'ecological areas' (p. 9).[9]

Contemporary researchers who are quick to attach the label 'descriptive research' to these early examples of eager empiricism ought to understand the historical context within which academic sociology began, as it is this context which bred the first studies of PAE. For many, it must be understood, there was a strong belief, harking back to the dramatic growth in statistical analysis in the mid-1800s, that the chief task of the social scientist was to collect the data. Truly, once gathered and correctly labeled, the facts would speak for themselves. Descriptive research, which it was not called then, was not simply a substitute for theory-building but was actually thought of as a necessary part of such production. It was indeed the scientific way to behave. It is within this context that the earliest research on motivation-to-learn must be interpreted. PAE research of the 1940s and 1950s combines the urge to discover 'what is out there' with a self-conscious application of the new methodologies.

Survey research has now become a fixed part of the adult education research scene. Clearly, methodological design as a whole has improved as have the variety and power of statistical procedures which may be applied. It should be noted, however, that arguably two of the best surveys in this area were both conducted in the 1960s, ironically, just as sociology began to lose its influence: London, Wenkert and Hagstrom (1963), and Johnstone and Rivera (1965). By contrast, and despite the new emphasis on statistical sophistication, recent surveys of PAE, most notably, Carp *et al.* (1974), and Aslanian and Brickell (1980) have lacked some of the rigor and depth of these earlier works (Courtney, 1984).

By the end of the 1950s, sociology had created the basis for an analysis of PAE within certain premises. PAE was, and is, linked with individual social status and with a lifestyle where involvement in a host of social or leisure activities, including education, is both desirable and frequent. Participation in adult education is not a phenomenon *sui generis* but the extension of a much more significant concept: participation in society at large, politically, economically and socially.

The overlap of sociology with adult education, and the belief that the dominant theoretical interests of the former could be applied to the more practical concerns of the latter, is nowhere more evident than in the chapter on participation in Brunner's (1959) landmark overview of research. Brunner was himself a sociologist, well-known for his studies of religion and rural communities and was, for most of his professional life, associated with the department of sociology at Teachers College.[10] It was thus natural that Brunner should have chosen John Newberry to draft the chapter on participation, when the latter had recently completed a dissertation on the subject of social participation.

Newberry, regretting the lack of studies specific to PAE in the adult education literature, turned instead to findings from the sociological literature and considered their implications for PAE. His rationale for doing so was interesting. Enumerating the ways in which agencies and institutions had approached the problem of engaging adults with their society, he cited their emphasis on community action and citizen participation: 'In this approach, participation in the community provides first-hand experiences in the practice of democracy. Adult education then becomes inextricably linked to social participation' (Brunner *et al.*, 1959, p. 90).

He referred to Kaplan's study, and to others belonging to the growing literature on 'social participation': Mather (1941), Anderson (1943), Komarovsky (1946), Davies (1949), Deane (1950), Dotson (1951), Axelrod (1956), Beal (1956), the more well-known survey of leisure patterns by Lundberg, Komarovsky, and McInerny (1934), and many others. A significant portion of these were dissertations, though similar doctoral research by adult educators did not start appearing in signficant numbers until the 1950s, e.g. Larsen (1953), Barron (1953), Canning (1955), Knox (1958) and Kindell (1959).

There appears, therefore, to have been a short but intense period, roughly from the 1940s to the end of the 1960s, in which the interdisciplinary focus was strong. Newberry, for example, collaborated with Coolie Verner on a survey which emphasized the link between PAE and social participation. Many of the studies they cited could be found in Newberry (1959). Similarly, a watershed study by Knox and Videbeck (1963), which called for a 'general theory of participation,' used almost exactly the same pool of references. Their approach to the problem was, and probably still is, one of the best examples of the interdisciplinary perspective in social science. Miller's (1967) attempt to combine Maslow's theory with then current perspectives on social class is also a case in point. Other studies in this vein are Havighurst and Orr (1956), Booth (1961) (who later co-authored a text on social participation with Edwards) and LeVine and Dole (1963).

These studies of PAE, while not theoretical in a deductive sense, could not have made serious headway or been of direct use to adult education without the injection of ideas, themes and hunches from the emerging discipline of sociology, which began to take hold in American universities in the late 1800s (Bernard and Bernard, 1943; Courtney, 1990). Even by this time, however, there were signs that a more psychologically oriented analysis was being considered. It was clear from the findings of Lorimer (1931), McGrath (1938), Kaplan (1945) and Komarovsky (1946), for example, that among those most inclined to participate there was a significant minority who did not, while among the least inclined there was a hardy few who did. This seemed to point to the importance of personality and individual differences. It was not long before the door was being opened further to admit a theoretical concern for personality, motivation, and a whole range of other, mostly psychological, variables.

In 1961, Cyril Houle, then a professor of adult education at the University of Chicago, published *The Inquiring Mind*, a short, highly readable account of attitudes towards continuing education.[11] Houle's thrust was psychological. He criticized survey research and pinpointed its principal limitation succinctly:

> It deals with single actions of individuals, not with their whole patterns of educational effort. It describes what men do, and not what they think about what they do or why they do it. (Houle, 1961, p. 8)

The limitations of this approach could be overcome by research which began with the individual participant rather than the act of participation. 'We would then not judge men by individual acts, but would judge such acts by the men who perform them' (p. 9). From this beginning and a close questioning of twenty-two men and women in the greater Chicago area emerged the now relatively well-known typology of the adult learner: the Goal-oriented, for whom knowledge was something to be put to use; the Activity-oriented, who took part in learning activities primarily for reasons unrelated to the purpose of these activities; and the Learning-oriented, for whom all considerations were subordinated to the desire for knowledge. Thus was born the concept of 'learning orientation' (Sheffield, 1962), or to call it by the name by which it is most commonly known today, 'motivational orientation' (Boshier, 1971).

From the middle of the 1960s on, theoretical interest in PAE, now beginning to expand, was largely psychological in orientation. London, whose important study correlating PAE with social class had appeared in

NORTHUMBERLAND COLL. LIBRARY OF ARTS & TECHNOLOGY

1963, published papers in the sociological vein as late as 1970. These, however, were isolated ventures which later researchers ignored. Two seminal papers on the concept of 'motivational orientation' were published in *Adult Education* in 1971, one by Roger Boshier, the other by Paul Burgess. It was to such ideas and their attendant methodologies that researchers – and the graduates of the new university degree programs – now responded.[12]

By the late 1960s and early 1970s, what was significant in participation research could be traced to the psychological perspective. In the hands of Boshier, it became synonymous with all that was seriously 'empirical' and 'theoretical' in the field. The single-mindedness of the new departure and its claims for scientific preeminence have, with few exceptions, rarely been challenged. The findings of Anderson and Darkenwald confirmed what many had probably suspected all along: demographic factors made important contributions to our understanding of educational participation without telling the vital parts of the whole story. What was needed was an investigation of motivation along the lines already being laid down by a newly developing psychology. What was needed was a more self-consciously theoretical initiative. What was needed were small-scale, experimental studies, the kind necessary to sustain that initiative. The psychological treatment of PAE and its causes, especially the version of it propounded under the banner of 'motivational orientation' research, seemed destined to fill precisely that role.

As we shall see, especially in Chapters 3 and 4, the psychological tradition has been fruitful up to a point. It has established a theoretical discourse within which much discussion has taken place and interesting, empirical work generated. What this historical account attempts to demonstrate, however, is that there is more than one scientific tradition which can lay claim to the problem of PAE, and more than one discipline of thought with the language and analytic tools to tackle it and produce answers.

## FRAMING THE QUESTION

Before leaving this chapter, two main issues of conceptual, as well as operational, definition require clarification. One concerns the distinction, made with increasing frequency, between 'adult education' and 'adult learning.' Is there a difference between the two? And, if so, how does this impact the subject of this study? Second, is PAE best explained by a theory of motivation or a theory of action? In other words, what kind of phenonemon is PAE?

## Adult education vs adult learning

Adult education terminology is notoriously slippery and its correct application very much a hit-and-miss affair. Few can agree on what exactly is the centerpiece of our discipline. Yet, in order to make sense of a theory of PAE clearly we need to have some sense of what it is that people are participating in. At the center of this study is the concept of *organized learning activities*, a phrase which has been used interchangeably with the more traditional, more ubiquitous phrase 'adult education.' If we are to take seriously the job of unravelling the complexities lying beneath people's motives and actions, then the first major task is to define what we mean by organized learning activities. What do we understand by the term adult education?

Almost every major figure in the field has at one time or another addressed this question and offered his or her own insights. Viewed historically, the concept has, at one time or another, referred to a variety of different entities and relationships (Courtney, 1989). It is the activities of special-purpose institutions, such as proprietary schools, or multi-purpose institutions such as colleges and universities (Griffith, 1970; Schroeder, 1970). It may describe the relationship between a learner and a teacher, as in the concept of andragogy (Knowles, 1980), or a special kind of learning, as in the distinction between 'adult education' and the 'education of adults' (Grattan, 1971). But it has also been used to describe the rise of spontaneous, mass social movements (Grattan, 1971; Welton, no date), a profession or discipline (Jensen, Liveright and Hallenbeck, 1964), and has been distinguished from other forms of education in terms of its societal functions or purposes (London and Wenkert, 1974).

For the purposes of this study, the term 'adult education' is being used here in two complementary senses. First, it is intended to refer to the activities of individuals or organizations as they behave in certain ways. Second, it is intended to reflect the functions or purposes which lie behind these activities. According to the first perspective, adult education is visible. It is something we can see if we look around us. Adults learn in social settings. There are places where learning takes place and where it can be observed taking place. These are contexts for action, 'learning sites' (Welton, 1986, p. 60), organizations in which individuals interact with others, with other parts of the world, for some purpose.[13] Often the process of learning, or the subject matter, or indeed the very nature of the clientele is tied strongly to some institutional base, to some organization or agency which sponsors the program. To understand why adults learn then, it is necessary, in the first place, to analyze where learning takes place and to identify who the learners are in those settings.

According to the second perspective, how we define adult education will have a direct bearing on how we conceive the question of motivation. Suppose we define adult education to refer to all organized forms of adult learning, forms which will tend to involve groups of learners, consciously constructed curricula, and so forth. Here, the question 'Why do adults learn?' translates as an inquiry into the factors which facilitate or inhibit participation in organized learning activities. According to this definition, nonparticipants will include not only those who are unable to participate, assuming that they would be willing, but also those who do not desire to become involved in activities that smack too much of formality and institutionalization, with its overtones of schools, exams, failure and the like. Thus, the reasons why some will not participate are already implied in the way the activity has been defined.

It may be this desire to avoid the associations with formality and regimentation that accounts for much of the use of the term 'adult learning' in place of – the more old-fashioned term? – 'adult education' in current literature (Brookfield, 1986, for example). Adult learning appears to include the formally organized activities but also those more natural, private affairs which are a part of simple living or the enjoyment of life. Again, however, whether defined to include or exclude these more ubiquitous forms of learning, the fact that they are at issue suggests that the factors responsible for PAE are also bound up with the context in which learning may occcur, and with the whole notion of formality, institutionalization and organizational base. Thus, at the very core of the question of why adults learn is the manner in which adult education is defined, and to what extent formality and organizational structure play a role in that definition. (These issues will again be addressed in greater detail in Chapters 5 and 6.)

## Is learning spiritual?

At any moment of historical time, men and women are engaged in various sides of the business of life, some of which includes the activity we call 'learning.' If every individual not now engaged in learning could – in terms definable by probability theory – be so engaged at a later date then much of the practical significance of the question 'Why do adults learn?' would evaporate. Similarly, if we were to make no distinctions of substance between different categories of learning activity, in other words if the very fact of learning was sufficient for us to say, 'good, he or she is learning,' regardless of what a person was learning or how the learning process was facilitated, then again the question of PAE would contain little to engage our attention as researchers. It would simply mean that all of us are learners at some time or other, a trivial piece of knowledge if empirically true, and tautological if analytically true. For, regarding this second point, behind all our discussion concerning adults and their learning or lack of it, lies the premise that all of us – all members of the *Homo sapiens* species – are, in some fundamental, psychobiological sense, learners.

Thus, when asking why adults learn we could be asking what it is about the nature of humans that makes them learning beings. This however would be an inquiry into the nature – spiritual? materialist? – of humankind and the relationship between ontology (the nature of being as such) and epistemology (the nature and scope of knowledge). Most people in the field of adult education, be they teacher, program planner or administrator, even the researcher who thinks he or she is raising fundamental questions, are rarely concerned with this more profound, philosophical aspect of the problem.

Philosophically, we take it on fiat that people are learning beings. Why they are learning beings we usually leave to others to ponder. Since most discussions of PAE and its causes, with few exceptions, take this philosophical premise for granted it will not, though important, be discussed again here. For the purposes of this discussion, and throughout what follows, I have premised my critique on the assumption that all humans share the propensity to learn and to confront the world existentially as learning beings. In its most basic sense, men and women learn because it is in their nature to learn. Kant pointed out that space and time are given as undeniable a priori in humanity's construction of the world. Though I cannot invoke the same authority here I assume for the purpose of this analysis that humans enter all existential situations as learning beings, whether or not they choose or are able to exercise that capacity in any one or all of these situations. What differentiates between people, groups, classes, organizations, communities and societies is how that capacity to learn and benefit from learning is actually realized in the lived world. That is what I take to be the primary rationale for pursuing the question of PAE.

It would be unsatisfactory, however, to leave this area in the grip of a grandiose assumption and not indicate some of the problematique to which it gives rise. For example, those inclined to an existential mode of thought, many of whom are not Christians, would take humans' 'learning-ness' for granted: it is a feature of their Being-in-the-World (to put it in Sartrean terms). They would not puzzle beyond that. Christians, however, indeed many people who espouse a religion, would interpret their learning-ness in terms of their spiritual *raison d'être* or reason for living. For in Christian discourse, learning is not simply the result of biological accident, that is evolution. It really is a demand – God's gift to us – of man's essential humanity. Learning prefigures the possibility of indefinite progress, human progress. It also implies choice. Choice revolves around the freedom to do wrong. And in Catholic eschatology, especially, freedom is a meaningless concept without the existence of evil. Learning therefore implies the reality of evil. Thus, within some religious discourse, talking about man's essential nature as learners means talking about their spiritual essence, in so far as it touches on their power to do good or evil.

## Is learning education?

Increasingly, in the literature of adult education, the phrase 'adult learning' appears to be favored more than the hitherto all-encompassing 'adult education' (Brookfield, 1986; Jarvis, 1987).[14] In this century, the term 'learning' has been, by and large, coopted by the science of psychology, according to which it connotes a process, morally and emotionally neutral, internal to the individual, according to which a significant change occurs in knowledge or behavior, not attributable to psychopharmeutical or maturational factors. There are other definitions of learning which distinguish cognitive from affective change and which query whether learning has taken place if it is not accompanied by behavioral change (Jarvis, 1987). However, for present purposes, what concerns us here is the fact that learning is assumed to be a psychobiological phenomenon of interest specifically to psychologists, while by contrast education refers to something outside of the individual, something social or sociological, and thus not essential to the structure of psychological discourse.

For other social sciences, however, the term itself is less crucial. For example, anthropologists see the concept of learning somewhat differently, though the psychological configuration is implicit in the usages of their linguistic community. They will often lump learning and education together, because for them the real distinction is between animals, who are identifiable as such, *inter alia*, by the substantially small role learning plays in their behavioral and survival repertoire and *Homo sapiens* for whom learning is the chief means by which they are socialized and achieve integration within their group. Thus, for an anthropologist, learning, education and schooling, while not synonymous, are not necessarily radically distinct terms, though they may be aware of disputes circling around them.[15]

Within the linguistic community of adult education, on the other hand, the term 'learning' occupies a niche somewhere between psychology and anthropology. Some adult educators are certainly thinking of psychological – internal – process when they use the phrase 'adult learning'. This is also the sense in which the phrase is used in the titles of graduate courses at many universities in the United States. For others, however, and increasingly among those who address the concept of 'self-directed learning' the term really means something quite different, something external, a visible activity, a type of behavior or form of action, though it may be far from public or even social.

It appears that 'adult education' has come to be synonymous with the aspect of education pejoratively called 'schooling.' While many will go on hurriedly to say that education and schooling are not the same thing and should not be taken to mean the same thing, nevertheless it is hard to turn aside the tide. Adult education has come to connote the institutionally based program, formal attendance in classes, certification, and the authority of experts. Adult learning, by contrast, connotes adults freely going about the business of learning in the context of the business of life. Adult learning means self-directed learning, the freedom to choose, to be a good consumer of educational products, to become involved or not depending on personally interpreted need, and so forth. Learning here carries the whiff of freedom from restraint, a sense of embeddness in life's day-to-day-ness. Education by contrast suggests the stiff and formal, the artificial chunk of life suspended from the real world. Adult learning suggests something which is 'natural' or 'accidental' meaning that the learning occurs in the pursuit of some other activity not explicitly educational in nature, while adult education suggests something organized, systematic, and planned.

We may even have come full circle on this point. Over half a century ago, we were told that adults learn in natural, societal settings: reading, watching TV, and so on. But this type of learning, according to Verner and Booth (1964), is both accidental and inefficient. By contrast, there is adult learning in the formal, instructional setting in which the element of chance is minimized. This setting comes into being when an educational agent designs a sequence of tasks using specific learning procedures to help an adult achieve a mutually agreeable learning objective. This is adult education. Whatever the form, content, duration, physical planning, or sponsorship, an activity is identified as adult education when it is part of a systematic, planned, instructional program for adults.

As the world moves towards a new century and Americans grapple with a changing economic and global role, there is some agreement that old ways of looking at reality will no longer suffice, that we need new ideas, new visions, and so forth. Such thinking permeates the world of education which increasingly finds frustration in outmoded notions of what it means to educate or train an individual. Some adult educators (Marsick, 1987, 1990; Welton, 1986) have begun to speak of new paradigms, and, again, within this discourse, the term 'learning' finds more favor than the term 'education.' It puts the emphasis back on the individual man or woman and the choices they make, freely or under constraint, while shifting it away from the educator or teacher and the all-pervasiveness of the institutional sponsor.

With this in mind, we will not be concerned here with 'learning' in the purely psychological sense, the sense whose grammatical space excludes 'education.' Rather will the focus be the *activity* of 'learning' which together with 'education' suggests a range of actions, some primarily individual and out of the public eye, some decidedly social, and involving complex forms of collective life. Learning, according to this context of usage, 'occurs in a variety of modes: formal, informal, non-formal, self-directed, open, distance, etc.' (Jarvis, 1987, p. 1). However, because of the history surrounding the definition of adult education a history which has often attached the label 'non-traditional' or 'informal' to what is now being reserved exclusively for the term 'adult learning,' throughout these chapters the phrases 'adult learning' and 'adult education' are used interchangeably, except, and this is a critical point, where the distinction hinges on formalism, institutional structures, and the traditional trappings of schooling which appear to cling to 'adult education' but are missing from 'adult learning.'

## THE FOCUS AND SCOPE OF THE PRESENT STUDY

In attempting to find answers to the questions posed here, more than fifty years of research activity have been located and analyzed. The problem encountered here was how to classify this research effort so as to make it intelligible to the general reader. Earlier attempts to classify and give some order to the enormous body of work in this area, work which naturally extends beyond the confines of the field of adult education are reported in Courtney (1984), which also discusses the other major classifications in this area: Newberry (Brunner *et al.*, 1959), Douglah (1970), Burgess (1971b) and Flinck (1977).[16]

There have been three major overviews of PAE research in the United States. The first, appearing in Brunner *et al.* (1959) and discussed in the previous section, consists of a summary by John Newberry of research up to the close of the 1950s. Though now naturally dated, it is highly significant in being the only extant review of research from a sociological angle. Many of the studies cited there promote the view of PAE as a species of social participation. (This perspective will be examined in Chapter 5.) The second, by Boshier (1976), reviews major studies – mostly dissertations – undertaken to test or refine Houle's typology. (This category of research is examined in Chapters 3 and 4.) Finally, in Cross (1981), one of the most cited publications in the field,[17] we find a review of theories of PAE which approach it as a decision-making process, theories which also include Houle's typology.

All three reviews, apart from the issue of timeliness, are in one way or another incomplete. It is believed that the present study is thus the first up-to-date review of both sociological as well as psychological research activity in this important area of adult education practice.

Initially, the plan was to examine every study which in some sense measured 'participation in adult education.' Thus, and subject to availability (a critical issue as far as United States dissertations are concerned),[18] my intention was to survey all of the literature bearing directly on the subject of adult motives or motivation for PAE. This leaves many hundreds of studies whose relevance to the current analysis is marginal. As Ozanne (1934), Brunner *et al.* (1959) and Cross (1978, 1979) make clear, even if an institution or agency conducts no other kind of research, it invariably collects statistics on its clients. At any one time, 'clientele analyses' (Knox, 1965) are being conducted by hundreds of organizations and state bodies across the country. Such research is, as Miller (1967) notes, conceptually easy to conduct and, while yielding a kind of census of a local area or program, renders serious analysis difficult if not impossible due to a lack of a comparison group, adequate sampling of the relevant 'hinterland,' or an explanatory framework to put the findings into perspective. Most of the research in this category suffers from one or more of these features, and has therefore been used selectively and only where it seemed to throw light on significant aspects of the problem.

Second, Boshier (1973) makes a strong case linking participation and persistence with drop-out and nonparticipation, and has advanced a model to this effect. Anderson and Darkenwald are typical of studies which have found it natural to examine PAE and persistence side-by-side. My intention was to focus exclusively on explanations of why people come to adult education in the first place, and while a complete picture of the causes and effects of PAE must include the element of persistence, only to the extent that it is necessary for larger explanatory purposes does this study include reference to studies of drop-out and persistence.[19]

Third, with respect to geographical coverage, a decision was made at an early stage to limit the study to sources within the continental United States, excluding Hawaii and the protectorates, e.g. Puerto Rico and Guam. Exceptions were permitted however. For example, because of the coverage of Boshier's work I have included reference to some Canadian and New Zealand studies. There is also selective reference to major surveys conducted in the British Isles (including Northern Ireland), and other countries of Europe with which I am particularly familiar.

Why is a study like this important? What can it contribute to improving the practice of our field? First, and most significantly for this author, adult education as a field of practice is moving towards some kind of professional status, both as a scientific discipline, no matter how applied, and as a form of technically based, social intervention, no matter how weak the technology. There is much debate and argument on this score: will lifelong learning become lifelong schooling? Nevertheless, while the desires of those who advance a more political and less bureaucratic approach to social problems, such as illiteracy, will continue to be felt, there can be no denying the increasing tendency towards credentialing, an activity which goes hand-in-hand with an increasing compulsoriness regarding the need for continuing learning in adulthood.[20]

Within this social and political context, the demand grows for a body of knowledge that somehow distinguishes adult education from other education disciplines as well as from the other major university disciplines.[21] The demand for a knowledge base is a demand for theory and research, nothing less. This study is intended to contribute to the solidifying of that knowledge base by presenting to practitioners as well as researchers the results of a substantial body of research which goes back to the earliest days of twentieth-century American adult education.

Second, despite increasing evidence to the contrary, adult learning is a voluntary activity, an activity of choice, in which adults may or may not engage. This is not to say, of course, that learning activities do not take place within an environment which tends to shape demand for them and which exerts a pressure in their direction. After all, we live in a highly consumer-oriented society which requires that we interpret learning as a regulated, norm-governed, consumer-type behavior much like other consumer-type behaviors. This society contains half-understood pressures towards and away from continuing learning, and it becomes our duty to understand the nature of these pressures the better to harness them and make them work not merely for ourselves and our programs but for the very clients whose learning we wish to facilitate. The present study is an attempt to put before the 'reflective practitioner' the results of this investigation into a special category of social behavior: adult learning and how it is facilitated, how it is prevented, and how it may be changed.

Finally, many adults, whether or not they ever encounter the official halls of institutional adult education, have a need to comprehend the rapidly changing environment in which they live. They have a strong need to understand where they are and why they got there. Researchers have been attempting to answer these questions for many years and will continue to do so. Elsewhere (Courtney, 1986), I have tried to make a case for increased support of the research enterprise, a fragile and anxiously regarded activity at the best of times, and non-existent at times of conservative and short-sighted retrenchment. Whatever claims adult education has for being judged an applied discipline will rest ultimately on its knowledge base. The planting and flowering of that base depends on research and creative reflection. Put simply, we would like other disciplines to take our work seriously. For them to be so inclined we must confront them with something that gives them some degree of pause, some reason to think there was thorny issues worth investigating. In the final analysis that is the hope for the present study: that it will be of value to those who regard themselves as adult educators and attract the attention of those who claim other professional and theoretical allegiances.

# 2 'Who are these people and why do they come to us?'[1]

There is a widespread impression that adult education is thriving on the middle class.

(Beals and Brody, 1941)

We are interested in the origins of needs and motives as they pertain to adult learning and in the conditions or factors which lead some to engage in formal education, others to choose informal learning activities, and still others to avoid, apparently, all contact with learning environments, formal or informal. The first place we might start is with the extent and shape of the phenomenon we are calling 'participation in adult education' (PAE). How widespread is PAE in American society, and how has the demand changed over the last fifty or more years?

As early as 1924, Morse Cartwright, then an officer with the Carnegie Corporation, had estimated a population of 15 million adult learners, or 18 per cent of the total adult population over 14 years of age. This estimate appears in a volume which includes a second estimate for 1934 of 'approximately 20 million persons, one-sixth of the total population and considerably more than half of the total school population of 36 million children' (Cartwright, 1935, pp. 60–61). Cartwright's calculation included thirty different categories of activities and organizations, many not normally associated with the traditional sites of learning, among them agricultural extension, radio and television, clubs, libraries, religious programs, the activities of business, labor unions and the armed forces, forums, lyceums, recreation and settlement programs for immigrants.

Surveys by Essert (1950) and Knowles (1955) followed in the Cartwright tradition, according to which PAE went from roughly one-fifth of the population in 1924 to one-third of that population in 1955. Knowles (1955), who provided these figures, estimated that by 1975 over half of the adult population of the United States would be involved in some form of organized learning. While certainly provocative in their way, these figures can hardly be sustained since they are not based on anything approaching a systematic sampling of the population. For that we must turn to Johnstone and Rivera's *Volunteers for Learning* (1965).[2]

It is to this study, based on a survey carried out by the National Opinion Research Center in Chicago, that we owe a special debt for providing us with the first systematic and nationwide attempt to see educational activity as a distinct and significant aspect of American social life. This is also the first study to go outside the purview of institutions to find evidence of educational involvement ('the whole institutional approach to the development of a definition [of PAE] was out of keeping with the spirit of a behavioral inventory of adult learning,' p. 25). Johnstone and Rivera calculated the overall level of PAE at 22 per cent or over one-fifth of the American adult population. Seizing on the significance of these findings, they wrote:

> These numbers are roughly equivalent to the total number of paid attendances at major league baseball games during a season, represent about one-third the number of persons who voted in the 1960 Presidential election, and constitute considerably more Americans than have their teeth cleaned by a dentist over a period of a year. (Johnstone and Rivera, 1965, p. 38)

Included in these estimates were activities sponsored by churches and synagogues, as well as schools and colleges, business and industry, government, the military and the many different varieties of community organization and voluntary association, for example museums, YMCAs, etc. Also included were on-the-job training as well as more formalized training and development activities, more educationally oriented radio and television programs, and independent study or private instruction. Owing perhaps to the influence of this study, the federal government, which began its own series of PAE surveys in 1969, adopted a similar definition, one which is still used by the Center for Education Statistics (CES), formerly the National Center for Education Statistics (NCES), the body which conducts these surveys.[3]

Most recent statistical surveys of the national population by Carp, Peterson and Roelfs (1974) and Aslanian and Brickell (1980), undertaken in the spirit of the Johnstone and Rivera study, have gone beyond the earlier study in their estimates of learning activities. Carp's study put the participating population at 31 per cent, Aslanian's study estimated it at 50 per cent; however, it is not possible to judge if this represents a real increase since the 1960s due to problems of comparability between all three studies.[4] The real proportion of those who have taken some course or studied some subject over a twelve month period appears to be somewhere between 15 per cent (*Trends in Adult Education 1969–1984:* NCES, 1986) and 50 per cent (Aslanian and Brickell, 1980). Beyond that it is difficult to be more precise. If the more informal modes of adult learning are excluded – and the most recent CES survey excludes 'self-directed learning without the guidance of a teacher or sponsoring agency' (Appendix III, p. 53) – then the national rate drops, holding steady as it has done over the past twenty years in the low- to mid-teens. If they *are* included there appears to be no potential ceiling. As London, Wenkert and Hagstrom (1963) noted: 'to speak of *a* participation rate . . . is deceptive; there are many ways of measuring the extent of participation, each of them useful for different purposes' (p. 185).

Apart from problems of definition and comparability, one senses an unspoken consensus among opinion-makers that the overall rate of PAE in the United States may be closer to the spirit of a definition proposed by Moses (1971). The latter spoke of the 'Learning Force,' defined as 'the total number of people developing their capacities through systematic education, i.e. where learning is aided by teaching and there are formal, organized efforts to impart knowledge through instruction' (p. 14). This included what he called the 'Core,' all those in mainstream, full-time education and the 'Periphery,' those in similar institutional settings who may be part-time or in some more informal context and thus much less accessible to the surveyor's probe.

According to this definition, there were 44 million people in the Learning Force in 1965 (of which 25 million may have been 'official' adult learners if Johnstone and Rivera's estimates are correct), while Moses's projection for 1975 was 88 million. If this number was extrapolated conservatively to the present time, it means that approximately half of the US adult population are active learners at any one point in time.

## CONTINUATION OR COMPENSATION? THE DEMOGRAPHICS OF PARTICIPATION IN ADULT EDUCATION

### The early surveys, 1931–63

Following here is a review of major surveys of PAE populations. Particular attention will be paid to early research, for the following reasons. First, it has often been assumed that there was little or no research on the causes of PAE prior to the 1960s, when this is not the case. Second, the problem of nonparticipation and how to solve it is still much the same problem it was when researchers first began to investigate it, so that the analysis of vintage studies does not invoke out-dated pictures of the past. Third, it is in this earlier phase of research activity that we find the strongest evidence of the sociological interpenetration of PAE research. Among the most prominent of the early surveys are Lorimer (1931), McGrath (1938), Kaplan (1945), and London, Wenkert and Hagstrom (1963).

## Lorimer, 1931

In 1929, Frank Lorimer was invited by the Brooklyn Conference on Adult Education to undertake an 'intensive' survey of educational provision in Brooklyn. The result was the first systematic survey of a potential adult learning population that we have on record.[5] Of a random sample of 1,166, Lorimer estimated that between 25 per cent and 40 per cent had taken part-time courses in adult education either since leaving school or since entering full-time employment. The estimate was based on participation in three types of activities and allowed for overlap between them: regular academic courses at night (9 per cent), English-as-a-second-language classes (8 per cent), and special part-time, mostly vocational, courses (27 per cent).[6]

Lorimer questioned a contemporary view which he found common even then that those who availed themselves of opportunities for adult education had been handicapped in some way while at school and had failed to complete their formal education. On this hypothesis, it could be anticipated that PAE would be highest among those with the least amount of formal schooling. He found, on the contrary, that of those with elementary schooling only, more than 75 per cent had taken no adult education courses; for those who *had* completed high school the figure was 45 per cent; and for those who had graduated from college, some 35 per cent had not taken further courses. Correspondingly, while only 6 per cent of those with the least amount of schooling took 200 or more hours of adult education, the figure for college graduates was 25 per cent.

Similarly, he found that the more skilled the workers and/or the less manual the occupation, the greater the likelihood that they would take courses. Again, however, the effects of earlier schooling were marked. When schooling was held constant and only those with a high school education or better were compared, there was little difference in educational activity between different occupational types. Therefore, formal schooling seemed to be the determining factor differentiating between groups of high and low educational involvement. Further, he noted a tendency for those who had *not* taken adult education courses to be out of work, and for those who had to be more likely to obtain pay raises in their current employment. He therefore rejected his original hypothesis, concluding that adult education was not a 'compensatory device' for those who had failed to avail of earlier schooling for later economic and social advance, but more the response of those who were already in the upwardly moving mainstream to current professional and occupational demands. Lorimer was also one of the first to uncover the interconnectedness of different species of participation:

> The idea that adult students are commonly unsociable fellows who compensate for the lack of society by devotion to education . . . appears to be fallacious if membership in clubs is used as the criterion of sociability. (p. 50)

In other words, those likely to be involved in adult education were also more likely to be involved with other forms of community activity (see Table 1). For example, he found that 48 per cent of those claiming no membership in clubs or associations compared with 57 per cent of those who did claim such membership had ever taken a course in adult education. In Table 1 we also see the relationship between level of formal schooling, involvement with educational programs and other types of leisure activity: reading magazines and 'quality' newspapers, attending the theater, and so forth. To Lorimer therefore must be given the credit for initiating a generalization about educational populations which has yet to receive adequate recognition among those charged with planning and marketing adult programs today: the idea that PAE is not a choice among other competing social activities but may overlap with them suggesting the existence of a general social participation syndrome.

Lorimer was suggesting, in other words, that when we find evidence of adults involving themselves in organized forms of learning we should also expect to find them engaged in other forms of organized social, lesiure-oriented, or even political activities. It might even be said that we should expect these adult learners to share with each other a general concern for participation as an obligation or aspect of their membership in their community. Some of the more significant dimensions of this 'general participation syndrome' will be examined more closely below.

## McGrath, 1938

McGrath's (1938) study was undertaken as part of the Regents' Inquiry into the *Character and Cost of Public Education in the State of New York*. Buffalo was chosen because a 'comprehensive' survey of adult education had been conducted there ten years before by Marsh (1926). Of the connection between former schooling and later PAE, McGrath was more detailed and analytical than Lorimer: 'One determinant of the student's ability to profit by further education is the amount of schooling which he has already completed' (McGrath, 1938, p. 11). Almost a half of his sample had completed secondary school; nearly one-fifth had gone to college. This

Table 1 Leisure-time activities, adult courses (vocational, cultural), and level of previous schooling

| | Elementary only | | | High School grads | | | College grads | |
| | None (1,152) % | Course type | | None (477) % | Course type | | None (117) % | Course type |
| | | Vocat'nal (258) % | Cult'al (42) % | | Vocat'nal (325) % | Cult'al (258) % | | Cult'al (67) % |
|---|---|---|---|---|---|---|---|---|
| **Use of Libraries** | | | | | | | | |
| None | 72 | 35 | 38 | 15 | 11 | 10 | 13 | 4 |
| Occasionally | 21 | 39 | 33 | 32 | 37 | 33 | 33 | 20 |
| Frequently | 7 | 26 | 29 | 53 | 52 | 57 | 54 | 76 |
| **Reading Mags** | | | | | | | | |
| None | 56 | 35 | 24 | 26 | 19 | 20 | 15 | 19 |
| Light | 37 | 35 | 43 | 21 | 26 | 23 | 17 | 6 |
| Serious | 7 | 30 | 33 | 53 | 55 | 57 | 68 | 75 |
| **Newspapers** | | | | | | | | |
| Tabloids | 15 | 6 | 2 | 1 | 1 | 1 | – | – |
| Serious (1)* | 19 | 26 | 31 | 10 | 11 | 6 | 2 | 1 |
| Serious (2)* | 18 | 43 | 55 | 69 | 74 | 73 | 81 | 79 |
| **Theater attendance** | | | | | | | | |
| Movies only | 21 | 19 | 17 | 12 | 14 | 8 | 8 | 6 |
| Vaudeville | 37 | 31 | 12 | 18 | 24 | 13 | 10 | 4 |
| Drama | 25 | 25 | 59 | 55 | 37 | 67 | 64 | 69 |
| Concerts | 22 | 24 | 50 | 44 | 41 | 56 | 59 | 58 |
| **Artistic activities** | | | | | | | | |
| Dramatics | 4 | 6 | 12 | 11 | 10 | 11 | 5 | 9 |
| Music | 16 | 20 | 38 | 35 | 33 | 41 | 21 | 24 |
| Art | 3 | 4 | 21 | 14 | 10 | 27 | 21 | 33 |

Source: Lorimer, 1931, p. 58.
* (1) N.Y. American, Evening Journal.   * (2) Herald, Post, Sun, Telegram, Times, World.

was in 1936, at the height of the Depression. Comparing the educational level of his sample with that of Marsh, McGrath concluded, despite misgivings about the representativeness of the former's sample, that there had occurred 'a pronounced improvement over the ten-year period in the educational equipment of adult students' (p. 12). While the high rate of participation among the least educated in 1926 could be explained by historical factors (this, after all, was only two years after the last great wave of immigration had been halted by the American Congress), how was the high rate of participation among the better educated in 1936 to be explained? McGrath answered as follows:

> During the past decade the Depression has sharpened the competition for desirable positions and classes for adults have been suggested to the student as a means of enhancing his occupational opportunities. Even high school and college graduates have found it necessary to supplement their systematic education through adult courses. (p. 12)

McGrath's conclusions tended to confirm Lorimer's 'compensation' hypothesis. Though distorted by the effects of the Depression, the overall level of education in the country had increased dramatically in the decade from the mid-1920s to mid-1930s. At the same time, the proportion of those with more education participating in programs of adult education also increased, suggesting that adults availed themselves of education not because they needed to make up for previous lack of education, but because obtaining more had made them aware of the link between a better education and a better job. What the experience of the Depression might suggest to the student of PAE is that when faced with enormous competition for a vastly reduced stock of jobs, educational credentialing substitutes for job experience. (Chapter 6 develops this point at greater length.)

## Kaplan, 1945

McGrath's study, while suggesting the relationship between prior levels of schooling and later PAE, did not make the case strongly. This was left to Kaplan (1945) and his survey of the population of Springfield (Mass.), which sampled equally from all major neighborhood areas within the city, a type of coverage that is as rare as it is exhaustive. Participation was measured by a range of activities available to the public at large: use of the public library, and attendance at Public Forums, concerts, art exhibits and educational courses. While distinguishing between educational and more cultural pursuits, it is interesting to see that his statistical analysis combines them, thus implying that adult education was but another side of the total cultural activity of the individual in his or her community.

Overall, Kaplan found the levels of participation throughout the community 'disappointing.' One-third of the sample reported not participating in any of the measured activities over a twelve-month period; 38 per cent reported engaging in one activity only. As far as library use was concerned, for example, 43 per cent of the sample (of 5,000) had not visited a library over a twelve-month period; only 29 per cent reported using it frequently.[7]

While participation on the whole was low, much more significant was the way it varied with 'ecological areas' or neighborhoods within the city. In Table 2, fourteen ecological areas are ranked for each form of participation. In column six, the ranks are summed and these sums are themselves ranked in column seven, under the heading 'participation.' Column eight shows the ranking of each area according to socio-economic status, measured in this case by a combination of income tax payment, automobile ownership and telephone possession. Columns seven and eight demonstrate an almost perfect correlation between participation and socio-economic status (SES). This can be seen clearly by comparing an area receiving a high ranking with one at the lower end.

Area B, for example, had the highest ranking on both participation and SES. It had the second highest educational level (11.5 years of schooling on average); was among the three areas with the highest priced apartment rentals; had the second highest number paying income tax (29 per cent), had the second highest percentage of automobile owners (61 per cent), had by far the highest number of telephone owners (85 per cent); and, finally, had among the highest proportion of those in professional, managerial and other high-status, non-manual occupations.

By contrast, Area N, which had the lowest rate of participation, tied for the lowest SES rank. It had the lowest educational level (6.6 years on average), and the highest number of individuals with no schooling (16 per cent compared with 1 per cent in Area B); no one in the area paid income tax, 19 per cent owned automobiles, while only 25 per cent owned telephones. The sample average for each of these categories was 10 per cent, 45 per cent, and 53 per cent, respectively. After Area L, N had the highest percentage of people in semi- and unskilled manual jobs (42 per cent compared with 7 per cent for Area B), and only 1 per cent in foreman and supervisory positions (compared with 23 per cent for Area B); and, finally, had the highest percentage of foreign-born residents (38 per cent compared with 15 per cent for Area B).

In a separate study of 250 of the original sample of 5,000, Kaplan examined the relationship between education, economic status, national origin and participation (he did not include occupational status as a separate variable). Education was strongly associated with both economic status and national origin, while neither of the latter was statistically related. Organizing the data into tables which strongly anticipated similar data

Table 2 Ranking of ecological areas (neighborhoods) according to participation in selected cultural and education activities and socio-economic status

| Ecological area | Use of library | Attend forums | Attend courses | Attend art exhibits | Attend concerts | Sum of ranks | Combined rank* P | Combined rank* SES |
|---|---|---|---|---|---|---|---|---|
| Column | 1 | 2 | 3 | 4 | 5 | 6 | 7 | 8 |
| A | 11 | 12 | 10 | 13 | 12 | 58 | 11.5 | 13 |
| B | 10 | 11 | 14 | 14 | 14 | 63 | 14 | 14 |
| C | 13 | 14 | 9 | 12 | 10 | 58 | 11.5 | 11.5 |
| D | 1 | 9 | 12 | 11 | 7 | 40 | 9 | 10 |
| E | 14 | 13 | 13 | 8 | 13 | 61 | 13 | 11.5 |
| F | 12 | 8 | 8 | 7 | 2 | 37 | 7 | 8 |
| G | 9 | 6.5 | 11 | 4 | 6 | 36.5 | 6 | 9 |
| H | 7 | 6.5 | 7 | 9 | 11 | 40.5 | 10 | 7 |
| I | 5 | 1 | 1 | 3 | 3 | 13 | 1.5 | 5 |
| J | 6 | 5 | 6 | 6 | 9 | 32 | 5 | 6 |
| K | 8 | 10 | 2 | 10 | 8 | 38 | 8 | 3.5 |
| L | 4 | 4 | 4 | 2 | 5 | 19 | 4 | 2 |
| M | 3 | 3 | 5 | 1 | 4 | 16 | 3 | 3.5 |
| N | 2 | 2 | 3 | 5 | 1 | 13 | 1.5 | 1 |

*Source:* Kaplan, 1945, p. 49.
* Refers to the ranking of the sum of ranks. The highest rank is 14, the lowest is 1.
P refers to all forms of participation combined.
SES refers to a composite of indexes used to measure Socio-Economic Status.

presentations by Johnstone and Rivera, Kaplan showed that holding educational level constant removed most of the variation in participation rates caused by economic status and national origin.

In conclusion he wrote: 'There would appear to be little doubt that amount of previous education is probably the strongest factor influencing adult participation in educational activities' (p. 90), and went on to quote from Lorimer to the effect that adult education did not appear to be a compensatory pursuit, but rather the continuing activity of those seeking occupational and educational advantage.

### London, Wenkert and Hagstrom, 1963

The last year of fieldwork for the Johnstone and Rivera study saw the publication of London, Wenkert and Hagstrom's (1963) *Adult Education and Social Class*, perhaps the most significant of the regional surveys ever conducted, and one of the most significant studies ever to be undertaken within the field. While similar in aim to the studies of Lorimer and others of the late 1920s and early 1930s, this study of Oakland, California, attempted to go beyond *description* to an *analysis* of the connections between different forms of participation and the style of working and social life in general. It also represents one of the more successful fusions of PAE research and the early Sociology of Participation.[8]

London, a sociologist by training, may have been the first researcher to note the independent effects of *age* and prior educational attainment on PAE. First, among those with four or more years of college the PAE rate was almost twice that of the total for the sample as a whole (23 per cent against 12 per cent). In all, those with twelve or more years of education accounted for almost three-quarters of all participants. Second, putting the findings on age and education together, London *et al.* echoed Lorimer's thesis that PAE seemed to be an extension rather than a substitute for formal education. Were it otherwise, they argued, the highest rates of PAE should have occurred among those with the least education and in the lowest occupational categories:

> To some extent, therefore, leaving school during adolescence is a basic deficit which locates an individual in the society for the remainder of his life and this location cannot be changed by the more informal channel of adult education. (p. 62)

Though the findings of Lorimer and Kaplan had hinted at it, London *et al.* was the first in the literature of the subject to explore a 'style of life' component which they thought contributed independently to variations in the rate of PAE. They found that the greater the frequency of television-watching, for example, the less the likelihood of educational participation. At first this looked simply like competition for free time: the more of it devoted to other kinds of leisure activity, the less there was to 'go around' for education. Not so, observed the research team. For among those most inclined to visit with relatives and neighbors frequently, PAE was highest. What seemed to be important here was an *active* as opposed to a *passive* attitude towards leisure.

Similarly, PAE varied with the 'content' of leisure activities. Despite the fact that about half of all participants cited vocational reasons for participation, among those who pursued art, music, or serious reading the PAE rate was 23 per cent, while among those engaged in 'aimless and frivolous' activities such as loafing, eating, driving, drinking or just sleeping, the PAE rate fell to less than 10 per cent. Was this variation a direct result of different educational levels?

In a separate examination, London *et al.* found that the more highly educated the respondent, the more activities in general he or she pursued. Furthermore, the relationship between education and involvement with organizations persisted even into informal associations: 'At least 50 per cent of the high school graduates participate at least once a year in the largest number of leisure activities compared with only 4 per cent of those with less than high school education' (p. 91). Those with less education tended to pursue a more passive lifestyle, around the home, in the neighborhood and with the extended family. They were 'connected' to the larger society through the mass media and entertainment. The better-educated, by contrast, engaged in more 'active' pursuits: reading, active sports and memberships in voluntary associations. At the same time, when groups were segregated according to educational level the differences persisted. Those most inclined to watch television were less likely to participate in education regardless of their level of education. Even when age was added to the equation the same differences emerged. London *et al.* concluded that there was a 'general participation syndrome' at work.

## National surveys, 1957–84

The various nationally representative studies which began appearing at the end of the 1950s all tend to confirm and expand in some way the major demographic correlations produced by the earlier regional studies. (See Arbeiter, 1977; Cross, 1978, 1979.) In studies as different as Carp *et al.*, Aslanian and Brickell, and the surveys of the NCES it is clear that the relationship between age, education and occupation *and* the tendency to participate in adult education has not changed down through the years, even if the overall social and economic landscape itself has undergone a profound transformation.

Participants continue to be younger, though there is now evidence of increasing involvement by those aged 65 and over. They continue to be middle-class, increasingly women more than men, mostly white, mostly employed, and mostly people who seem to be taking advantage of educational opportunities for career advance or continuing professional upgrading in an increasingly stratified job market.

### Johnstone and Rivera, 1965

Johnstone and Rivera (1965) was the first national study to establish a frame of reference for later independent and federal research. It calculated a national PAE population of 25 million or one-fifth of the adult population. At the same time, close questioning of respondents revealed that close to two-thirds had taken some kind of educational course since leaving high school or college. Most of the courses were non-credit and 'over-whelmingly non-academic' (p. 2) in nature. It appeared that 'the major emphasis in adult learning is on the practical rather than the academic; on the applied rather than the theoretical; and on skills rather than on knowledge or information' (p. 3).

More than half of all courses were taken in a non-classroom environment, such as churches, business premises, and, despite the strong showing by public schools and universities, by a ratio of 2:1 more adults studied outside of the school system than within it. The authors estimated that more than half of all educational involvement was in institutions whose primary function was not education, for example YMCAs, armed forces, churches, etc. Overall, more adults in the sample had studied in religious institutions and organizations than in any other single institution.

Who were the participants? For a start they were younger than the general population: 'Over half were under forty, and nearly four out of five were under fifty' (p. 6). Second, they were better educated than the general population. For example, the rate of participation for those with no formal schooling was 4 per cent compared with a rate of 47 per cent for those with sixteen or more years. The effects of schooling were truly striking. Dividing participants according to occupational prestige, income and level of schooling (a typical index of 'socio-economic status'), they found that while occupation and income correlated positively with PAE (11 per cent of those with the highest income compared with 7 per cent of those with the lowest, for blue-collar workers), both variables were relatively insignificant when compared with formal schooling.

A white-collar worker with the highest income, but without a high school diploma, was far less likely to participate in education than a high school graduate in a blue-collar occupation with the lowest income (14 per cent as against 20 per cent). More dramatically, for those with the most education and occupying the best jobs and highest income levels, PAE rates approached 50 per cent (over a twelve-month period), whereas there were insignificant differences between the PAE rates of those who had not completed high school, regardless of their occupational status or income level. In conclusion, the authors echoed the Lorimer thesis:

> Adult education today does not cater primarily to those who are trying to complete an unfinished formal education; ... In this sense, the field cannot be said to play a primarily remedial or rehabilitative role ... Adult learning in America ... can be better characterized as 'continuing education.' (p. 21)

Has this situation changed with time? Has the correlation of socio-economic status and age with PAE tended towards a more equal distribution over time or have the differences between those most likely to participate and those least likely increased? Important as they are, single, non-replicated surveys like *Volunteers for Learning* and the surveys of Carp and Aslanian cannot reveal trends. For these we must turn to US government sources, which, despite a more exclusive definition of adult education activity, remain the only source of information on changes and trends.

### Participation in Adult Education Reports, 1957–84

Government interest in this subject first surfaced in 1957 (Holden, 1958). This was the year of the first PAE survey by a federal authority. It showed that participants in adult education contained disproportionate numbers (compared to their numbers in the general population) of the better educated, those in higher status occupations, and generally those in the younger age categories[9] Really comparable surveys of the adult population began in 1969 and have continued to the present time, the most recent occurring in 1984. (As of this date no survey has been conducted since 1984, though it was proposed to conduct one in the late spring of 1991 [Rosalyn Korb, CES, personal communication].) The most significant trends occurring over this period are reported below.

### Gender

While the general characteristics of the PAE population have not changed noticeably over the fifteen-year period, 1969 to 1984 (the year for which we have the most recent information) the contribution of women to this population has changed, and changed dramatically. This trend appears to be unique and was not noted in any previous study that has come to our attention. Moreover, it appears to be part of a more general trend favoring women's participation in community and economic life. Thus while the proportion of males remained stable at 47 per cent of the general adult population from 1969 to 1984, their participation in adult education decreased from 52 per cent to 45 per cent. For women, also with a static population growth, PAE went from 48 per cent to 55 per cent. Similarly, focusing only on college enrollments, for the period of 1973 to 1983, for example, while male enrollments jumped 12 per cent, enrollments by females leaped by 52 per cent (*Digest of Education Statistics*, 1985–86, p. 95).

## Age

With respect to age, one of the two major demographic variables known to correlate highly with measures of PAE, a number of important changes have occurred since the late 1960s. First, it is important to note that those under 35 still account for *half* or more of all participants, with the age group 25–34 containing the largest percentage of participants, a fact which is true for both men and women. Organized adult learning is still very much a young person's game, which makes sense in the light of remarks by London *et al.* that adult education activity may be judged in part as a kind of 'half-way house' for those anxious to get into the job market and establish social status on their own terms.

There is evidence, however, that this representation of the population is changing. Among those 55 and over, there appears to be signs of a dramatic improvement in PAE rates: for those aged 55 to 64, from 4 per cent in 1969 to 8 per cent in 1984; and from 2 per cent to 4 per cent for those over 65, over the same period. It is also worth noting that in the period 1973 to 1983, the biggest increase of all in higher education enrollments has occurred among those 35 years and older: an impressive 90 per cent (*Digest of Education Statistics*, 1985–86, p. 95).

This trend is also evident when gender is combined with age, though here we must rely on a comparison between 1975 and 1981 figures, since the CES did not break out similar figures for 1984.[10] For example, PAE among those aged 17 to 24 declined from 20 per cent in 1975 to 16 per cent in 1981. However, among males of the same age the decrease was 2.6 per cent, while among females it was only 1.8 per cent. A more startling fact emerges among those aged 25 to 34. Between 1975 and 1981, the overall rate of PAE for this age group remained the same, around 36 per cent of the total participating population. However, this relative stability hides a real decline of 2 per cent among males and a real increase of 2 per cent among females.

Schooling

Despite the effects of age and now gender on PAE rates, schooling continues to be the dominant demographic influence on PAE. In 1969, those with less than four years of high school accounted for a substantial 44 per cent of the total adult population, but only 15 per cent of participants in adult education. By contrast, those with college degrees and more accounted for about 10 per cent of the population but more than one-quarter of all participants. By 1984, PAE among those with less than four years of high school had fallen to 8 per cent, while among those with college degrees and more, it had risen to a remarkable 36 per cent, an increase of 11 per cent.

It appears then that the majority of those who participate in organized forms of adult learning have already availed themselves of college-level experience. At the same time, high-school graduates, the single most popular category of participants, had dropped from 39 per cent of the participating population in 1969 to 30 per cent in 1984. Nor should this decline blind us to the real significance of educational attainment. As Johnstone and others have noted, a phenomenon going right back to the 1930s, PAE is a relatively uncommon activity among those who have not obtained any kind of educational credentialing. Once the most basic level has been passed, that is obtaining a high school diploma, PAE rates increase dramatically.

Occupational Status

Regional surveys have shown a strong tendency for those in the better jobs to be more likely to undertake further education and training than those in jobs of lesser status. How does this connection fare at the federal level? Here it is necessary to introduce a note of caution, for of all of the demographic categories likely to change over a period of time, occupation is probably the most susceptible to change. This reflects an extraordinary dynamism in the American economy, both for good and ill, in the period since the Second World War, though it had begun long before that time. (See Chapter 6 for relevant statistics.)

Those who occupy the professional and technical stratum of the work world constitute roughly one-third of all participants, almost twice as many as clerical workers, the nearest occupation category. This figure is impressive, though it had fallen from 33 per cent in 1969 to 31 per cent in 1984. For operatives, service, and unskilled laborers the rate of PAE is very low indeed. Farmer and farm laborers constitute the least involved occupational group, a situation which has not changed in the past fifty years.

The connection between job status and later PAE is particularly striking in those occupational categories most closely identified with higher levels of education preparation. Take, for example, teachers and allied health workers. In 1969, teachers constituted 2 per cent of the total adult population, but their contribution to the PAE population was five times greater: 10 per cent. Overall, the proportion of teachers participating in educational activities in 1969 was a remarkable 43 per cent. Allied health workers also constituted 2 per cent of the total adult population in 1969 while their contribution to the PAE population was almost twice that. Though not as high as teachers, fully 23 per cent of all allied health workers took part in some form of continuing education in 1969.

Twelve years later, however, the figures had been almost reversed reflecting perhaps the levelling off in the acquisition of higher levels of credentialling among teachers, and its continuing growth among health professionals. In 1981, only 37 per cent of teachers were becoming involved with adult education compared with 43 per cent of health workers. In this twelve-year period, while teachers' share of the population had grown from 2 per cent to over 3 per cent, their share of the PAE population had fallen from 10 per cent to 7.5 per cent. Over the same period, while the total contribution of health workers to the national population had hardly changed (from 2 per cent to 2.3 per cent), their share of the PAE population had increased by 50 per cent: from 4 per cent to 6 per cent.

## Race

With respect to race, the CES estimated that of the 23 million people participating in adult education in 1984, 91 per cent were white (compared with 81 per cent of the national population); 6.5 per cent were black (10.8 per cent of the national population); while 2.5 per cent were 'other' non-Hispanics (2.6 per cent of the national population). (Hispanics are not treated as a separate category here as they were not broken out of the white classification until 1981.) Fifteen years earlier the proportions respectively were 91.5 per cent white, 9.7 per cent black, and 1 per cent 'other'. Thus, whereas white PAE has remained high, relative to its share of the adult population, and other minority groups have more than doubled their rate of PAE, though this still reflects their share of the national population (and can thus be accounted for as a result of natural increase), black PAE has declined absolutely.

Johnstone and Rivera, who recorded a black sampling proportion of 12 per cent, noted black PAE at 9 per cent in 1962. Allowing for sampling variation between the NORC and CES studies, black PAE seems to have been at its highest at that time. The precise reasons for this decline are far from obvious. For example, despite signs of a leveling off or even decline in black enrollments in higher education at large, enrollment among blacks and other minorities increased by an amazing 85 per cent in the period 1973 to 1983 (*Digest of Education Statistics*, 1985–86). It may be that, in the past, adult education served as a conduit into the professional mainstream for many blacks, otherwise blocked from entering traditional avenues of higher education. Now, with increased emphasis on recruiting blacks and other minorities to universities, black PAE would be expected to decrease as the traditional routes are opened up. According to this scenario, however, it would also be expected that as significant numbers of blacks enter the educational mainstream they would also be expected to 'rejoin' the ranks of adult education, on the assumption, according to London *et al.* that higher levels of professionalism bring out higher levels of PAE. This does not appear to be happening, though the reasons for it are as yet hard to determine given that the trends involved have yet to play themselves out.

Other recent trend data of significance are as follows. According to the CES report, adult education for credit constituted over half of all courses taken in 1969. By 1984, however, this had fallen to one-third. By contrast, courses taken for some form of certification or licensure increased dramatically. From 1969 to 1975, the number remained stable, but then doubled between 1975 and 1984, from 3.2 million to 6.4 million. This in part, the report argued, could be accounted for by the fact that every state now has a mandatory continuing education requirement for many professions.

With respect to the providers of adult education, the report noted that while schools and other postsecondary providers remained the majority provider this proportion had slipped from 63 per cent in 1969 to 53 per cent in 1984. Business and industry now accounts for almost as many courses as the main school provider, the four-year college or university. Second, the two-year community college which accounted for a half of the four-year college total in 1969, equalled the latter's total in 1984, and may already have overtaken it.

Finally, the CES calculated that persons paying for their education spent a total of 3 billion dollars in 1984, and this accounted for about 47 per cent of all courses taken. How much was spent by the other sponsors of adult education is unknown. This led the CES to calculate an average of $152 per course, paid by participants or their families. In conclusion, the report notes that:

> the monetary and time expenditures for adult education represent a
> significant investment in education which is not a part of the formal

education system in this country . . . This reflects a slowly changing concept of 'education' – one in which education does not stop after high school or college graduation, but continues throughout life, often related to work or to personal interests. (NCES, 1969–84, p. 16)

## Conclusions

While this comparision of national statistics contains many points of significance, the following are important to the present investigation. Overall, it appears that much of what is listed in the literature as adult education, and thus distinct from the formal system of secondary and higher education, is in fact a continuation of formal schooling for certain categories of occupation and the general population. Second, it appears that formal adult education results from rather than leads to economic mobility: men and women pursue adult education because they have been successful, so far, rather than want to be successful.

Third, both of these points contribute to the remarkable durability of a phenomenon first uncovered back in the 1920s and 1930s, namely that formal adult education remains the domain of the younger adult with better levels of prior schooling and income. Fourth, and a factor which up until now has not been highlighted, though reasonably well documented in earlier surveys, PAE appears to be a species of a larger genus. There is a factor which we might call 'general participation' which comprehends various forms of community or societal participation, all of which appear to be related to each other. PAE, according to this hypothesis, is related to the other forms of participation in that the tendency to undertake learning activities in adulthood correlates with the tendency to have more formal social commitments and to have a leisure agenda which includes more formal types of pleasure consumption, for instance going to the theater or concerts, reading 'quality' magazines and periodicals. This phenomenon and its causes, unremarked in the traditional PAE literature up until now, will be examined more closely in Chapters 5 and 6.

Finally, the fact that formal PAE appears to be a function of general social and economic status and that it is by and large the pursuit of the younger adult population suggest that adult education has a strong link with the world of work, the chief means by which that status is maintained and elevated. This leads to a consideration of what precisely it is that men and women say about why they learn and what we can deduce from these statements as to their real motives for learning.

## KNOWLEDGE OR UTILITY? MOTIVES FOR ADULT EDUCATION

### The early surveys, 1931–63

It is sobering to realize that though the field has grown in statistical sophistication and conceptual complexity, the categories of motive uncovered by Lorimer in the late 1920s, and his comments upon them, are as apropos to today's research context as they were sixty years ago:

> Motives for adult study are commonly less idealistic than some educators would like to believe. Poets are eager for an increase of beauty, and social scientists are interested in the intelligent social control of public affairs. And many men and women in all walks of life share these hungers. But, by all odds, the largest percentage of [adult students] in Brooklyn . . . are motivated by a sense of economic or social insecurity and a concern to advance themselves vocationally or in social status. (Lorimer, 1931, p. 51)

In his sample, vocational motives accounted for almost two-thirds of the reasons for PAE endorsed by men and a half of those endorsed by women. Moreover, these applied to current rather than new jobs. Approximately 45 per cent of all men reporting vocational motives had their present job in mind when making their endorsements. This is in line with national studies, with the significant exception of the Johnstone and Rivera study, about which more below. In general, among those giving job reasons for participation, the bulk of the motivation reflects current occupational concerns, rather than preparation for future, new jobs. For example, the latest government survey shows that of the job-related reasons for PAE (in themselves accounting for two-thirds of all reasons for PAE), 'advance in job' made up nearly 50 per cent of that category compared with 12 per cent for 'get new job' (NCES 1969–84).[11]

Why is the vocational motive so strong in Lorimer and McGrath? Remember that McGrath (1938) too had found job-orientation to constitute the single most important motive for PAE (among eight other reasons for participation and accounting for over one-quarter of all reasons). Lorimer did not attempt an explanation; McGrath sought to explain it by reference to the Depression. But where were the effects of the Depression in the Lorimer study when his fieldwork was undertaken in 1929, just before the beginnings of that great catastrophe? By an extraordinary irony, Lorimer's respondents spoke quite frequently of the effects of the 'the Depression' and of the need for adult education if they wanted to get on in the new era. They were referring to the economic dislocation of *1921!*

London *et al.*'s question regarding reasons for PAE simply asked respondents whether their reasons for participation were work or non-work related. Exactly half claimed a vocational motive for participation. Since his sample consisted of males only there are no data here on sex differences. In an important set of findings, London *et al.* (1963) demonstrated that the strong decline in PAE with age, a feature of all survey research undertaken on this subject, could be traced to the lessening importance of the vocational motive. While job preparation or advancement was very important to younger age groups it lessened significantly with age. Participating for educational and intellectual reasons, however, hardly changed with age. Moreover, this trend operated regardless of educational level. At the same time, London *et al.* were surprised that more than 50 per cent of all those with college experience participated for job-related reasons, compared with just over 40 per cent of those who had not graduated from high school, a finding which exactly mirrored McGrath's a quarter of a century earlier. To explain these results the Berkeley researchers pointed to the influence of age. The better-educated were also younger, and it was among this group that vocational motives were strongest. 'It appears likely,' they argued, 'that the educated who are interested in liberal learning provide themselves with such an education in their spare time, while using adult education for vocational purposes' (London *et al.*, 1963, p. 70).

Speculating further on the relationship between age, formal schooling and reasons for PAE, London *et al.* developed the following argument, which goes some way to explain the connection between job status and PAE discussed earlier:

(1) The better educated are more likely to be professionals; (2) in-service training continues throughout the professional career, while it is either non-existent or confined to the early stages of non-professional occupations; (3) [PAE] for vocational reasons is therefore equally probable for the professional as for the non-professional during the early years of a career, but is more likely to continue for the professional; (4) therefore, vocational participation should be higher among the better educated than among the less educated within the older age groups, but should be about equal within the younger age groups. (p. 75)

This is still one of the better explanations of the dominance of the vocational motive as a reason for PAE.

But what of other motives for adult learning? Is the vocational or 'utilitarian' motive so strong that it minimizes the influences of other more 'liberal' motives? And is the vocational motive to be considered synonymous with utilitarian goals? In other words, if there are other

practical reasons for PAE are these to be considered educationally equal
and as educationally suspect as are vocational motives by some leaders of
the field? To consider answers to these questions we turn to a group of
studies which over the years have come to constitute the bulk of PAE
research, even if they have varied widely in quality.

## Clientele analysis, 1950–87

Regional and national surveys represent but a small fraction of the total
output in this area over the last half century. Most of that output consists of
localized studies, what Knox (1965) called 'clientele analysis,' a significant
minority of which began and have remained as dissertations, their value to
the field depending by and large on their availability.

Researchers have studied the correlation between demography and
motivation-to-learn among students in local institutions and agencies,
including the Community (Barron, 1953; Dowling, 1963), the Museum
(Nedzel, 1952; Dimmock, 1985), the Great Books Program (Deane, 1950;
Davis, 1957), University Extension (McLaughlin, 1951; Hagelberg, 1960;
Carter, Kerr and York, 1962), the Public School (Philips, 1958; Pattyson,
1961; Burnett, 1976), the Community College (Hartig, 1962), and
Voluntary Associations (Newberry, 1959; Douglah, 1970).

Many have focused on the demographic identities and motivational
backgrounds of adult students, both full-time and part-time, in a variety of
school and college settings: Deane (1950), Nicholson (1955), Canning
(1955), Knox (1958), Chapman (1959), Franklin (1960), Sworen (1960),
Zeman (1960), Smith (1962), Dugger (1965), Ross (1978), Strange (1979),
Grigsby (1980), Keogh (1980).

Researchers have been interested in the reality or likelihood of PAE
among special populations: the poor, welfare or other economically
disadvantaged groups (Burman, 1959; Hymon, 1960; Jack, 1969; Divita,
1969; Lewis, 1969; Burnett, 1976), farmers and other rural Americans
(Kindell, 1959; Davis, 1960; Waldron, 1968; Conrad, 1974), the military
(Larsen, 1953; Bennet, 1968), drop-outs (Savides, 1960; Scharles, 1966;
Garrison, 1987), African-Americans (London *et al.*, 1963; Cunningham,
1973), nonparticipants (Morrill, 1960), and women (Sitts, 1960; Hall, 1965;
Giffis, 1982).

Some few studies derive their significance from being longitudinal in
nature, an approach to the problem which is truly underrepresented:
Snyder (1951), Carson (1965), Boyle (1967), Waldron (1968). Still others
have developed new methods of measurement. Litchfield (1965), for
example, constucted a widely used instrument for measuring the

frequency and importance of different forms of educational and cultural participation.

What major national surveys like those of Johnstone and Rivera, Carp *et al.* and the NCES have attempted to do on a national level, the best examples of clientele analysis have tried to do on a local level: to describe the demographics of participating and nonparticipating populations; to analyze their reasons for participation; and in some cases to give explanatory accounts of the motivation behind PAE.

In what follows we consider the major findings of these studies as they reflect on the central question of why adults learn. Many of these studies make the point that was made eloquently by London *et al.* that formal adult education attracts mostly those with vocational motives.

## Dugger, 1965

In a survey of 1,567 adult part-time students attending extension classes at Drake University, Dugger began with the hypothesis that the major reason why adults bother with education is because they are 'interested in preparation for a type of job they do not hold or to prepare for career advancement in their present occupations' (Dugger, 1965, A-5195). While the author does not say whether vocational motives are related to job change or job promotion, he did find corroboration for his hypothesis in an analysis of the most frequently endorsed reasons for PAE. At the same time, and contrary perhaps to commonsense expectations, the strongest 'vocational motive' was held by those *already employed*; those who were unemployed tended to choose 'socio-cultural motives' as reasons for attending evening classes. In other words, those who on the surface appear to be most in need of employment participated in educational activities less for work-related reasons than those who are already employed. Though this runs counter to the conventional wisdom (see e.g. Rubenson, 1978), it is a point which was made by McGrath and more recently by Conrad (1974). This is an important point and one to which we will return.

Dugger's findings are supported by others, especially those who focus on full-time or extension students in college environments, who conclude that, despite the prominence of 'liberal' motives, adults attend classes for vocational or other pragmatic reasons (Knox, 1958; Franklin, 1960; Hagelberg, 1960; Carter, Kerr and York, 1962).[12]

Two points are worth pursuing from these findings. First, there is the fact that not all of the findings with respect to vocational motives are in line with expectations, as we saw in the case of Dugger. Second, though often dominant, the vocational motive does not hold exclusive sway. Other motives are present and on the face of it (and in the absence of a more sophisticated statistical treatment) interact with the vocational motive to produce PAE. But the issue of motivation appears to be even more complex than that, as the following examples illustrate.[13]

### 'Surveys of the Great Books Program, 1950, 1957'

In a comparative profile of adult students enrolled in college credit and non-credit evening classes and participants of the Great Books Program, Deane (1950) found that those in college credit classes were most interested in the practical aspects of their school work and enjoyed it; they liked competitive activities and sought vocational success and financial security as lifetime goals. Those in the Great Books Program, a slightly older group, sought cultural broadening with no relation to their vocational interests; they expressed dislike of competitive activities, and reported greater interest and activity in community affairs as a result of the course.[14]

In a later survey of Great Books participants, Davis (1957) gave his subjects a checklist of twenty-four reasons for participation and asked which of them they 'definitely had in mind as a reason for joining' (Davis, 1957, Table 17). Using 'cluster analysis' to analyze responses (and anticipating Boshier and Collins, 1985), he classified the twenty-four reasons into four categories. Cluster A (Stepping Stone) was characterized by an emphasis on the person's job and social life, for example, 'to improve my ability to carry out my job through the intellectual training of reading Great Books'. Cluster B (Content) was characterized by an emphasis on what Davis called the 'official motivation' for the program, for example, 'to learn what the greatest minds in history have to say about the basic issues of life'. This statement, incidentally, was endorsed by 64 per cent of the sample, compared with 44 per cent for the next most frequently cited reason. Cluster C (Self-Help) was characterized by a need to acquire the intellectual or technical skills associated with the study of Great Books, for example 'improving my reading skills', 'gaining the equivalent of a college education'. Cluster D (Cosmopolitanism) was characterized by 'pushes and pulls' (Davis, 1957, p. 32): the need to escape boredom and the narrow confines of the everyday world, which Davis saw as a push; and the hope that by joining something like Great Books the person will meet people who are alert and stimulating, the pull.

Davis showed that the most common motive for PAE seemed to be 'content,' followed by 'cosmopolitanism,' 'self-help' and 'stepping stone.' Most important of all, however, Davis's study brings out very clearly a feature of most research which classifies varieties of motivation-to-learn: that while a single motive may dominate an individual's consciousness of why she acted as she did, that motive is usually not alone in the total matrix of considerations. Other motives are also present.

Is the utilitarian/vocational motive for PAE equally strong among all of the major demographic groups? Few of the studies classified here as clientele analysis focus on differences between the sexes or pay attention to groups not normally seen among the ranks of adult learners in any great numbers. The differences among them, however, are instructive. Take the issue of gender.

## Nicholson, 1955

Nicholson collected demographic information on 5,211 students (a 58 per cent response rate) in day colleges, business and trade schools, and part-time evening classes 'in different sections of the United States' (p. 6). Subjects were administered a checklist of thirty statements of reasons for PAE and asked to indicate for each one whether it was important as a motive for participation. The author grouped responses into three clusters, labelled 'economic-occupational', 'intellectual-cultural' and 'personal-social.'

Students had one or more dominant motives for attendance; few were attending for a single all-encompassing reason, a finding which emerges ever more clearly from these studies. But Nicholson noted important differences between the sexes. The three vocational reasons which appeared in the top five places received the highest rankings from men, while the two intellectual motives were ranked first by women. For men education would increase income and was necessary for success in life; for women it would provide mental stimulation and familiarity with liberal education. Women also ranked personal-social reasons higher than men did. That was in 1955 and many years before the onset of feminism and the Women's Liberation Movement. Clearly, if the same study were done today we could anticipate an assimilation of men's and women's views of the importance of adult education. Yet in a recent survey of community college populations near Chicago, Keogh (1980) found, first, that economic factors did not appear to be a 'significant motivator' in the decisions of either sex to return to college. While the men and women in his sample exhibited similar levels of self-esteem, women indicated that adult education was an important source of self-confidence for their re-entry into the work world. And Keogh concluded that while the male sample was more interested in improving career opportunities by PAE, the female group appeared to have intellectual stimulation as a major reason for the return to school.

## Adult education and disadvantage

A number of studies have appeared directed at discovering more about PAE and perceptions of adult education among lower socio-economic classes and those least likely to undertake formal educational endeavors during the adult years, such as rural populations. The study of such populations has been a natural by-product of the rise of social science in universities of the Midwest and urban areas like New York, towards the end of the nineteenth century. Indeed, the very first surveys, as we saw in Chapter 1, were of rural and urban communities and their various social strata. Nevertheless, the specific focus on PAE among lower socio-economic populations, with significant exceptions like Kaplan (1945), has not been frequent and this may have much to do with the ultimate pragmatism of the survey's goals, with its intention to boost PAE among those more likely to participate than among those traditionally absent from the classroom.

Two studies, both produced out of Indiana University, are of interest therefore because of their specific focus. Burman (1959) investigated the aspirations of fifty adult men and women (evenly divided) from lower socio-economic levels. He looked at aspirations, the difficulties standing in the way of fulfilling these aspirations, the opportunities sought to achieve them, and the implications of his findings for adult education. Of eight aspiration categories, the most pronounced concerned family, material and occupational betterment. Education came halfway down the list (Burman, 1959, Figures 1 and 2, p. 88). The sources of difficulties in the way of fulfilling the aspirations were socio-economic and personal. No one, in other words, saw lack of education as the reason he or she was not more successful. As for opportunities, those listed under the heading 'social' were the most important. For both men and women it was the desire for more interaction with others and 'some way for poor people to get together to see what can be done' (p. 136). Second came education: often very specific desires concerning how education might improve their lot.

Hymon (1960) appears to have studied a population drawn from the same census tract in Indianapolis. She set out to discover how those of lower social status perceived adult education and its relevance to their lives. She surveyed fifty adults sampled from a list provided by a local educational agency. Among her conclusions, she noted an overall 'paucity of participation' among a majority of the sample, though, interestingly enough, more 'non-users' of the educational agency in question indicated involvement in other organizations and were interested in ways to improve leisure-time. Overall, not only did adult education play little part in the lives of these individuals but also it was by and large peripheral to their thinking.[15]

A much larger sample of 6,710 adult men and women was studied by Lewis (1969) in North Carolina. He measured 'participation orientation' as a combination of past and current PAE activity and interest in future participation. Approximately one-fifth of his sample had participated in some form of adult education or job training in the past, a figure which is much higher than national estimates of a similar population. On some of the major demographic variables reviewed in the first half of this chapter, Lewis found that his population was similar to the general PAE population. PAE and interest in it were functions of age, educational level, income, and place of residence (urban vs rural). The study does not throw light on attitudes and perceptions outside of the immediate realm of PAE and there are no data on personal and social lifestyle issues, such as we find in Burman, Hymon and in the next study.

In a further study of rural disadvantaged adults Conrad (1974) came to conclusions which surprised him but are in line with Burman's. Most of those in his sample ranked feelings for others, a desire for knowledge and their own emotional stability as being more important than education for vocational or practical ends.

Further discussion of the reasons why we might expect the reality of adult education to be different for different social groups must await the introduction of psychological and sociological theories of PAE in later chapters. It is important to note at this point, however, that apart from scattered references here and there this study does not include extensive discussion of populations and motives for PAE among those pursuing programs in Adult Basic Education (ABE) or the test of General Education Development (GED), populations traditionally considered to be disadvantaged though better off than the 'underclass' populations, for whom the option of adult education appears to be as close as Alpha Centauri. It would be important for future researchers to study this population at closer quarters.

## Surveys of motivation-to-learn at the national level

Have the varied findings of these local studies been replicated at the national level? Regarding motives for PAE, Johnstone and Rivera asked their respondents: 'In which of the following ways had you hoped the course would be helpful to you?' (1965, p. 143). Their sample of 4,603 was given a checklist based on a number of 'popular interpretations of why adults enroll [in courses]' (p. 142). In providing the checklist, Johnstone and Rivera noted, as have others (e.g. Davis, 1957), that even when subjects are allowed to generate their own categories of reasons for PAE, very few do so. Statements of motive were endorsed in the following order of importance: become a better informed person (37 per cent); prepare for a new job or occupation (36 per cent); on the job I held at that time (32 per cent); spend my spare time more enjoyably (20 per cent); meet new and interesting people (15 per cent); in carrying out everyday tasks and duties (13 per cent); get away from the daily routine (10 per cent); everyday tasks away from home (10 per cent).[16]

With regard to age, Johnstone and Rivera replicated the findings of London *et al.* (1963) and others. Like London *et al.* also, they noted the decline of the vocational motive with age: 'Job centered reasons most frequently propel younger adults into education and, by comparison, the uses made of education by older adults are much less pragmatic and utilitarian' (p. 156). Johnstone and Rivera also observed that for both sexes, adult education was more likely to be used by 'low' SES persons to enter new jobs, while among those of 'high' SES, advancement in one's current position was a more important reason. Second, the pursuit of education as a leisure-time activity tripled as one moved from low to high SES, for both sexes. Incidentally, at each SES level, educational leisure was almost three times as important a motive for women as for men.

McGrath (1938), on the contrary, found that the best educated also displayed the greatest instrumentalism: education was being pursued primarily for job-related reasons, or in order to fulfill educational requirements. London *et al.* were surprised that more of the higher SES seemed not to be involved with education for 'cultural' or leisure reasons. How can these differences in interpretation be reconciled?

First, it must be recognized that all three were asking different questions. By all accounts both McGrath and London et al. tried to elicit the most important reason for PAE, whereas Johnstone and Rivera allowed their respondents to select more than one, and on average they chose almost two each. Second, and most importantly, it is likely that, at least in McGrath's case, when those in the lowest educational category gave educational more than vocational reasons for PAE they were acknowledging that they had a lot of educational 'catching-up' to do, and that before they could begin to use adult education in the pursuit of a career they had to compensate for earlier deficiencies. Hence education served a more diffuse personal as well as vocational objective. Third, unlike McGrath, Johnstone and Rivera did not include a category tapping the need to fulfill educational requirements (an absence noted by Houle, 1974). Given the prevalence of this motive in other studies it seems odd that it should be missing from the Johnstone and Rivera sample. Is it possible then that the category 'become better informed' contains those who were pursuing adult education in order to fulfill other educational requirements, since, as the authors note, this category 'could be a meaningful rationale for studying practically anything' (p. 144)? If this were the case it would bring Johnstone and Rivera's findings more in line with previous research.

Finally, the tendency for 'clientele analysis' or regional surveys to find that motives for adult education tend to be more utilitarian than not, are confirmed in the latest Trend report from the NCES. Noting that 'adult education has become closely related to the world of work,' (NCES, 1986, p. 5), the NCES reports that in 1969 a little over half of all courses were taken for job-related reasons; by 1984, this figure had risen to two-thirds. Much of this increase, they pointed out, appeared to be due to the increase in the numbers of women seeking education in connection with work. At the same time, over the same fifteen-year period, women outnumbered men two-to-one in the number of courses taken for 'personal or social purposes,' an interesting figure which bears out Keogh's findings cited above and which again suggests the inner complexity of the motivation issue.

## WHY ADULTS LEARN: THE CASE FOR SURVEY ANALYSIS

The studies examined in this chapter were selected, classified and analyzed because of the light they might throw on the question, 'Why do adults learn?' Before considering how these questions have been answered two important caveats should be borne in mind, caveats which limit the explanatory power of survey research.

First, remember the findings of Anderson and Darkenwald discussed in Chapter 1 who concluded that, though significant, demographic variables appear to leave out a great deal in the explanation of PAE. So no matter how strong the correlation between age and PAE, or formal education and later PAE, for example, other factors of unknown dimension are stronger determinants of PAE and survey research is not in the best position to analyze these underlying factors without some general theory.

Second, survey research takes the expression of motives or reasons for PAE at their face value. It assumes that if someone is asked why they participate, the reason they give is that which is actually responsible for them being in a classroom. But, as will be discussed in Chapters 3 and 4, we ought to distinguish between the need or desire for learning and the factors, many conditional, like for example the availability of funds, which coupled with the need for learning can lead to PAE. Need for learning, on its own, may not result in the action of PAE, nor need it even be necessary as in those cases where enrollment is compelled by an organization of its employees regardless of felt need to learn. That is to say, the 'need to learn' has more than one 'promoter': apart from the individuals involved, organizations and communities, even whole societies, as in the case of

AIDS, may 'experience' a need to learn, which gets translated into individual 'mandates' to learn.

These caveats aside, what may we conclude from this analysis of survey research concerning adults' reasons for learning? In the first place, what the earliest surveys revealed continues to be a dominant characteristic of today's PAE population. There is a perception that those who pursue adult education are really making up for earlier deficiencies, having failed to learn to read in school, having dropped out of college or being prevented from going to college, and the like. What has emerged again and again, however, from studies as diverse as Lorimer's and the NCES, is that adult education is more likely to be a 'continuing' rather than 'compensatory' venture, pursued for practical or vocational reasons connected with the world of work, rather than for the pure love of knowledge. This is clearly connected with the most enduring finding of the entire literature: that those who have already reached the highest levels of formal schooling are those most likely to be represented among the ranks of participants in adult education.

Taken collectively, this seems to point to the function of adult education as an extension of formal schooling. For the youngest age categories, it is as if adult education is really no more than higher or third-level education. While for those who have been out of school for five or more years, it is perceived in much the same way as higher education is perceived: as the means to occupational and social advance. (These are important points and will be dealt with at length in Chapter 6.)

Second, survey research reveals a number of motives to be at work for most participants, even where the vocational motive is dominant. A classic alignment of both the vocational and nonvocational orientations is revealed in the Johnstone and Rivera study, where getting ahead in the world vies with becoming better informed as important reasons for PAE. However, as Houle (1974) points out, even for those subject matters, such as nursing, where only a vocational motive might seem appropriate, non-vocational motives, for example the desire to meet people, may also be operational.[17]

Third, there is a relationship which is not touched upon in the most well-known of the PAE surveys but may ultimately prove far more important than the most popular findings connecting PAE with age and formal education. This relationship was first uncovered by the more sociologically oriented studies (e.g. Lorimer, Kaplan, London *et al.*) and subsequently lost from the literature. It says in effect: do not look at PAE in isolation from other species of social involvement. When a man or woman undertakes formal learning during the adult years, it is likely that they are also involved in other types of formal cultural activities, from concert or museum attendance, to organized social activities like group sports, and organized community activities like local politics and professional associations. Indeed, a point made by the prominent anthropologist Bourdieu, and one which will be examined in more detail later, PAE itself may be seen less as an educational activity leading to certain desirable social goals than as itself a form of cultural 'consumption,' enjoyed for its own sake because it goes with a certain social role and standard of living.

There is another side to this finding, though less well documented. Kaplan (1945) discovered that those involved in some educational agencies within their particular community were also more likely to be involved in other educational agencies. It was just such a 'fear' – namely that adult education agencies were siphoning off members from each other rather than recruiting new clientele – which motivated the Dowling (1963) study cited earlier. PAE populations overlap. This finding can be explained by London et al.'s 'general participation syndrome.' It appears, in many cases, that adult education is a social activity which fits more comfortably with some lifestyles than with others. For one, the potential learner has to be engaged in society, occupying a number of recognized and valued roles. He or she invariably has a job and an income that is above the national median, while his or her occupational status is more likely to be professional or technical or some occupation which stresses formal schooling. Adult education is more often pursued by those with a more 'active' orientation to life, people who are more apt to be involved with other formal organizations besides the school, more active in community life, more in touch with world affairs, more likely to use the library and to read the 'quality' newspapers and magazines, to be active in and have opinions about politics, and so forth.

In other words, a participant in adult education is more likely to be an active and productive participant in his or her community, and in the society at large, than someone who is not. This might be summed up by saying that adult education is a form of cultural engagement, a form of consumption or expression, that is ideally suited to the educated middle class. It appears to capture the essence of the bourgeois mentality and attitude to life, an orientation that many participants may not be eager to reveal![18]

If this proved to be the case it would also explain the lack of involvement of the most disadvantaged groups in our society. How else to explain low participation by the unemployed, the older and less well-off citizen, certain ethnic groups and minorities, even farmers, traditionally low participants?

# 3 Adult learning and the psychology of motive

No other subject is more widely pondered and discussed by people interested in the education of adults than the motives which lead men and women to introduce systematic learning into the patterns of their lives.

(Houle, 1974)

Why are motives so important? Why do we always seem to come back to this point when attempting to understand the factors behind the phenomenon of adult learning? Most obviously, perhaps, it is because PAE appears to be, and with important exceptions, a voluntary activity. People do not have to participate. But many do. How then are we to distinguish betweeen those who do and those who don't except in the language of 'motive' and 'motivation'? Thus, it is not hard to see that over the years, the problem of PAE has come to be synonymous with the identification and classification of people's motives for learning, on the assumption that once we know a motive we know all of the reasons – causes – behind a person's decision to become involved: we know precisely what made that person act. Houle, as we shall see shortly, attempted such an analysis with his classification of learner types. Boshier, who has based much of his professional life on the testing and extension of the Houle typology, went further and attempted to link expressions of motive to underlying personality types.

Cross (1981) devotes two chapters of her popular book, *Adults as Learners*, to the analysis of reasons and motives for adult learning, in which she details models which attempt to mirror and explain what is involved in the decision to undertake organized forms of learning. Missing from these chapters, however, is an overarching sense of what is meant by the concept of motive or motivation (is there a difference between these terms, for example?). While connections are shown between the elements which make up the individual models we find no critique which might help the reader evaluate their relative worth or help a researcher decide which of them might be worth testing. The present and following chapters are intended to fill the gaps left by the Cross analysis, and in particular to offer a more complete account of the psychology of motive as an explanation of PAE.

We commence this task by considering the meaning of the question, 'Why do adults learn?' Reflecting on this question for a moment, it will soon be apparent that there are at least two ways in which it has meaning. First, it may mean a quest for the presence and origin of the need to learn: why are (some more than other) adults interested in learning? What are their attitudes to learning? What do they believe that learning will accomplish? Second, it may mean an examination of the conditions under which some people embrace formal types of education, or become involved in the more informal varieties, while still others do not seem to get involved at all.[1] A good theory of PAE would be one which accounted for both meanings of the question: it would account for the origins of learning need as well as being a depiction of the steps leading someone to become involved in a learning project. We turn now to an examination of the various theories of PAE which have appeared over the years and consider to what extent these theories approach or depart from this idealized structure for a theory of PAE.

## PSYCHOLOGY AND ADULT LEARNING

Research on motives for PAE in the United States has been dominated, since the 1960s, by the focus on the individual and his or her motives for educational involvement. Within this paradigm, there are, roughly, three groups of theory: decision models, life cycle theory and motivational orientations.

### Decision models

Decision models are, more or less, independent conceptualizations which break down the conditions governing the act of participation into different elements, some personal and psychological, others social and sociological.[2] Here the focus is on the decision which leads to the action called participation, rather than on motives as such. Hence, all explanatory theories under this heading pay more attention to the conditions influencing action (element two of the idealized theory of PAE) than to the origins of learning need (element one) though some attempt to take account of both phenomena. While personality factors play a role in some of these models they are not necessarily the dominant factors, since social structure and environmental considerations are also expected to play a role. Studies characteristic of this approach include Love (1953), Boyd (1960, 1965), Miller (1967), Boshier (1973), Rubenson (1978), Grotelueschen and Caulley (1977), Cross (1981), Darkenwald and Merriam (1982), and Cookson (1983, 1986).

## Life cycle theory

Life cycle theory denotes a small number of independent studies which borrow ideas and concepts from prominent life cycle theorists, e.g. Havighurst, to explain participation. Here the basic idea, found prominently among the assumptions of andragogy, is that life stage or developmental changes in the life of the individual create needs, especially during so-called 'transitional' phases. These needs become translated into the need to learn new knowledge and skills to cope with change factors. Life cycle theory is a theory, *par excellence*, of the origin of learning need and, in specific cases, it attempts to account for the conditions influencing the decision to act (or not to act). Examples of adult developmental theory applied to adult education include Havighurst and Orr (1956), Havighurst (1963), Knox and Videbeck (1963), Phifer (1964), Marple (1969) and Aslanian and Brickell (1980).

## Motivational orientations

Motivational orientations research arose from Houle's (1961) typology of learners, and was elaborated by Boshier and others in a number of publications. Here it is on the personality or temperamental precursors of the act of PAE that emphasis is placed. PAE, according to this perspective, is a direct result of individual personality traits, temperament, or dominant motivational orientations. Thus, motivational orientations are clearly attempts to account for the origin of learning need, rather than the factors governing the actual decision to participate. Over the years, various elaborations of this theory have been produced and will be examined here. Examples of studies in this area include Houle (1961), Sheffield (1963), Boshier (1971, 1976, 1980), Burgess (1971a), Grabowski (1972), Morstain and Smart (1974), Dickinson and Clark (1975), Ordos (1980), Goodnow (1982), Boshier and Collins (1985), Clayton and Smith (1987). (For a fuller bibliography, up to 1983, see Courtney, 1984.)

## Early theory, 1952–69

One of the first attempts to go beyond the surface analysis of survey responses to the question of motive was a study of museum attendance by Nedzel (1952). She wrote of a basic attitude which distinguished participants from nonparticipants: 'The educationally motivated are those [in] whom some strong influence caused identification of excitement and adventure with education, while for the unmotivated it is a bore' (Nedzel, 1952, p. 13). Based on an analysis of responses to thirty questions by British and American researchers, Nedzel could find 'no consistent or pronounced contrasts in social and family background nor in general attitudes between those who were educationally motivated and those who were not' (p. 14). The most that she could say was that motivated types seemed generally 'more active and imaginative and identified education with adventure, whereas the unmotivated identified education chiefly with salary, and made frequent and specific mention of having disliked school and homework' (p. 14).[3]

Love (1953), too, noted the importance of an underlying orientation towards education, but went further than Nedzel. As an administrator of extension programs in the New York City College system when the GI Bill[4] began to take effect, Love addressed the question of how to attract more veterans back to school. He began with a sense that students did not differ from non-students merely in terms of their stated reasons for participation. Rather, it had something to do with a person's 'underlying attitudes towards education' (Love, 1953, p. 211). He interviewed a small sample of veterans representing a cross-section of student types in regard to sex, age and socio-economic status and a similarly matched group of non-students. (This, incidentally, is one of the few published studies to compare participants with nonparticipants).

While not designed to test a specific theory the study was guided by the need to determine 'the process through which the individual must go before he decides to enroll for evening or extension studies' (p. 212). From in-depth interviews there emerged a 'sequence of enrollment' based on two preconditions: first, to become a student a person must have an awareness of education as a positive value in the solution of problems; second, he or she must equate education with success and happiness. To participate a person must (a) have a current problem for which he or she seeks a solution, and that problem must be acute and well-defined; (b) be aware of a specific course or field of study; (c) be directed towards specific schools or programs; (d) actually enroll (pp. 210–13).

Love's is the first theory of PAE, and in some respects the only one, to account for both the origin or nature of learning need and the conditions under which learning activity is conducted. His is one of the few studies to conceive PAE, not as a single action which appears out of the blue and is located in a sea of inaction – an image that is implied in many current psychological theories – but as a *series of actions*, each of which is preceded by another action and each stage of which is accompanied by reflection and analysis. He also anticipated the concern of Houle, Boshier and others with underlying orientations to learning. He may possibly be the first and only researcher who has juxtaposed in the same study both the decision to participate and the learning orientation underlying that decision; in other words, taking account simultaneously of underlying psychological factors which are necessary in order for PAE to take place (the primary focus of those engaged in research on motivational orientation) but also of the circumstantial factors which are necessary for learning orientation to be translated into action. Love's study is important for another reason. Despite the promise inherent in the approach, his study has never been replicated or followed up, a condition which says much about the importance of research to the practice of adult education in the United States (Courtney, 1986).

Boyd (1960, 1965), who approached the study of PAE through the writings of Maslow, Erikson and Havighurst, may also have been the first to suggest a model explicitly combining a psychological perspective with that of sociology. The first dimension of his two-dimensional model consisted of factors, both psychological and sociological predisposing the individual to participate: internal, psycho-physiological conditions and also external, socio-cultural factors. The second was a series of incremental steps from 'source' to 'arousal' to 'expression' to 'reward and punishment.'

In 1962, a group forming the National Seminar on Adult Education Research convened in Chicago to discuss motivation to learn. At that meeting, Knox and Sjogren (1962) distinguished between 'motivation to participate' and 'motivation to learn.' According to the first, which they termed 'initial motivation,' the individual is guided by expectations (Rubenson, 1978) and motives of 'disequilibrium' (Boshier, 1971). The second took account of those aspects of general motivation – not however made explicit during the Chicago conference – which led to success in learning. Despite its suggestiveness, there is no evidence that this distinction became a rallying point for later research. (See Knox and Videbeck, 1963; Knox, 1977.)

LeClair (1969) is also an example of an early decision model theory in the tradition of Love, which is significant because it ties in learning with a particular social environment: the world of work. LeClair characterized the factors influencing PAE as both psychological and situational or social. He studied the relationship between 'perceived need deficiency,' the importance of need fulfillment, and the perception of education as a 'mobility facilitator' with a group of workers drawn from companies in Fort Wayne, Indiana. His findings revealed that participants, who tended to occupy higher positions within the company, showed a higher 'perceived need-deficiency' than nonparticipants, and differed also from them in the importance they attached to education as a factor in mobility. LeClair's study is important in that it directly anticipates two of the very limited number of studies of PAE in relation to the world of work: Devlin (1977) and Bergsten (1980).

This early body of work provides us with important insights. First, it says that in order to understand why adults learn, why they take part in learning activities, there must exist some underlying orientation to learning which portrays learning in a positive light and which predisposes the individual to take part in education-related activity. More specifically, those who appear eager and willing to participate in organized learning activities are distinguishable from those who are not by an underlying attitude which sees education as a positive force, to be equated with happiness, and finds in it also a mechanism for solving 'acute' problems. The various accounts differ, or are silent, on where these orientations to learning come from or how they might be related to other aspects of the personality.

Second, the more sophisticated accounts say that it is not enough to posit orientation to learning; account must also be taken of real-world, current circumstances which may or may not 'activate' the motive to learn. This is where the sociological or social component of the theory comes into play. Here PAE is conceptualized as a sequence of steps, some of which may be visible only to the participant, which eventually leads to the kind of act normally recognized as PAE, that is enrollment in a course. According to some, the person must be in a situation calling for the solution of a particular problem. This could mean situations such as obtaining a promotion, changing jobs or taking on new responsibilities in the family or the community, or it could refer to the need to learn a new set of work skills, such as might arise in situations like divorce or unemployment.

## DECISION MODEL THEORY

The title 'decision model' has been used to cover a number of otherwise independent theories which focus on PAE as the result of a conjunction of forces, conditions or factors, either of a purely psychological or quasi-sociological nature. These models are not theories of rational decision-making in the usual sense, in that they do not involve an indiviudal reviewing alternative courses of action and evaluating each course with respect to its consequences. They are decision models in so far as they attempt to imitate the conjunction of forces which might be expected to operate during a decision-making process.

What follows is a summary and analysis of six models of PAE, chosen for their currency, their general degree of explanatory sophistication, and the fact that in almost all cases the model is derived from a more generalized theory of motivation or behavior. These models are Miller (1967), Grotelueschen and Caulley (1977), Rubenson (1978), Cross (1981), Darkenwald and Merriam (1982) and Cookson (1983, 1986). The essential points of each model are summarized below. Readers are also referred to Cross (1981) for a summary of Miller, Cross, Darkenwald and Merriam.

## Miller, 1967

Love (1953) told us that a person who becomes involved in learning activities first experiences some deep-felt attitudes towards education. Learning begins with the existence of a need to learn. But where do needs come from? According to Miller, personal needs do not operate in a vacuum, they are embedded within social structures which determine and share their expression. Miller borrows Maslow's need hierarchy to offer an account of how learning needs arise and links them by implication to adult life stages. In this scenario, the early stages of life are concerned with satisfying the basic needs of physiological existence, security and love. Increasing age brings a concern with status and achievement, needs which schools and the world of work nourish. Finally, sometime in middle-age or later, the person strives for some kind of self-actualization: 'It is a rare person who begins to think about the meaning of his life and the value of self-hood before he reaches 40' (Miller, 1967, p. 7). This observation has received interesting support in Pritchard (1979), one of the few studies to apply motivational orientation theory to an older age group.

Miller's account is particularly unique in its attempt to assimilate sociological concepts – Herbert Gans's analysis of social class – within the framework of what is essentially a psychological model. Otherwise, and apart from Maslow, most of this model owes its justification to Kurt Lewin's distinction between 'driving' and 'restraining' forces (the concept of 'force-field,' in the title of Miller's monograph, is also Lewin's). Driving forces are those acting on a situation pushing it away from the status quo; restraining forces act in the opposite direction. (See Figure 1.)

PAE results when the driving forces win out over the restraining forces and nonparticipation is the result when the opposite occurs. In the case of the lower-lower class, there are more restraining than driving forces so there is little incentive to participate in adult education, which accords generally with the facts as observed by other researchers. By contrast, the lower-middle class are better-off; with them the forces all point in one, positive direction. Most of the monograph consists of tables which show,

*Figure 1* Education for vocational competence (a) Lower-lower class level, (b) Lower-middle class level

**Positive forces**

1. Survival needs
2. Changing technology
3. Safety needs of female culture
4. Government attempts to change opportunity structure

**Negative forces**

5. Action-excitement orientation of male culture
6. Hostility to education and to middle-class object-orientation
7. Relative absence of specific, immediate job opportunities after training
8. Limited access through organizational ties
9. Weak family structure

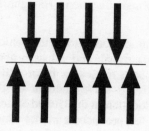

(a)

**Positive forces**

1. Satisfied survival need
2. Satisfied safety need
3. Strong status need
4. Changing technology
5. Access through organizational ties
6. Acceptance of middle-class career drives
7. Familiarity with educational processes

**Negative forces**

(b)

*Source*: Miller, 1967, pp. 21, 23.

for each social class, the 'forces' which impede or facilitate that class's involvement with education.

The problem with this analysis, despite its intuitive appeal, is that it does not square easily with the facts, as they have been uncovered in a great many of the surveys discussed in Chapter 2. The implication in Miller's model is that the higher social classes have a need for a form of learning which will satisfy the 'higher' needs, as outlined by Maslow, while among the lower classes, whose needs are tied to brute survival, educational needs, where they exist, will be tied to jobs and the market place. Yet, Miller's model shows no negative forces standing in the way of middle-class participation when we have already seen that nonparticipation in this category is significant. Furthermore, the argument that the middle class want enlightenment is contrary to most of the major survey findings in this category, e.g. McGrath, Lorimer, London. And consider the following observation:

> Middle-class people generally regard education as *instrumental*. They make up a vast majority of those who pursue education as adults. Their jobs require their continual education. They tend to raise their children, to look after their business and to conduct themselves as citizens with the aid of reading, study, and formal and informal education. (Havighurst, 1963, p. 23; emphasis mine)

The thrust of this argument is that adult education appears to be the vehicle *par excellence* for the promotion of middle-class goals and values, a point that Miller (1967) and Cross (1981) have both missed, a point which continues to be missed by those who offer a naive account of the relationship between social class and adult education in the United States.

Miller, on the positive side of the ledger, has produced a model which accounts for both the origin of learning need and the conditions which influence the decision to participate. Furthermore, the depiction of educational involvement as a function of the balance between driving and restraining forces is a particularly dynamic one, permitting an ever-changing configuration of these forces, sometimes pushing mostly one way, the next pushing the other. It is also incidentally a view of reality that might be presented to research subjects for their reactions and elaborations.


## Rubenson, 1978

If the experience of need is a critical factor in beginning the 'drive' to participate then this appears to place the weight on *current circumstances* rather than *past history*. This is the emphasis in Rubenson's model. This Swedish researcher (1978) has written extensively on the subject of recruiting minorities or otherwise disadvantaged groups to 'recurrent' education. It is within this context that he has formulated an 'ahistorical' model of PAE which depicts participation as a decision arising out of current circumstances rather than past events. Thus, indirectly he is offering an account of how Miller's 'status quo' might change, something Miller himself does not do. This theory rests on the finding of significant amounts of educational involvement among people normally judged to be nonparticipants provided the researcher is willing to go far enough back in time, for example five years. In other words, over the long run, a majority of persons undertake some form of organized learning making it easier to predict participatory behavior from a person's current personal and social status than from longer-term 'stable values or psychological configurations.'[5] Within such an account, participants could be distinguished from nonparticipants better in terms of current differences in lifestyle and occupational status than in terms of more abiding psychological variables. This is also in line with Love's hypothesis that basic orientations towards learning are necessary but not sufficient to explain PAE.

Needs, as such, however, do not lead unerringly to the pursuit of education. As we saw with Love's study there must be a linking of a current 'problem' (or need) with education. Miller speaks about the changing nature of the life cycle giving rise to different (Maslovian) needs, but makes no case for why the experience of these needs should become 'learning' needs. Rubenson accommodates this distinction with his category, 'perception of needs,' but basically, apart from his concepts of 'expectancy' and 'valence,' leaves the distinction between 'current needs' and their 'perception' unexplored. (See Figure 2.)

Rubenson, like Miller, places strong emphasis on social structure and the degree to which an individual's decision-making may be determined 'from above.' PAE is not the single act of a single individual but the result of accumulated experiences as a member of a group. Drawing on Newcomb's concept of member and reference groups he points to differences in perception among white-collar and blue-collar workers, perceptions towards activities like education which are much more determined by group norms in the former than in the latter.

How does need get translated into action? The decision to participate, according to Rubenson, results from the interaction of 'expectancy' and 'valence,' terms drawn also from the work of Lewin. Expectancy, in this context, is a combination of a person's expectation that education will bring benefits and that he or she will be able to participate and complete the program. Valence means the individual's sense of the value of education. Expectancy is determined by 'perception and interpretation of the environment,' a deeper and more generalized sense of one's place in the world which is shaped through actual properties of the environment (the degree of 'hierarchic structure' and the values of both member and reference groups), as well as institutional policies which tend to facilitate or inhibit participation. Perception of the environment is also influenced by the individual's experience of needs as well as by an 'active preparedness,' in part determined by temperament and other biopsychological conditions over which the individual presumably has little control. The experience of needs will determine the value an individual places on education; this and 'expectancy' make up the 'force' which is 'the strength where will determines behavior' (p. 22).

Rubenson is in good company in his adaptation of 'expectancy-value'

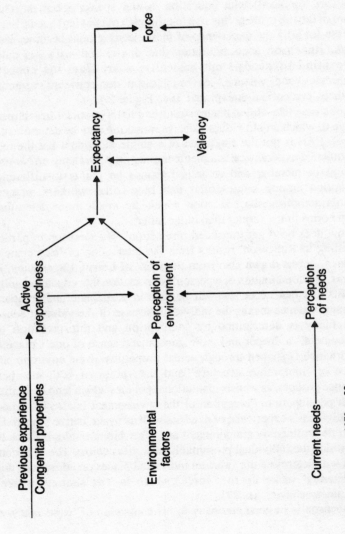

*Figure 2* Rubenson's paradigm of recruitment in recurrent education

*Source:* Rubenson, 1978, p. 22.
By permission of the author.

theory. Much has been made of this close-to-commonsense account of why people act as they do, applicable in contexts as diverse as the world of work or collective social action (for example, the work by Klandermans in the area of 'mobilization theory'; Klandermans and Oegema, 1987). In contrast with the earlier drive theories (Cofer and Appley, 1964), the charm of this theory lies in its ability to deal with actions such as PAE as forms of rationality rather than the outcome of hidden drives which appear not to be under the control of the individual. In Rubenson's account, however, the precise ways in which the 'early' elements fuse with the 'later' elements is left unexplained. What, for example, is 'previous experience' experience of? If it means experience of the world in general, it is clearly too broad. If, on the other hand, we took it to mean experience of learning at some other point in time, this would indeed be an important asset to the model since it would capture an important insight of other research in this area (Sjogren, Knox and Grotelueschen, 1968; Ray, 1981), namely, that current PAE is more strongly predicted by previous PAE than by almost any other psychological factor.

Despite its native appeal, however, Rubenson's account has not received the attention it deserves. Nor would it be very difficult to test, assuming that the 'early' elements of the model, as suggested above, could be made more precise and translatable in terms appropriate to the discussion of learning.

## Grotelueschen and Caulley, 1977

Miller and Rubenson are juxtaposed to show the degree to which two models can be similar when based on an identity of theoretical origin and yet quite different in what either researcher sees as significant in the phenomenon under scrutiny. Two features distinguish the work of Grotelueschen and Caulley (1977) from most of the decision models discussed here: their exclusive concern with 'professional' participation, and their adaptation of the ideas of the social-psychologist, Martin Fishbein, to the analysis of PAE. It should be noted, however, that Fishbein's own work is also based on an expectancy-value model, so here again the association with Lewin's work is strong.

The Fishbein model depends on a distinction being made between belief, attitude, intention and behavior. The particular rationale for this derives partly at least from a general concern among psychologists of the 1940s and 1950s, that while they had come close to defining and measuring attitudes scientifically, they were not finding a clearcut relationship between attitudes and behavior. It became clear that beliefs and attitudes might set up predisposing conditions to behave in certain ways, but that behavior itself was governed by other factors also. Beliefs and attitudes, in other words, determined intentions to behave but not behavior itself.

According to Fishbein, 'behavioral intentions' were determined by three factors: an attitude, a social normative factor and a personal normative factor. In the case of PAE by professionals, a person's attitude is a function of his or her beliefs about the efficacy or inefficacy of further education or training. It is the relationship between belief and attitude which calls forth the notion of 'expectancy-valence.' The social normative factor refers to what the professional thinks most people who are important to him think about his participating in continuing education; the personal normative factor reflects the person's beliefs about whether or not he or she *should* participate, and his or her motivation for complying with this belief.

One of the few attempts to test this model, however, has not been positive. Ray (1981), of the University of Wisconsin, applied the model to 'therapeutic recreational professionals' attending a three-day symposium in the Midwest. Questions which measure 'behavioral intention' were embedded in an evaluation instrument. Unexpectedly, Ray's findings ran counter to his hypotheses: 'Prior experience appears to be a much more reliable estimate of future behavior [rather than intention to behave], and more parsimonious' (p. 74).

Nevertheless, there may yet be promise in this approach. Nowadays, Fishbein's original analysis has evolved into what has been called the 'Theory of Reasoned Action' (Young and Kent, 1985; Pryor, 1990), according to which the decision to participate in a learning experience may actually be a series of decisions each involving discrete sets of behaviors, for example reading a catalogue, registering for a particular program, listening to a lecture. The link between PAE as a set of decisions and as a series of actions is clearly too obvious to be ignored.

## Cross, 1981

While Miller and Rubenson appear content with PAE as a single act resulting from a conjunction of forces (though Rubenson does have a category 'previous experience' which may imply previous acts of learning), PAE as the result of a series of actions or 'chains of response' is central to Cross's (1981) model. (See Figure 3.) An essential element in Love's model and implied in Boyd (1965), it means that PAE is not so much an isolated, single action beginning linearly after a period of thought, as a change within an ongoing set of actions from one *form* of action to another. For Cross, drawing on recent work in the area of 'social motivation' (Brody, 1980; Atkinson and Birch, 1970), PAE occurs within a stream of action, much of it habituated, and thus competes with other forms of action

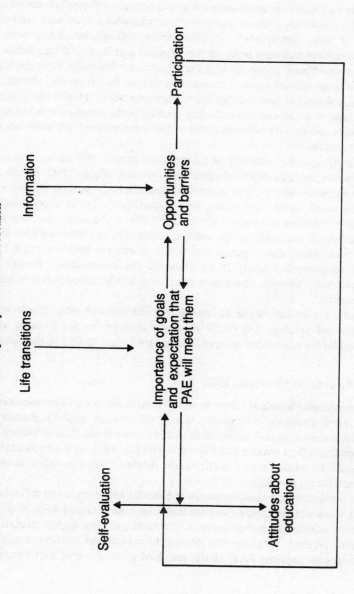

*Figure 3* Cross's chain of response model for participation in adult education

*Source:* Cross, 1981, p. 124
By permission of the publishers.

because it may be an unusual or less common alternative to habituated forms. Apart from Love, this is perhaps the only place in the literature that the character of PAE as a complex rather than simple action is described, and where the distinction between learning as a habit or as a unique, not-repeated act is hinted at.

Her model also contains Rubenson's 'expectancy-valence' components which she combines into one category, 'attitudes about education' and the notion of 'life transitions' borrowed from Havighurst. Also, where Darkenwald and Merriam separate out 'stimuli' and 'barriers' (see below), these become Cross's 'opportunities and barriers.' Similarly, both she and Cookson (see below) have a component called 'information,' meaning awareness about the possibilities for further education. This is the second step in Love's sequence, and reflects a finding in the survey literature that individuals and groups differ in terms of the information each holds about adult education.

Cross stresses the ordering of factors. The positioning of barriers and opportunities suggests that while their removal will 'trigger' PAE for many people, for many others it will make no difference because their motivation has been weak in the first place; this is due, possibly, to a poor 'self-evaluation,' the first element in the chain. While Rubenson suggested the applicability of his model to an understanding of why people of low SES fail to participate, Cross points out that research on PAE over the last decade supports her analysis by showing the tremendous growth in participation by women, now that many traditional 'external barriers' have been removed.

Cross's model has begun to receive the attention of other researchers (Dolphin and Schrage, 1989). Of all of the decision model theories, this may well be the one which receives greater study and testing in the future.

## Darkenwald and Merriam, 1982

Darkenwald and Merriam have chosen to emphasize social-environmental forces, particularly socio-economic status, not because 'individual traits or attitudes are unimportant but because less is known about their influence on participation' (Darkenwald and Merriam, 1982, p. 142). In this respect they are closer to Miller's and Rubenson's themes than the other models discussed here. (See Figure 4.)

The pre-adulthood components of the model are intended to reflect the current wisdom that family environment, especially IQ and SES, strongly determine aspirations and attainment in school and later higher education. 'Learning Press,' meaning the degree to which the current situation encourages or requires PAE, is the result of general social participation,

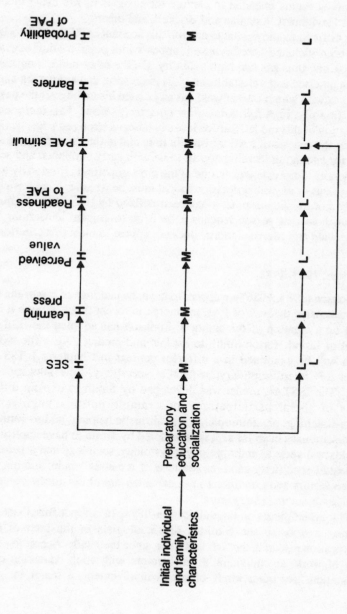

*Figure 4* Psychosocial interaction model of participation in organized adult education

*Source:* Darkenwald and Merriam, 1982, p. 143. By permission of the publishers.

The figure shows a flow from "Initial individual and family characteristics" to "Preparatory education and socialization" leading through the following stages, each marked at High (H), Medium (M), and Low (L) levels:

- SES
- Learning press
- Perceived value
- Readiness to PAE
- PAE stimuli
- Barriers
- Probability of PAE

occupational complexity and lifestyle. The value of PAE as perceived by the individual resembles Rubenson's 'valence' factor. Participation stimuli are 'triggers' such as job change or the need for self-expression, which will prompt PAE in the absence of 'barriers,' which will block it. In this regard, their model seems intended to capture the insights of life cycle theorists such as Havighurst, Aslanian and Brickell, and others.

It is difficult to know what to do with this account of PAE and its origins. It has been included here because it appears in a popular adult education textbook and thus has had high visibility. On the other hand, it appears to be both untested and untestable, and it is interesting that among the harvest of studies with which Darkenwald has associated his name over the past ten years (mainly in *Adult Education Quarterly*) none has included an elaboration of this model. Suffice it to say here, its strongest point lies in its pushing the genesis of PAE far back in time and in thus suggesting that the seeds for later adult learning appear to lie with early childhood and school experiences. Surely, however, one of the most important criterion by which to judge this or any other decision model must be whether it depicts within the logic of the situation, as it has been defined by the individual man or woman, how that person reaches a decision to engage in learning. The Darkenwald and Merriam model does not appear to meet this criterion.

### Cookson, 1983, 1986

In Cookson (1983, 1986) we appear to have the makings of one of the more comprehensive theories of PAE to emerge in recent times, though it is not based on a creation of the author's. Cookson has adopted the 'ISSTAL' model of David Horton Smith to explain and predict PAE. (The work of Smith will be examined in a different context in Chapter 5.) 'ISSTAL' stands for 'interdisciplinary, sequential specificity, time allocation, life span.' The ISSTAL model was developed by Smith to explain different forms of social participation, for example political involvement, media-watching, philanthropic giving, altruistic helping, and so forth. It is interdisciplinary in so far as it is considered by Smith to have applicability to fields as diverse as anthropology, physiology, sociology and psychology. Sequential specificity captures the idea of a causal 'chain' linking more remote factors and conditions to ones which are closer to the context in which PAE occurs. (See Figure 5.)

With his emphasis on time-allocation-life-span components, Cookson is opening a door to the findings of sociologists in the area of social participation research, the first invitation since the 1960s. According to this body of work, an individual's involvement with adult education carries implications for other kinds of social involvement, a major insight of

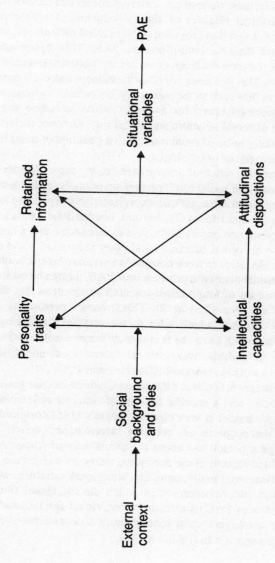

*Figure 5* Cookson's adaptation of the ISSTAL model of participation in adult education

**External context** → **Social background and roles** → **Personality traits** / **Retained information** / **Intellectual capacities** / **Attitudinal dispositions** → **Situational variables** → **PAE**

*Source:* Cookson, 1983, p. 70.
Copyright - D.H. Smith, 1980. By permission of the author.

London *et al.*'s and one to which Cookson responds here: '[PAE] is thus conceptualized as part of an overall behavior pattern of social participation' (Cookson, 1983, p. 70). And elsewhere: '[PAE] is treated as a form of individual discretionary behavior, a consequent of the combined and interactive influence of six classes of ... variables' (Cookson, 1986, p. 131). What are these classes of variables?

At the furthest remove are 'external contextual factors' which consist of actual physical features of the environment, for example climate and geography, as well as cross-national, cultural differences, whose combined effects set limiting conditions on PAE. This list would also include disparate factors such as government policies towards investment in education. This is a category of extraordinary catch-all proportions, whose usefulness has yet to be seriously defended. Rubenson's category of environmental factors, for example, while including the not-unfamiliar concepts of social structure and social role, does not include topographical factors likely to be of more interest to a geographer or a climatologist than to a sociologist or psychologist.

Second, in order of importance, come those factors termed 'social background and social role': perception of one's health, perception of early schooling experience, unique experiential history, socio-economic status, position in the life cycle, current occupational status, organizational membership, and leisure style. It is in this sector that Cookson locates the influence of formal education and other indexes of socio-economic status on PAE. He refers to work designed to measure how schooling may interact with personal history to produce later PAE, though he omits interesting and rare examples of longitudinal research pertinent to this topic, e.g. Suyder (1951), etc. (see Chapter 2). Third, come 'personality and intellectual capacity' factors, which refer to the relatively enduring aspects of the individual which he or she brings to different situations. Such factors might be said to underlie motivational orientations, and Cookson discusses Boshier's work on personality in this context.[6]

Fourth are 'attitudinal dispositions,' which include both a 'general value orientation,' and a specific attitude of 'interest in learning' (p. 73). Here Cookson's model is very close to Houle's (1961) original typology. Then comes the property of 'retained information,' which may reflect the knowlege a person has about the availability of resources for learning (a highlighted feature of the Johnstone study, as well as the models of Cross and Rubenson). Finally, there are 'situational variables' which arise within the immediate environment in which the individual finds himself. Here Cookson sees PAE as a 'form of individual discretionary behavior most directly contingent upon [one's] immediate awareness and definition of situations specific to [PAE]' (p. 73).

Cookson concludes his report by insisting, significantly, that the ISSTAL model brings together previously unrelated bodies of research, while testing the premise that PAE is a species of social participation in general. To date, however, no one has accepted Cookson's challenge to test this rather cumbersome and statistically daunting theoretical package, and there are serious doubts as to whether it may ever be truly put to the test.

## LIFE CYCLE THEORY

Life cycle theory, as the term is employed here, refers to those research forms and methodologies whose central concern is the outline, investigation and analysis of adult development, in all its various phases and stages (Lasker and Moore, 1980). It also goes by the label 'adult psychology' or 'lifespan developmental psychology' (Bischoff, 1976; Baltes and Lipsitt, 1980). The central project of this branch of psychology is to discover underlying but distinct regularities occurring over the lifespan, especially after the end of the first two decades. Issues of stability and change dominate the agenda, with researchers studying, in turn, personality change, patterns of socialization, responses to major life events, and the overall mode of dealing with life's developmental tasks (Clausen, 1986). Names commonly associated with this field include Erikson, Levinson, Gould, and Vaillant.

Life cycle theory got a relatively late start. For many years the notion of 'development' was synonymous with the growth of the child, both biologically and psychologically. Second, with the influence of figures such as Freud, and also through the influence of adolescent psychologists such as the great Stanley Hall, research stopped at the gates of adulthood, confident there was very little to interest it without. Gradually the picture changed. First came Jung, a contemporary of Freud whose interest, encyclopediac at the best of times, ranged over the entire span of the human life. Then, with more deliberateness in the writings of Buhler, Neugarten and others, there occurred a tilt towards the adult years and a growing belief that here too could be found growth and patterns of significance.

Havighurst, practically unique in this field for his ability to write confidently in both psychology and sociology, went so far as to say that '[adulthood] is a developmental period in almost as complete a sense as childhood and adolescence are developmental periods' (Havighurst and Orr, 1956, p. 1). It was Havighurst also who popularized the phrase, 'developmental task,' which he conceptualized as midway between an individual need and a societal demand ('a task which must be achieved at or about a certain phase in life, if a person is to be judged and to judge himself as a competent person' – Havighurst, 1973, p. 19). Havighurst's position is that life consists of a long series of tasks, the successful learning of which brings rewards and social approval, while the failure to learn draws to it unhappiness, social disapproval and difficulty with later tasks. Relevant to the subject of the present study and an issue to which we shall return in the following chapters, developmental tasks reflect the two fundamental functions which, Havighurst believed, education fulfills: the *instrumental* function, according to which the person uses education to accomplish an external goal, and the *expressive* function, where the goal lies within the act of learning. Tasks connected with the instrumental functions include preparing for an occupation, rearing children, making a comfortable home, and so on (p. 20). Those connected with the expressive function include becoming a member of a friendship group, choosing a marriage partner, becoming a club or association member, etc.[7]

Thus, while Havighurst has contributed significant amounts to our understanding of the motivational factors behind learning in adulthood, he has also insisted that we interpret PAE within the broader scope of a society and its functions and not simply as a reflection of individual motivation alone. During the middle and later 1950s much of his work interwove both themes (Havighurst and Orr, 1956; Havighurst and Neugarten, 1957; Havighurst, 1963, 1973).

In recent years, lifespan developmental psychology appears to have gravitated around two distinct approaches to the adult years. According to the first, the so-called 'phase' approach (Lasker and Moore, 1980), adulthood is characterized by relatively stable periods or phases, interspersed by more turbulent periods of 'transition.' Both phases and the transitions between them are age-related (Levinson, 1978; Gould, 1978). According to the second, the so-called 'stage' approach, researchers claim that, irrespective of age, the human organism goes through a definite sequence of developmental stages of increasing complexity. The concept of maturity is more easily associated with this approach than with the first.[8]

Though use of the term 'development' to refer to patterns of regularity and correlated behaviors in adulthood seems to suggest that the same kind of biological factors are at work as in childhood, sociologists like Clausen (1986) have insisted that adult life stages are really *psychological* (concerned with adaptation), *sociological* (concerned with socialization), and *historical* (concerned with the effects of culture over time), rather than *biological* (concerned with physical development and maturation of the organism). That is the position taken here. I accept the view that major forms of biological development have reached a natural end by the time the person nears the customary age of adulthood (though it is of course important to avoid circularity of definition here). However, this does not mean the absence of major changes, both in life situation and perspective, through the adult years. It does, however, mean that we should not seek the causes of such change in biological destiny.

The idea that adults continue to grow and change over the lifespan and that this may require or create an interest in learning is the kind of straightforward relationship which would be expected to appeal to those interested in adult motivation for learning. Educators such as Knowles have been quick to oblige. Across a considerable array of writings (Knowles, 1980, for example), we are told that the motivation to learn in adulthood arises from the developmental tasks which adults are expected to perform, the social roles they occupy, and the changes which they encounter in occupation, family and life position. And yet, oddly enough, the direct test of such a relationship has been rare. Despite its obviousness, too often the idea that adults learn because they have entered transitions or are responding to developmental tasks is easier to assume than to prove. Isolated exceptions have been Phifer (1964) and Marple (1969).

Phifer examined changes of interest between young and later adulthood among participants in adult education programs, applying Jung's concept of the life cycle and Havighurst's developmental tasks. Marple (1969) analyzed factors governing the desire to participate in adult education using Buhler's four basic life tendencies: creative expansion, maintaining internal order, need-satisfaction, and self-limiting adaptation. Despite the innovativeness of the study and the correlation of life-tendencies with other psychological and social variables, few of the findings were statistically significant. Perhaps the most well-known effort to correlate theories of the life cycle with motivation is a study done by Aslanian and Brickell at the end of the 1970s.

## Aslanian and Brickell, 1980

The paucity of studies linking PAE to the life cycle gives Aslanian and Brickell (1980) exaggerated importance to this category of research. Drawing on major lifespan theorists such as Gould, Levinson, Neugarten, Vaillant, and Knox they developed a theory, central to which is the notion of a transition. According to this, adults experience problems of disequilibrium as they move from one stage to the next. Transitions may be provoked by internal, psychobiological factors, or precipitated by social and economic forces, such as the period of rapid change experienced by contemporary generations of Americans. Whatever the source, however, it appeared to Aslanian and Brickell that transitions might be periods which call for additional or new learning by the adult.

This led them to a general formulation: 'Moving from one status in life to another requires the learning of new knowledge, new skills, and/or new attitudes or values' (p. 34). At the same time, adults cope with transitions differently, due to the occurrence of 'life events' (Levinson's 'marker events' and Vaillant's 'stressors') which 'triggered' the 'latent desire to learn.' This led them to a second general formulation: 'Some identifiable event triggers an adult's decision to learn at a particular point in time' (p. 37).

In an analysis which suggests Tough (1968), the adult sees a benefit to be gained from the move from one status to another; the purpose of learning is the securing of that benefit. Triggers, on the other hand, are actual events like having a baby, joining the Army, getting fired or having a heart attack. The model to emerge from this defines the occurrence of learning as a chain, with the following elements: all transitions are periods of the life cycle which require learning; certain visible events or conditions signal the arrival of those transitions; and it is during these conditions that learning is most desirable or likely to occur.

In a national study by the authors of those who had participated in adult education over the previous twelve months (some 50 per cent of the sample, as reported in Chapter 2), 83 per cent acknowledged that their learning experience was connected with a transition or 'life change'; 17 per cent said it was not. From their analysis, it further becomes clear that the minority were those whom Houle would have described as 'learning-oriented': they learned for the sake of learning, and the activity itself was both the benefit and the end sought. For the majority, however, learning was a means, not an end; the satisfaction would come later and not from the learning experience; and learning was 'utilitarian' rather than 'its own justification' (p. 51).

Even allowing for the flexibility of its major constructs, life cycle theory faces substantial problems. Typically, for example, studies like that of Aslanian and Brickell do not provide a detailed anatomy of the movement from the transition phase to the act of participation. We are told, for example, that a woman who experiences a divorce and has a need to reenter the job market will engage in adult education in order to replenish old job skills or learn new ones. Why then do not all divorced women behave in the same way? What is it that makes some more inclined to PAE than others? How does that person get from her experience of divorce – incidentally an extraordinarily complex emotional trauma that, like most human experiences related to learning, receives only the thinnest of treatments in the literature as a whole – to contemplating adult education, rather than suicide for example, and from that 'experience' to actually getting involved? If the notion of universal developmental tasks can account for the origin of the need to learn, why is it that not everyone who is passing through a particular transition actually engages in visible learning activities? Why is visible learning still a minority affair?

Answers to these questions require other dimensions than those provided by Aslanian and Brickell. There is speculative research like that of London and Ewing (1982) which attempts to prove that developmental priorities and subsequent tasks vary with different age 'cohorts,' groups which have lived through different historical periods. Compare, for example, those now in their '70s and '80s who experienced the full effects of the Depression during what would normally have been their most productive work years with the 'organizational man' who began his career during the suburban 1950s. Could we expect the developmental priorities of these respective groups to be the same? (Again remember McGrath's and Lorimer's findings on the strength of the vocational motive in times of adversity.) Thus, while it is certainly the case that there are internal, age-related forces pushing people along certain life paths, there are also social, historical forces which may exert a greater effect. On top of that there are *cultural* differences which affect whole groups and classes of people and which result in different groups reacting to life cycle forces in different ways. Compare, for example, differences in the experiences of Blacks and Hispanics in the US in the last hundred years, a topic which would take us beyond the scope of the current treatment but which clearly belongs in any discussion of adult learning in the United States.

## MOTIVATIONAL ORIENTATION RESEARCH

Motivational orientation (MO) research, as expounded chiefly in the writings of Roger Boshier, commands our attention because it is the only approach to PAE where there has been a sustained effort to replicate and develop the findings of others. In other words, it is one of the very few areas of adult education research to exhibit a defining feature of the scientific enterprise in general: the collective analysis, replication and elaboration of empirical findings. Second, it is currently the only area of PAE research where we can see played out the relationship between the expression of motive and the tendency to become involved in learning activities. Finally, through his work on participation, Boshier has brought a microscope to the research enterprise in a way which has raised serious questions about its quality and relevance to practice.

If we include Boshier's work around persistence and dropout also within this context, then MO research is probably the most highly developed theory of PAE, which is why it demands our attention here. As such, it occupies the research stage more centrally than any of the others by commanding the interest and allegiance of other researchers, so that today a fairly substantial body of knowledge exists in and around the MO concept. Interested readers are referred to Courtney (1984) for a detailed examination of its history.

## The influence of Cyril Houle

MO theory is a collection of studies which all grew out of Houle's seminal study of 1961. Much has been made of the typology which this former professor at the University of Chicago formulated to describe the differences between the educational goals of a small group of continuing learners in the Chicago area. Prior to this no one had offered an 'internal' theory of PAE. That is to say, no one had offered a theory of adult motivation to learn that appeared not to borrow major theoretical constructs from outside of the field of adult education. What Houle accomplished in his influential study was to show that the many superficially distinct reasons and motives for PAE which appeared with regularity in national surveys and the many examples of clientele analysis were really reflections of a smaller number of fundamental 'learning orientations.' To achieve this Houle focused on the conscious world of the individual participant and his or her values and beliefs.

The result is the now famous typology of 'goal-oriented,' 'activity-oriented,' and 'learning-oriented.' Epitomized by the phrase, 'knowledge for the sake of knowledge,' the learning orientation appears to capture the essence of the liberal tendency in education where the motivation for engagement with the learning process is internal to it: learning is the end, not the means. The goal-orientation reflects the idea that most people have some specific purpose or objective in pursuing education. The activity-orientation defines those who seek in education an opportunity to pursue non-educational objectives, for example the need to establish personal relationships, to be with others of like mind, to escape a boring home or job environment, and so forth.

Since the publication of Houle (1961) a considerable – by adult education standards – body of work has grown up around the typology and attempts to prove or disprove it. From this body of work the following generalizations can be drawn. First, with some few exceptions, most of factors discovered by researchers investigating MOs appear to conform to the structure of Houle's original typology, even if the fit is occasionally rather forced. Second, every researcher since Houle has discovered more than three factors.[9] At the same time no one has claimed to have refuted or 'falsified' the typology. Third, which factors are uncovered and how they are named depends on which scale is being used and whose theory is being followed.[10] Houle's learning-oriented has become Sheffield's (1962) learning-oriented and Morstain and Smart's (1974) Cognitive Interest. His goal-oriented divided into Sheffield's Personal Goal and Societal Goal, while these, respectively, became Morstain and Smart's Professional Advance and Social Welfare. Similarly, Houle's activity-oriented became Sheffield's Desire-Activity and Need-Activity oriented, and these, respectively, became Morstain and Smart's Social Relations and Escape/Stimulation.

The learning-orientation, named Cognitive Interest by Boshier and those who have followed his theory, has been the most consistently discovered of all factors. Simply put, there are no studies which have not found it. Of all of the orientations distinguishing among participants with different motives, this had the clearest identity in Houle's eyes. The goal- and activity-orientations have not remained unchanged, however, a development partly suggested in Houle's original description of the types. Goal orientation, for example, appears to contain two somewhat distinct or complementary halves: a *personal* side whereby the goal in question benefits the individual and no other, and a *social* side whereby the expected beneficiary is the community or society at large. The personal goal-orientation has often emerged as an occupational or professional factor, suggesting reasons and motives connected with the world of work. The activity-orientation, likewise, appears to contain two complementary sides: the more 'negative' need to get away from boredom, and the more 'positive' desire to cultivate new friendships. In Boshier's writings, the first of these sub-orientations becomes a classic example of what the author, following Maslow, calls a 'deficiency' motive, while the latter resembles the 'growth' motivated.

Besides these major orientations, others have been located which do not fit any of the above categories. The most important is a factor, variously named 'External Expectations' (Boshier, 1977; Boshier and Collins, 1985) or the 'Desire to Comply with Formal Requirements' (Burgess, 1971b) which suggests that the individual is being compelled to participate in response to outside influences or pressures, rather than from any self-generated feelings of attraction or necessity.

## Motivational orientations as an explanation of PAE

MO studies have been, in the main, attempts to describe and refine the structure of Houle's basic typology. The question which naturally arises here is, Are MOs in themselves sufficient to cause PAE? Is there a direct relationship between dominant types (of motivation) and actual involvement with educational activities? To some extent, answers to these questions have been attempted by Sheffield (1962), Bennet (1968), Burgess (1971a), Sovie (1972), Dickinson and Clark (1975), King (1980) and

Hawes (1981). In most of the studies which correlate MO with PAE, the latter is never directly measured. Instead, a respondent is given a scale and asked to indicate for each activity on it, whether he or she has partaken of this activity over a specified period. One of the more popular of these scales, Litchfield's *Leisure Activity Scale* (LAS), was developed at the University of Chicago as part of a dissertation and intended for measuring the kinds of educative activities which people voluntarily undertake in their spare time. Sheffield (1962) found learning-orientation to have the highest correlation with PAE as measured by LAS. Next in rank came the personal goal orientation. While the other orientations did not correlate significantly with PAE, 'greater percentage of the Social Goal oriented were in the two higher [activities] quartiles . . . than was the case with those holding other orientations' (p. 85).

Bennet (1968) using Sheffield's scale measured the relationship between MOs and the extent of PAE over a five-year period. Comparing participants and nonparticipants among a group of Air Force nurses, he found that both held the Need-Fulfillment orientation as their 'major orientation.' Analyzing correlations for participating nurses only, Bennet agreed with Sheffield that the learning and personal goal orientations were better predictors of PAE than any of the others. At the same time, he noted that the values of the correlations for these two were so low as to be of little practical value. Incidentally, with regard to the main reason for conducting the study, Bennet found no relationship between the extent of participation and officer effectiveness ratings, raising questions about the accepted wisdom of some forms of continuing professional education.

Sovie (1972), who correlated her orientations with twelve continuing education activities on a sample of nurses, both participants and 'potential' participants, came up with a similar finding. Only the learning and personal goal orientations significantly distinguished betweeen both groups. Dickinson and Clark (1975), who also studied nurses, distinguished between 'self-education' and 'continuing education.' Correlating measures of both with their seven discovered orientations they found that the most significant relationships occurred between self-education and three orientations: Interaction, Learning, and Occupational Goal. Unlike other MO researchers, Dickinson and Clark uncovered three rather than two activity factors, two of which resembled Sheffield's factors. The third, Interaction, was made up of four items borrowing from both of the other activity-oriented factors.

The most unusual finding, apart from the correlation of the 'Interaction' factor with 'self-education,' concerned what the authors termed 'professional goal' orientation. The latter, which Sheffield termed 'personal goal,' has usually shown one of the highest correlations with PAE. In this study the correlation was high, but the direction was not. Professional Goal was negatively correlated with PAE: 'Thus, those nurses whose reasons for participating were more related to professional competence were less likely to participate, suggesting that learning activities may be perceived as having little effect on the quality of professional practice' (p. 13).

Burgess (1971a), in one of the most comprehensive surveys of the typology, found that approximately one-third of his entire sample of over 1,000 could be characterized by a single dominant orientation, with the Desire to Know being the most prevalent and the Desire to Escape being the least so. (Nicholson, 1955, incidentally, found something similar.) This means that over two-thirds of the sample exhibited two or more dominant orientations for PAE. Burgess constructed twenty profiles based on 'factor scores,' that is how highly a respondent rated an individual item as being influential in his or her decision to participate. The most prevalent profile was a pairing of personal goal with social goal. Of the twenty profiles, the highest activity score – more frequent and intense participation – was achieved by a combination of the Desire to Know and Desire to Reach a Social Goal. The combination of Desire to Know and Personal Goal ranked a distant second. Generally speaking, profiles composed of more than one orientation were more likely to have higher activity scores than those composed of a single orientation only. This suggested that while particular orientations may reflect a stronger interest in learning than others, it is really the combination of orientations which produces PAE, rather than single orientations in isolation from each other.

Thus, in all of these cases where a direct test of the relationship has been conducted, the results give but lukewarm support to the reality of MOs as causes of participation. If it can be assumed, and all the indications favor this viewpoint, that Houle intended to isolate individual dominant orientations which underlie the act of participation, the evidence suggests that a majority of participants are characterized by more than one orientation, and that it is combinations of orientations rather than dominant orientations taken separately which have the greatest power in predicting PAE.

## COMMON THEMES AND PROBLEMS

Concerns for the individual rather than the larger social unit characterize the major psychological approaches to participation. With the exception of Houles's interpretation of orientations, however, most of the studies encountered here are more *social*-psychological than psychological. That is to say, while the models of Miller, Rubenson, and others focus on individual perceptions and interpretation of the environment within which learning is to take place, sociological considerations appear to play as important a role as psychological factors in finally determining the likelihood that people will try to learn. Indeed, in Cookson's model there is a clear recognition that PAE is but one example of a host of participatory relationships, so far not specified.

In general, each of the major types of psychological explanation measures a fraction of the total reality. Decision models depict the relationship between the various factors which researchers feel are important in determining PAE, but they do not spell out the content of these factors. For example, Cross has a component called 'life transitions' but it is left to the life cycle theorists to describe and analyze what is involved here. Various models share a view of the importance of perceptions and expectations concerning the value of education as major determinants in the PAE calculus. What they are talking about here may be orientations, though they appear to be reluctant to invoke personality theory.

On the positive side, it looks as if decision models could benefit from inclusion of the MO concept. MOs may be what Rubenson had in mind when he spoke about perceptual 'filter,' that which comes between actual reality and the factors of expectancy and valence, determining the mathematical values of both, as it were. If so, we have moved much further along the road in now being able, at least tentatively, to answer the question: what is meant by 'perception and interpretation of the environment' (Rubenson), 'perceived value of education' (Darkenwald and Merrian), 'attitudinal dispositions' (Cookson), or 'attitudes about education' (Cross). In all of these cases, we would be talking about a single psychological reality: orientations towards learning.

Both decision and life cycle theorists see PAE as a form of action resulting from contemporary pushes and pulls. On this they are all agreed. At the same time, and with the exception of Cross, they are more preoccupied with the antecedents of PAE than with PAE itself as a form of action. Yet, as we saw in that important but underused study by Love (1953), PAE was not a single, dichotomous action – whatever that might be – but a chain of actions, or a *change* of action (as in Cross's model), each subject to some type of decision-making, however rudimentary. The notion that PAE is a 'sum' of activities rather than a single action is also part of Cookson's model. Of all of the psychologically oriented models of PAE the one that focuses most on PAE from the perspective of participation rather than motivation is Knox and Videbeck (1963), a study which is also important for its framing of the problem in sociological terms as we shall see later.

Ambiguities and puzzles concerning how we are to get – theoretically speaking – from thought to action, from motive to participation, dog most psychological approaches to this problem. It is essentially the problem of how do we derive a set of behaviors or actions based only on our knowledge of motives and motivational antecedents. The problem is not new to psychology. (See Atkinson and Birch, 1970, for example.) From its earliest days, researchers have found it difficult to predict behavior on the basis of attitude or belief. Hence, as we saw above, the concept of a 'behavioral tendency' or 'reasoned action' which stops short of action but would definitely result in it, were the circumstances right. Naturally, this kind of reasoning begs many questions, not the least of which is the question of what kind of evidence would satisfy our basic question, Why do adults learn? Does a question like this always require the concept of motive or are there other ways of framing it which might satisfy the intention behind the question without invoking the concept of motive? This is one of the key questions to be addressed in the following chapter.

# 4 Adult learning as motivation and action

Many surveys and analyses have been made . . . [There are] statistics on achievement; census data; information on motives for study . . . Interests and needs are commonly recognized. But when do they become motives – movers – in the literal sense of the term?

(Beals and Brody, 1941)

The quest for the causes of adult learning can take us in either of two directions. It may be a search for the origins of learning need or orientation. It may be a search for the conditions under which adults are likely to participate or not participate in organized forms of learning. Survey research, as examined in Chapter 2, is in reality both searches without the surveyors being aware that they are so engaged. For the isolation of demographic variables, such as education, age, which correlate strongly with measures of PAE, is in reality a quest for the conditions which are responsible for adult learning. Similarly, asking respondents why they participate – their reasons for learning – carries the implication that the origins of learning need and orientation may be found in people's expressed motives. In both cases, the survey approach is inadequate without a theory of motivation and action. For demographic variables in themselves cannot do justice to the panorama of social and environmental factors which in some way facilitate or inhibit adult learning, while expressions of motive may confuse real motives and goals with facilitating or inhibiting conditions.

The case for and against psychologically-based models is much more complex. To make this case, while at the same time preparing for a transition from one way of talking about PAE (the language of motivation) to another (the language of action) it is necessary to look more closely at the concept of motive, its major themes and variations, and to judge to what extent this concept illuminates the question, Why do adults learn?

## MOTIVE AND CAUSE: THE PSYCHOLOGICAL CASE FOR PARTICIPATION

The philosopher Collingwood (1940) enunciated three basic senses in which the word 'cause' might be used. According to the first, the *historical* sense, that which is caused is the free and responsible act of someone. According to the second, the *practical* or *productive* sense, an event in nature is caused by another event over which we may exercise control. The third, or *theoretical* sense, refers to the one-to-one relationship between an event which is a cause and an event which is an effect, and over which there is no human agency. It is in this latter sense, incidentally, that Collingwood speaks of theoretical *science,* for example physics, chemistry.

For Collingwood, explaining PAE would mean specifying causation in the historical sense. Here the concept of motive is critical. When someone undertakes an action or series of actions in a free and responsible way, we explain his reasons for doing what he did by specifying his motive for doing so. According to this view, the question Why do adults learn? becomes the question What affords people a motive for participating in organized learning activities? Collingwood specifies two conditions whose presence is both necessary and sufficient for us to speak of a motive: an *efficient cause* which is an existing state of affairs; and a *final cause* which is a state of things to be brought about. An efficient cause is not however a mere situation as it exists objectively for all to see, for example high unemployment, a blighted neighborhood, lack of educational credentials. It is rather one which is *perceived* or *interpreted* by the person as something which directly affects him or her and from which he or she may suffer. This distinction is made by Rubenson, 'A person's actions cannot be explained only in terms of the actual situation[;] one has to take into account how the individual person perceives and interprets his situation' (Rubenson, 1978, pp. 22–3). Existing states of affairs are what they are. To be causes of PAE they must be embraced and interpreted in some way relative to the actor by the actor. In other words, many people in this society 'lack' college degrees. But not all interpret this to mean they should do something about it, or that they cannot get on in life unless they close the educational gap with a potential competitor.

A 'final cause,' in Collingwood's terms, means the intention to act. For someone to enroll in a class, she must not merely desire or want to; she must intend to. It is difficult to get intentionality into scientific models of behavior, and in general, it is missing from most psychologically-based models of PAE, though it is here that we might expect to find it. The exception is the Fishbein-inspired program, where Grotelueschen and Caulley (1977) speak of a 'behavioral tendency' which suggests the likelihood of action, though not the actual act itself. Rubenson speaks of 'expectancy' and 'value' combining in some way to produce 'force' ('the strength where will determines behavior,' p. 22) but nowhere discusses intentionality. Strangely enough, up to the point where the concept of force comes into play, Rubenson's model is essentially a rationalist account of the motivation to act, in this case to take part in learning activities. With 'force,' however, we enter a more a-rational domain, with its connotation of drive or compulsion.

In Cross's model, a person's perceptions of the importance of educational goals combines with opportunities and the removal of barriers to bring about PAE. But is intentionality driven merely by this combination? Perceptions of existing states of affairs, according to Collingwood, are necessary but not sufficient to cause PAE. If Cross sees PAE as a change in the behavioral stream, what brings about the change? As Love might have analyzed the situation, for the change to occur the potential participant must somehow make a connection between the existing state of affairs (an 'acute problem' or Aslanian's 'trigger', such as promotion at work) and a final state of affairs (some vision of competency or lack thereof). Intentionality is needed here to establish the link between the current situation and the situation which is desired.

There are, however, problems with measuring intentionality. We are rarely in a position to measure intention to act until the action has taken place. And even then we usually infer backwards, not to the *intention* to act but to the *motive* behind the intention, because normally we assume that for an action to take place the person must have had an intention to so behave. What the motive for the action might have been, however, may remain unclear, as, for example, in cases of crime where the ability to detect a perpetrator may hinge on the ability to construct a motive.

In Collingwood's scheme a motive is the single, sufficient and necessary, cause of action, implying that it is unnecessary to look elsewhere for factors other than motive when examining the causes for a particular example of action like PAE. But what about learning orientations or personality traits (as in Houle's and Boshier's work)? What about facilitating conditions such as the existence of opportunity (as in Cross's)? In specifying these we might, in our own minds and that of our colleagues at least, be discussing what we believe to be 'causes' of PAE. But are these motives? Take this example. A man is asked his 'reason' for enrolling in a degree-program at a local four-year college. Suppose he responds: 'I am doing this because my boss finally gave in and gave me the green light.' Now we may go on to inquire as to this man's *goals* for joining the program. In this case, I would argue, the inquiry after goals would, in Collingwood's rationale, be a quest for motive, and goal would be considered to be a legitimate cause of action. But is not the 'boss's' permission also a legitimate cause of action? Is not the man's 'reason' for enrolling in this program, therefore, really a combination of motive and something else: motive and opportunity to act, goal and the removal of a barrier? This allows us to say, following Peters (1958), that motives are reasons but not vice versa. That is why asking people their reasons for participating may be ambiguous. People may talk about opportunities and other enabling conditions which gave them the freedom to act on a particular occasion, without specifying their motives or goals and vice versa.

Merely seeking out people's reasons for enrolling in courses, therefore, may yield only a listing of goals, without at the same time yielding up an adequate view of opportunities for or barriers to PAE. If we were to probe a little more deeply, we might even find that this conceptual confusion could go some way to explain why the reasons which PAE people disclose to surveyors often do not correlate with the selection of subject matter or program (as Houle, 1974, discovered). It might also help explain findings by researchers (London *et al.*, 1963; Ordos, 1980) that participants and nonparticipants are often close together in terms of their goals and what they would like from education. Goals and benefits are not sufficient in themselves to distinguish between those who do and those who do not participate, or between those who regularly do, and the rest. What distinguishes between them may in fact have more to do with a *tendency to action*, an attitude towards action, being generally passive or active, and the like, rather than the fact that one had a motive for PAE and the other did not.

Remember, the last step in Love's 'sequence of enrolment' is not the step prior to enrolment (thus making PAE an automatic dependent variable) but the actual act of participation. This says that the overall reality being described is not adequately captured by a theoretical narrative which begins with a person's thinking about learning and ends with his actual participation, but rather one which goes on to embrace further acts, on the assumption that one 'act' of participation, one act of learning, does not an adult learner make. The narrative also recognizes that a person's 'thinking' about participation includes a weighing of considerations concerning an overall *program* of PAE and not the mere act of 'turning up for class the first night.' This account further implies that further action is prompted or pushed, not by abstract or once-off triggers, but by other actions lying further back in the chain, an implication contained in the findings of several researchers cited in Chapter 3 (Sjogren *et al.*, 1968; Ray, 1981).

The typical decision model, for example Rubenson and Cookson, details all those antecedent conditions, such as physical states, personality characteristics, social factors, which occur prior to the act of participation.

The act itself, however, is endowed with a certain uniqueness and irrevocability. It is the end point in the chain of decision-making, and thus not part of the overall analysis. When we ask for the causes of participation we automatically disengage the act from its causes assuming that all causes are non-acts. Discussions of participation tend to begin with this conceptual split. But there are awkward facts to deal with. Someone may well have participated in adult education prior to the time at which the matter is being investigated, making it difficult to decide who is a participant and who is not, as London discovered. Clearly, that person's willingness to engage in a new act of participation owes something to the fact that he or she was once involved. Similarly, if people enroll in a course but then decide to drop out, how is that action to be interpreted? Are they participants just because the statistics say so? Or are they nonparticipants, and does this make them closer in genus to all those who rarely or never enroll in courses?

## Motives and motivation

Collingwood's analysis of causation in the historical sense permits a motive to mean something which can induce, persuade, urge, or compel someone to do something (p. 290). Thus, embedded in the very idea of motive is the notion of compulsion. Someone who is compelled to enroll in classes also has a motive for PAE. A model of PAE then should include a variable, some kind of continuum ranging from freedom to act on one end and compulsion to act on the other. This brings the discussion to another element normally missing from discussions of PAE: the issue of motive versus motivation. Often when we use the latter term we mean something akin to staying-power, drive, ambition, tenacity, and the like. Motivated behavior means behavior which is the result of conscious motive. This does not imply, however, following Peters (1958), that all behavior is caused in this sense. It will be necessary, for example, to distinguish, as Houle does in his characterization of the activity-oriented, between PAE which is the result of *habit* and PAE which is the result of a definite and deliberate choice.

The force of this distinction should not be underestimated. The population of participants may include, at any one time, those who are regular or continuous participants from those who are not. We may spend a great deal of time and effort trying to classify all participants in terms of motives or orientations, while the variable of significance may in fact be behavioral rather than motivational. Indeed, it may turn out that what schooling imparts to would-be participants in adult education is not appropriate motives or orientations so much as *habits* of involvement with learning which make later PAE a *continuous* experience, that is where motive is less important than orientation. On the contrary, those who participate on a once-off basis may be more like those who never do, an important hypothesis first suggested in Boshier (1973). What the quasi-participants and nonparticipants may have in common is the failure, for whatever reason, to acquire at school, the habit of learning.

## Rationalizing action

Apart from problems specific to each category of theory and arising out of the way in which that category delimits its universe of discourse, more general problems remain common to all. Discussions of motives and motivation, though they often imply rationality, are rarely discussed in those terms. Actors are more often seen to be doing precisely that: acting (to someone else's configuration but their own), rather than engaging in a dialogue with their lives, the kind of process which has many ragged edges and lines blurred. Why motives? Why not real plans, ideas, goals or other symbols of the individual's effort after meaning and rationality? And is PAE the rational act that we, researchers committed to rationality at all costs, make it out to be?

People may engage in learning activities not because they have certain goals but precisely because they lack them, and educational involvement is seen as a way of obtaining or rediscovering goals. Moreover, goals may change, a consideration rarely addressed by any of the psychological models. Indeed changing goals may be one of the most important 'side-effects' of the experience of education. The phenomenon of goal haziness or goal change suggests strongly that concentration on reasons for beginning participation may in the long run be unproductive or disappointing. When we talk about reasons for participation we should really be talking about the whole experience and perception of the value of education to particular individuals, about the experience of education and how it changes or does not change individuals, and what its effects are in creating a basis for further participation or in bringing about the desired objectives sought in the first place. After all, one of the best predictors of later PAE, apart from earlier schooling, is previous PAE.

This shortsightedness is partly due to the tendency to lump together *motives* which reflect deliberate plans, goals, or other attempts at rational processes, and *motivation* which reflects deep-rooted, basically non-rational drives. For example, two people may share the same motives, while one may lack the drive or ambition of another. Drive may be something a person experiences but about which he or she can do little. A motive or goal, on the other hand, is an attempt at reconstructing the environment – in this case a set of life options – over which the individual may assume control or may be *taught* to gain control.[1]

Finally, what about the idea of goals or motives in conflict, an issue on which all psychological models of PAE are silent? Are people who do not participate really uninterested in learning or really unable to do so because they cannot extricate themselves from a situation in which goals, dreams and motives vie with each other for supremacy. The theories and models surveyed here rarely depict situations in which motives for PAE are in conflict with each other. They do not conceptualize the act of PAE as being a see-saw between opposing tendencies. Indeed, while ultimately the act of participation may be free, it may come about only through long and hard personal and social conflict and at many points along the way may bear no resemblance to a free and voluntary act.

While there are clearly areas of promise within the social-psychological paradigm, to date it has failed to produce a sustained body of systematic research on this problem of involvement with organized learning in the adult years. Researchers have shown no inclination to talk to each other, to spell out what they see as the most significant dimensions of the problem, and have shown no real willingness to follow-up on each other's work or to replicate each other's findings, thus spurning one of the most basic tenets of scientific inquiry: that it is a cooperative, collective enterprise (Courtney, 1986). Thus, through the appearance of fragmented and often unrelated studies, they have failed to make a convincing case to practitioners, or even to each other, that here is a problem worth pursuing.

## FROM MOTIVE TO ACTION: REFRAMING THE QUESTION OF PARTICIPATION

It appears then that while motive has its place in the theory of PAE and has played a useful role down through the years, we cannot now make significant advance without a stronger sense of what is involved in the *action* of PAE rather than the *motive* for it. What is at issue here, however, is not so much the integrity of the theory to explain or in some sense account for the phenomenon of PAE. More important to this discussion is the perspective or 'frame' which the researcher brings to the task, a frame which embodies a theory, and a theory which carries with it its own vocabulary, linguistic rules and discursive practices. To shift the frame, to reconstitute the discourse, we need to make a problematic out of that which hitherto we have taken for granted. Consider the following example based on a real event.

A few years ago, on an Amtrak train bound from Florida to New York, a man shot and seriously wounded his wife and child. During the incident, widely reported in the media, the train was surrounded by police, and, after a brief siege, the man surrendered. Most people will find an incident of this kind interesting almost by instinct and in the same instinctual fashion no one reading the account in a newspaper will be satisfied without learning of the man's reasons for behaving as he did. All will ask, 'Why did he do it?' and will mean, by their question, 'What were the causes of the action?' But were they looking for his motives?

Suppose the man spontaneously replies that he did it to 'shut that damn baby up; he's been howling since we left Miami.' It also comes out in later police reports that the wife tried to intervene when she suspected what the man might be up to and she too was shot. The question we might raise is whether or not the man intended to kill his child, assuming that he did not have this intention with regard to his wife. If after some psychological distancing from the act the man offers this explanation: 'I didn't really intend to kill anyone only to stop all that crying; it was driving me mad,' we may feel a temporary relief that we now understand why he did what he did. But it would only be temporary. For we could still ask, even if the child was as bad as that what could bring a man to the point of anger or frustration that he would lose control of himself and attempt seriously to harm a helpless infant? This is nearer to the idea of causality that people are really after and it is not satisfied by the elaboration of motive.

Notice here, also, that the explanation of an act in terms of momentary loss of control does not seem to conform to a commonsense idea of motive. Suppose after many months it turns out that the man really intended to kill his wife and not his child, that he did so in order to get out of his marriage and thought that by shooting both parties he could claim temporary insanity. People would then say: 'So that was his real motive in doing what he did.' Here we are applying the concept of motive to that which is done deliberately, consciously, under control, and for some perceived gain. That is what we tend to mean by motive, and probably why detective novels and thrillers are so popular.

Under the concept of cause on the other hand we would include, besides motives, acts which appear to be the result of unconscious or driven forces. Cause, in other words, implies both an unconscious as well as the conscious, the irrational as well as the rational, the unreasoned as well as the reasoned, the apparently spontaneous as well as more deliberate types of action. It also permits, a significant allowance in the case of PAE, that the goals or end of the action – its final purpose – may not be clear. With motive, on the other hand, the goals are always clear to the individual who had them.

In this case, then, we seek more than the clarification of motive. For we believe that even if the Amtrak man did have a motive for his action, we still do not understand how he could come to act as he did. We are told that he behaved as he did because he had had enough; he couldn't take it any more. Does this explanation satisfy us? No. What we really want to know is why did he feel like he did. Why was the situation so bad for him that he was able to overcome resistance to one of society's strongest taboos and attempt seriously to harm his child. Think further. Everyday we are faced with wanton acts of savagery, cases of child abuse, incest, and so forth: the perpetration of acts which society regards as among the most evil or most forbidden. It is rarely that we will be satisfied with explanations which limit themselves to single individuals and their life histories. What we are seeking is a general explanation which will tie all these acts together into some understandable – and comforting – whole. What we are seeking is an explanation which tells us how it is that men and women overcome the resistance – which they must surely feel – to the execution of acts which they must surely realize are repugnant to the norms of society.

What I am proposing here is that PAE may be interpreted, on a much less dramatic scale to be sure – though here too there is sometimes drama (remember the enthusiasm for the film, *Educating Rita?*) – as a function of the overcoming of resistance to action rather than the outcome of motives. Explaining PAE in terms of the goals of participants means merely focusing on motives. It is a theory of the kinds of motives people hold and an explanation of why they hold these motives. A theory of this kind is important and throws light on aspects of the need to learn. It does not, however, focus on the act of participation nor is it concerned that participation has certain social and personal consequents. It does not confront the fact that the act of participation has a certain social significance: it, like the Amtrak incident, is accorded meaning by society at large.

The action which offends a taboo reflects a failure to realize some other goal by some other action, the inability of a personality to copy with certain limitations, alignment with certain values or identification with certain groups, and implies that the actor desires to change things in radical ways. That the act offends a taboo should not blind us to certain characteristics of all acts which carry with them social or value-oriented implications, of which PAE is one. They are not easy to carry out, and the more difficult they are to carry out the more they are likely to be done suddenly and with apparent lack of reason or deliberation. Once carried out the actor is changed in various ways. Indeed, to the extent that the action may be difficult to carry out, for example an older adult enrolling in a class suggests that the actor is at least partially aware of the extent to which that act may carry profound implications for his or her ordinary way-of-life. (This, incidentally, I take to be part of the significance of 'perspective transformation' as detailed in Mezirow's work.) By the same token, the opposite will hold: the idea of education may carry with it a certain mystique and may be embraced eagerly precisely because it is hoped that the actions thereby will bring about decisive and permanent changes to one's life situation.

Moving back now to the subject of this study, what implications might this concept of action have for our understanding of why adults learn? It is surprising to see how few studies of PAE and tests of theories and models of PAE compare participants with nonparticipants. Were they to do so they might find that it is not easy to distinguish between them on the basis of motive, on the basis of answers to the question: Why did you enroll in this course? Why were you interested in pursuing this program? What did you hope to get out of it? If we focus only on participants, be they older adults in leisure-type activities, or young adults returning to college, and take their description of goals at face value, we should be surprised not to find them replying along predictable lines, as I believe they do in most of the government-sponsored studies examined in Chapter 2.

There are, of course, genuine reasons for PAE connected with the enjoyment of leisure, efforts to vary the daily routine, and the desire to change careers. If we ponder these responses a little, however, we shall discover that they are ultimately unsatisfactory, and for this reason. For every displaced worker who is learning to become a computer operator, there are many more who sit at home and growl inwardly at the television set. For every displaced homeworker who attempts to learn new skills and return to the world of full-time employment there may be many others who cannot or will not take that path. And yet if we talk to these non-learners, we shall soon notice that they could have the same motives for learning as their counterparts who are learners. People who are not visible to us as learners could have the same reasons for learning as those who are. Men and women who do not participate in organized learning activities could or may have the same motives, or nearly the same motives for learning, as their counterparts who do. Simply put, the existence of nonparticipants (in organized forms of learning) raises questions about the importance of motive to an understanding of participants.

If not motive, what then? Perhaps it has something to do with the tendency to action, the ability or willingness to act on information, on belief, on assessments of the situation. If we admire the woman who suddenly returns to school to get her degree, and if we think of ourselves in a similar way, then what stops us from doing the same thing? If we are both seething with the same inner turmoil, the same call to do something to change the current state of things, what is it about her that suddenly fires her to action while we are content-in-discontent to sit it out and take the consequences? It is these questions which make adult learners and their existential call to action of interest. We are less interested in their motive than in their ability to take action. We admire the will to act. We see and are dazzled by action. That, it seems to me, is what makes the adult learner unique and a definite curiosity for social science.

Suppose now that instead of assuming our major focus to be learning as a form of accomplishment or some kind of internal psychological process resulting in cognitive change, we approach it as a form of normative, social action, a notion already embedded in our free use of the term 'participation.' Nor should this shift-of-focus be necessarily counter-intuitive. While it is natural for us to use the term learning to refer to the accomplishment or *result* of actions – as when we say of someone, he has learned algebra or she is a learned person – notice how we already use the word 'learning' to refer to real, on-going activities in their own right. We say of someone that she is learning math when we point to her sitting at a desk, her head in a book. While she is not moving about and acting in that sense of the term, she could show us that she is doing certain things which will result in a goal being accomplished. She is performing actions which will result in her learning something. The actions she is performing we legitimately call learning or learning activities. In all of these cases we are talking about actions, some social and public as in school classrooms, some private and less visible, as in the quiet solitude of a study. In this case, it is the process not the product that is significant.

Viewed within a framework of action theory rather than motivational or personality theory what might a theory of PAE look like? What would it need to include? First, and at the very least, the question of voluntariness itself would become an issue. One of the first questions we might ask about any kind of action is whether it is voluntary or compelled. Adult educators in their writing and general thinking are apt to premise all discussion on the idea that adult learners are 'there' because they want to be. No one is compelling them. And what distinguishes adult education from other forms of higher or mainstream education is precisely its voluntary nature (for example, the quote which prefaced Chapter 1). But how true is this? I am sure there are many educators, as well as students themselves, who would argue that going to university is much more a reflex, conforming activity today, then it was a generation ago. When 40 per cent or more of the eligible population enters college straight after high school, where is conscious choice in all of this? Where is voluntariness?

By the same token, many forms of adult education, especially those forms of Continuing Professional Education which are tailored to an ever fickle job-market, are populated by students who while they might verbalize motives and goals along conventional lines, when pressed, are more apt to talk in terms of 'needing to get a degree if I am to stay competitive in the job market; there is no one hiring today unless you have a college degree,' and so on. Nor should we omit the small but growing sector of the field which caters to two extremes of the national population: the so-called 'learnfare' programs which compel welfare recipients to enter literacy programs if they want to collect welfare checks, and those in many technical and professional occupations who must undergo mandatory 'continuing education' for relicensure.

These cases are illustrative of the broader problem of approaching PAE as if it were just a question of motivation. There can be no doubting the fact that much of what is traditionally called adult education is an activity performed in leisure time for leisure purposes. Here it would seem a contradiction to speak of compulsion, since the very essence of a leisure pursuit is the freely-chosen use of free time. (Research around this topic is discussed in Chapter 5.) Yet, most of the adult education activity cited in federal and independent surveys is related to some kind of job or occupational domain. And while much of this activity (we have no good figures here) may be free of legal compulsion, we cannot overlook the compulsion which arises from the need to conform, to be in the mainstream, to stay competitive, or whatever the phrase might be.

A theory of PAE then ought to begin with voluntary action as a question rather than assumption. Following that we must look at the nature of action itself. Returning to the more general question, Why do adults learn?, we see that it can be rendered validly as the more specific, 'Why do men and women return to pursue a degree after they have been out of college for some years?' If we wish, we can frame our answer to that question in terms of Houlian orientations. In this case, the activity-oriented individual, for example, is not so much interested in learning a specific subject matter as in being with others of like background and personality. Or, as Houle also points out, that individual may have been pursuing credits for so long that she has forgotten why she got started in the first place. The goal-oriented individual, on the other hand, is not interested in the subject matter but wants to get a degree in his hand. Finally, the learning-oriented individual is really fascinated by a particular subject and has always had that fascination, and now at last has acquired the time to devote to it.

We could, however, answer the same question using a different frame of reference. In place of motives we would talk instead about PAE in terms of *general constraints on or encouragements to perform certain actions*. This we saw above in the example of the employee 'given freedom' by his supervisor to enroll in a degree program. His being in class requires that he have some educational goal, some kind of learning orientation. But that, as was argued already, will still not account for his presence in the classroom. What is needed is the removal of a constraint on his ability to act as he would like to act. His action or actions are explained less by motive or even by intention to act than by the overcoming of resistance or obstacles to action.

A theory of PAE appears then to be a theory of action in disguise.[2] As such, it shifts our focus to the act of participation not as an isolated act of learning so much as a social act embedded in a matrix of many other social actions, the majority of which are habitual and routine and some few of which rise above the others and are in some respects out-of-the-ordinary. This now gives us a way of distinguishing between participants and nonparticipants. Participants are those people for whom PAE does not mean an act requiring the overcoming of resistance: they are willing to act. Of them may be people who, experiencing resistance to their acting in a particular way, are able to overcome that resistance. Nonparticipants, by contrast, may be those for whom PAE appears too far removed from their sphere of common actions to appear as a reasonable option; it is not something which they feel the need to concern themselves with. For them the question of overcoming resistance does not arise. Nonparticipants may also be those who, while they are aware of PAE as an act with certain social consequences, and who are desirous of acting in certain ways, are not able to overcome resistance to that act.

## Adult learning, participation and social action

Focusing on forms of action requires that we consider the kind of action implied by the concept of participation. Considered abstractly, the word 'participation' means involvement or commitment. It is an activity accompanied by orientations and beliefs, feelings and ideas. To participate is to take part or to join in. To participate is also to partake or to have a share of. It also means to possess or enjoy in common with others, to take on the qualities of other participants: those which are related to goal-seeking or the reason for setting up the group in the first place. In the context of adult education, participation implies the involvement of men and women in organized activities which have knowledge or skill acquisition as their major purpose. There is involvment with a social process and a commitment to some goal shared among members of the group who may also be expected to share other orientations, beliefs or values.

Over the years, the concept has easily become operationalized in terms of class registration and attendance. It is obvious, however, even without invoking research findings, that participation is less an all-or-none activity than a continuum of involvement, some parts of which are more significant, long-lasting and of enduring value to the participant than others. Cookson

(1983), for example, proposed a definition which would include 'the sum total of behaviors (activities) performed by men and women (alone, in groups, or institutional settings) while engaged in the process of seeking to improve their knowledge, skill, or sensitiveness' (p. 71), a definition which is also implied in Cookson (1986). While this, and other definitions like it, have the value of directing our attention beyond institutional settings and mere singular acts, they remain somewhat flat and abstract, suggesting no underlying link between diverse types of activities apart from their enumeration. This was the problem also faced by Knox and Videbeck (1963), at a time when the problem of PAE was ceasing to be interpreted as a problem for sociology. Hence, their attempt to introduce a dynamic element by proposing the notion of a 'participatory domain' which they defined as a 'cluster of participatory acts and social relationships' (p. 104).

The idea of a participatory domain implies chains of meaningfully linked actions. The concept of social participation implies something which is irreducibly public, since the concept of interaction appears critical to its definition. It is something which takes place in a public domain according to rules of behavior, norms and conventions, and within a context of roles which sociologists have long spent time dissecting (as in the work of Erving Goffman). In the domain of sociology, participation can mean all kinds of activities, from visiting one's parents on Sundays, to attending symphony concerts, or to becoming an officer in the Kiwanis Club. Despite this elasticity of meaning, however, participation at all times implies a social dimension to human action, an interaction to some end, however diffuse, an organization of others for some common purpose.

At the beginning we argued that the meaning of a person's actions is not exhausted by an analysis of motives. Nor is it something that takes place in a social or collective vacuum. As Peters (1958) points out:

> *Man is a rule-following animal.* His actions are not simply directed towards ends; they also conform to social standards and conventions . . . A man who is ruthless, selfish, punctual, considerate, . . . does not have any particular goals; rather he pursues whatever goals he has in particular sorts of ways. (p. 5, emphasis in original).

Adult learning is not something which is confined to the lives of individual men and women acting alone. Adults act or chose not to act with respect to each other. Often the reason for not acting in a way that seems desirable and in the interests of the individual is simply because no one else appears to be taking action either. The most dramatic example of such consideration is the 'whistleblower,' that singular, moral superman or superwoman of the modern era. Many of us find areas of our worklife that run contrary to our moral code. We feel a strong need to resolve such situations, especially where the corruption is significant. If we look around us, however, we find that while many of our colleagues are involved in the same situation no one appears willing to speak out on the subject and risk the serious consequences that must surely follow.

In such situations most of us would have the same motives for acting if we chose to act. The real issue, though, is not motive but the ability and willingness to overcome inaction: the great fear of acting alone. In other words, though this example may seem somewhat out of the ordinary it does illustrate an aspect of the phenomenon we are investigating. People are rarely willing to act on their own and in accordance with their own feelings, beliefs or conscience. They look for support in others' behavior. They witness each others' actions and when they do act it is within a context that has already set a precedent for their action. It was not for nothing that Pope, the great English poet, wrote: 'Be not the First by whom the new are tried, nor yet the last to lay the old aside.'³ Whether he means it or not Pope is cautioning against individualism and isolated action. Do not be the only one to act in a particular way. Wait until others have had the courage to act first and then follow their example.

Thus it is with PAE. While yet a minority affair, it is not so rare that becoming involved constitutes an isolated action. Someone who chooses to return to school to obtain a degree may be the only adult in his family ever to have done so, may be the only one in his job who has done so, or finally, may be the only one among his squash partners to have done so. In that respect, he is acting alone and is 'the first by whom the new is tried.' Nevertheless, at least in today's world, if he has read any literature on the subject he will realize that he is not alone. Many others older than him, with fewer advantages, greater fears, have chosen to become adult learners. When finally he chooses to act and become an adult learner too, he has gauged the behavior of others and can find in their action the basic strength for his own.

This is not to say that all men and women will act only once they have seen others do so: that they will enroll in degree programs, or attempt to obtain their GED, (High School equivalency exams) only when a neighbor has shown that it is possible. As we have suggested above, men and women do act alone, and many are unique for that reason. What I am arguing is that the tendency to focus on individuals and their individual personality or motives for learning tends to mislead us into viewing all action as the result of individual factors. PAE is as much a social as it is an individual act. To deny this social, this sociological, dimension is to ignore what may well turn out to be the most significant aspect of the problem.

A sufficiently rich account of adult learning ought then to allow room for interpreting PAE as a normative or rule-conforming act, and the actions or states which precede it as likewise subject to rule-following consider-ations. People act – behave socially – according to rules or norms of action. These norms will be established not by individuals as individuals but as members of groups or classes. People conduct themselves in tune with their membership or perceived membership of groups. Much of this action actually takes place in organizational contexts, as when people involve themselves or are involved in the workplace. Work is the classic example of this kind of involvement. Most work is conducted within organizations and people's actions within these organizations are guided, facilitated, constrained or otherwise shaped by their roles within them.

If organizations shape people's behavior or conduct, then it is natural to assume that people's decisions to become involved with organizations outside of the work milieu will be predicated not only of merely on issues of motivation and personality but more precisely on their understanding of what these organizations are about and how they can help people accomplish what they want to accomplish. It is to this larger concern, a concern for the social and organizational dimensions of people's actions, that we now turn.

# 5 Adult learning and the concept of social participation

The problem of participation is not confined to adult education alone, for it is present in every aspect of the social life of the community. Since participation in any one activity is related to participation in all other social relationships, the problem cannot be studied adequately by isolating one form of association from all others.

(Verner and Newberry, 1965)

We have said that explaining why adults learn might have more to do with a theory of action rather than a theory of motivation. What do we mean, in this context, by adult learning as a theory of action? I am interpreting this question to mean learning as a function of one's relationship to others or one's membership of social units whose essence is defined by their ability to shape or determine how we behave or conduct our life.

It is easy to lose sight of the fact that almost all significant acts of learning are conducted in the context of other people's activities. Learning is a 'compresent' (Forsythe, 1983) phenomenon. We may achieve our most important insights, our breakthroughs, as it were, while in silent contemplation or in the solitary reading of a book. Nevertheless, except in those cases where learning naturally accompanies the doing of some other activity – and this phenomenon of 'natural' or 'incidental' learning is receiving new attention (Marsick, 1990; Marsick and Watkins, 1991) – most learning activity takes place in the direct company of others engaged in a similar task, such as a class, or the indirect company of others, for example a correspondence course, and/or is aided, promoted or facilitated by another person according to some external standards of others or, at the very least, through the agreement or assent of another. Thus it may be assumed that the willingness, determination or motivation to engage in learning activity has something to do with one's integration within or membership of a larger social unit, with one's relationship to others and, overall, with one's pattern of socialization within the larger community of others.

This does not mean that all of learning is a social act or that we are forswearing the 'creation' of learning by the science of psychology as a science of individual achievement, personality and cognitive functioning. Certainly, learning is something which individuals do, is something which happens 'within' them, and is something which by and large appears to an outsider as an invisible process or accomplishment. Nevertheless, for every aspect of this process which appears invisible or unconnected with others, we can find another aspect where others are involved, either in creating an opportunity for the learning to take place, or enforcing standards according to which achievement is judged or simply because they are all doing something which individuals come to feel that they should be doing though they may articulate other reasons which appear to give preeminence to the self. We have ignored the social dimensions of learning at some cost to adequate theory-building.

In this and the following chapter, we shall examine these social dimensions from three specific vantage points. First, there is the idea that significant learning often takes place in organizational settings, be they schools, work sites or where people gather for leisure purposes. Thus, to seek motivation for learning we might seek for those factors which motivate people to join or be a part of organizations or for reasons why organizations compel as well as encourage forms of voluntary participation. Second, there is the idea that learning is a discretionary act, a function of leisure time, or time away from work and essential personal needs, such as sleep. Thus, in seeking reasons why adults learn or 'fail' to learn we are concerned with the total 'distribution' of life's activities over the day, week or some other convenient temporality. Third, there is the idea that all learning somehow involves the socialization or integration of the individual within the larger social whole, and that therefore reasons for learning might be sought in the 'function' played by education in giving or denying the individual access to social roles and rewards.

## THE CONCEPT OF PARTICIPATION

Whatever else it may be construed as, and it has been construed as many things (Courtney, 1989), adult education suggests activities in which a man or woman engages for some purpose, activities outside of the ordinary business of life. Even adult learning, the now more popular phrase, carries with it a connotation of activity, something external engaged in by the would-be learner for some definite end. That notion of activity, action, behavior or conduct, whichever term is preferred, is embedded, I would submit, in the term 'participation.' It is not for nought that the term has been traditionally conjoined with 'adult education.'

We are accustomed to this conjunction without paying too much attention to the fact that 'learning' and 'participation' may not mean the same thing. The purpose of the present chapter is to draw attention to the distinction between them by exploring the notion of participation, especially as it has been used beyond the field of adult education, to see what light it may throw on the causes of adult learning. In particular, we are interested in the idea that it is within the total matrix of activities of men and women interacting with each other, formally and informally, that we may locate the reasons why adults learn.

It was Newberry (Brunner *et al*., 1959) who noted the tendency for organizations to attract their own kind of client, for educational institutions to attract a particular kind of student who would not be attracted to a 'competitor' especially if they were offering a similar kind of program. This observation, though easily tested, has been overlooked in recent times. It tells us, at the very least, that factors responsible for a person's decision to engage in a learning activity has something to do with the organization which sponsors that activity. Concern for such factors as organizations and their philosophy or culture take us beyond the normal considerations of motive and individual goals. It requires that we pay attention to people as social animals and to the kinds of activities, mostly associational and involving interaction with others, which make up much of their day-to-day lives.

'Educators,' noted Douglah (1970, p. 90), 'use the term [participation] in reference to involvement in events, activities, or programs whose primary purpose is educational in nature.' Other uses are also possible. In the context of political science the term has meant the various ways in which individuals signal involvement with the political process, for example voting, marching in protest. Sociologists have used the term to refer to memberships in clubs, community involvement, as well as the most casual neighborhood encounters. The term has also typically meant involvement in decision-making processes, and the degree of influence carried by different members of a group, as in the concept of 'workers' participation' used in discussions of industrial democracy. Despite this variety of uses, however, the concept has certain 'universal properties,' according to Douglah, and it is these properties which will be analyzed here.

First, the act of participation is both an individual and group phenomenon. For too long now we have emphasized its individualist orientation in the PAE literature. Second, it is associative, meaning PAE is a species of societal participation in general and researchers should be concerned with seeking explanations for it in those factors responsible for other forms of participation also. Third, it is qualitative, in that it reflects not only the degree of involvement but, also, less easily enumerated properties such as an individual's understanding of the organization, attitudes towards its operation, beliefs about his or her influence within it, and so forth. Finally, participation is almost always a means to an end, and not an end in itself. People who become involved in organized learning activities almost always have a goal they wish to accomplish. Thus, according to this view, learning-for-its-own-sake – Houle's learning-orientation – is not so much a goal as something which accompanies a goal by enhancing the learning process.

## The concept of participation in American sociology

Participation comes to adult education via the discipline of sociology. It is a term which received its earliest and most robust exposition at the hands of sociologists. Because American social science first took hold in the newer universities of the Midwest and in major metropolitan areas such as New York, e.g. Columbia University, it was natural that 'urban sociology' and the 'community study' should become the 'two leading lines of development of research and speculation' (Shils, 1948, p. 7). We find this emphasis on urbanism and community life in some of the better known introductory textbooks of the time, e.g. Robert McIver's (1937) *Society* (for whom sociology was the 'relationships of social beings as they cohere into systems and as they change in response to all the conditions that affect human life'), and Park and Burgess's *Introduction to the Science of Society*. We find it also in many of the ground-breaking empirical studies of the time, e.g. Lynd and Lynd's *Middletown*, and Lundberg, Komarovsky and McInerny's (1934), *Leisure: A Suburban Study*.

A theme running through both urban and community studies was that of 'social participation' in all its many and varied forms. Researchers were keen to subject any and all forms of organized public life to scrutiny: church congregations, farming communities, trade unions and professional associations. Immigrant and working-class populations in particular were described and classified, as were the various aspects of cultural and artistic life, all for the purpose of understanding how and why people formed into groups and larger collective entities, and what were the factors responsible for societal 'solidarity' and dissolution.[1]

Concern for the origins of community life were not, however, merely driven by scientific curiosity. Mirroring the evolution of social science in this country (Courtney, 1990), in its initial phase the study of social participation was a tension between the urge to reform, change and improve the human lot and the urge merely to classify and understand. This mixture of sentiment and science is evident in many of the early works, for example

Queen, Chapin and Anderson in the 1930s and 1940s. For Queen, obstacles to social participation were symptoms of 'social pathology' and needed to be treated much as a doctor might a sick patient.[2] Since then, the concern of researchers has stretched far beyond the original preoccupation with community life in all its diagnostic and prescriptive variety. Today the concept includes sophisticated attempts at theory building (Edwards and Booth, 1973; Smith, Macaulay and associates, 1980), a highly developed study of political participation (Verba and Nie, 1972; Milbraith and Goel, 1977), the study of philanthropic giving (Macaulay and Berkowitz, 1970), mass-media consumption (Jeffres and Robinson, 1980), time-budget analysis (DeGrazia, 1964; Szalai, 1972), leisure research (Kaplan, 1960; Kleemeier, 1961) as well as the traditional focus on membership of and participation in voluntary associations (Defee, Schultz and Pasework, 1974; Smith, 1975; Smith *et al.*, 1980; McPherson and Smith-Lovin, 1986).

For present purposes, the social participation literature is important for two reasons: (1) it directs our attention to other forms of participation which it suggests are similar to PAE because the factors most significantly correlated with PAE are those same factors influential in shaping these other forms; (2) it directs our attention to how the individual relates to the society through the organizations which he or she constructs, voluntarily participates in and uses to give expression to his or her social, political, educational and economic needs.

## SOCIAL PARTICIPATION AND VOLUNTARY ASSOCIATION

One of the most prominent of those foundation blocks which undergird the American psychic edifice is the notion of voluntary association.[3] It is one which neatly combines both the idea of philanthropic giving and that of the free and voluntary interaction with others of like background for common goals and purposes. It is an idea, rather than a reality, that goes all the way back to Tocqueville for whom voluntarism expressed a true realization of the democratic principle: where injustices, social ills or simple inconveniences exist, under the democratic mode of government, people will come together for the purpose of eradicating them. It epitomizes the American preoccupation with the nature of the 'interstitial glue' (McPherson and Smith-Lovin, 1986) that has made its social and political institutions possible. In a very basic sense it is the obsession with democratic form – hence the periodic St Vitus dance around Americanization – that which has given the American ideology its krypton of pride, and its power to harm others in the name of a political ideal. At its most fundamental level, it is the universal quest for the 'constituents and conditions of order in social life, [and] the nature, conditions, and consequences of the "identification of interests" – problems which had long been central to political philosophy, . . . and which now . . . constitute the central problem of sociology' (Shils, 1948, p. 6).

Traditionally, social participation has been measured according to (1) its degree of formality, (2) the kind of organization involved, and (3) the type of activity (Brunner *et al.*, 1959). There has been no enduring consensus on the significance of these dimensions, however. Brunner, for example, defined social participation as

> interaction with others in a socially defined relationship wherein the roles of those participating are more or less structured and mutually understood. The relationship must involve some exchange or transmittal, although direct personal contact is not always required. Social participation also implies some degree of purposive effort and ego-involvement on the part of the participant. Casual contact and routine 'transaction' are, therefore, excluded as is interaction in the course of gainful employment. (Brunner *et al.*, 1959, p. 99)

Informal and casual interactions are, however, an essential aspect of some definitions. Booth and Edwards (1973), for example, cite as episodes of social participation activities like 'team bowling, card-playing, voting as a member of a committee, belonging to a neighborhood improvement association, protesting racial discrimination, interacting with kin and friends, contributing to the Community Chest, and many other activities' (p. 1). And in Smith *et al.*'s (1980) encyclopedic examination of 'voluntary action,' we witness a highly abstracted attempt to explain all forms of participation from the most casual to the most formal via a single framework, the ISSTAL model, adapted by Cookson and described in Chapter 3.

How much America really is a 'nation of joiners' (Hausknecht, 1962) has been the subject of dispute among social scientists from the very beginning. The opinion of Toqueville has been held by many influential writers including the Beards, Gunnar Myrdal and others. Others have been less convinced, finding that while memberships are often high, real active participation, as we shall see, may be low (Wilensky, 1961). Moreover, as researchers have also been quick to point out, participation where it does occur is very often skewed. Among the better-off sectors of the community, participation is concentrated in degree both of intensity and variety. The working-class tends to avoid the more formal structures and to seek opportunities for learning and friendship within more informal patterns of association, while the poorest classes tend to shun even these less structured modes, effectively cutting themselves off from any source of organization and power. Mather (1941) summed up the situation as sociologists saw it on the eve of the Second World War:

> The implications of [my] findings are not pleasant for the lover of democracy . . . [they] indicate that 65 per cent of the 6,264 people living in [Franklin, Indiana] this typical farmers' town, are rather completely dominated in their recreation, politics, religion, patriotism, and culture – every phase of their organized life – by the remaining 35 per cent . . . The people of Franklin do not form one group in the sociological sense. (pp. 382–3)

Few studies coming after Mather's have disputed the thrust of this finding:

> The most nearly universal relationship found in studies of participation is the consistent positive association of formal participation rates and patterns with variables which are either correlates or measures of socio-economic status. (Brunner *et al.*, 1959, p. 102)

Since 'socio-economic status' is usually a code for income, occupation and formal education, it is clear that social participation, like PAE, is associated with a cluster of 'status configurations' (Knox and Videbeck, 1963), of which formal schooling has proved the most potent.

From the early days there has been a long line of research to demonstrate two key points of American social life. First, most forms of voluntary, social participation are really a minority affair affecting overlapping populations of the same or similar people and, second, social participation is a class-dominated phenomenon: Lorimer (1931), Dotson (1951), Foskett (1955), Bell and Force (1956), Scott (1957), Wright and Hyman (1958), Hodge and Treiman (1968), Defee, Schultz and Pasewark (1972). Typical of the earlier body of work are Komarovsky (1946), Reissman (1954) and Axelrod (1956).

In a study focusing on social class differences, Komarovsky (1946) surveyed over 2,000 residents of New York City. She found that 60 per cent of working-class men and 53 per cent of white-collar men 'did not have a single organized group affiliation with the exception of, perhaps, a Church' (p. 687), thus giving an early emphasis to the idea that social participation was confined to minorities within the community. Of 146 unskilled laborers in her study, approximately 70 per cent indicated no affiliations, while 25 per cent were members of one group. By contrast, of 295 professionals, just over 20 per cent belonged to no organizations, with over 60 per cent belonging to two or more groups. Furthermore, she observed, the 'organized life of the professional is dominated by his profession' (p. 692). (See also, Wilensky, 1961, 1973.) When associations were classified into categories, economic, political, masonic, religious, social, etc., almost all the affiliations of the professional group belonged in the 'economic' category. This was also true for the skilled worker category. For those who were unskilled, participation was confined to the 'social and athletic club,' while for those who were classified as office or clerical workers with a high school education their participation was spread over the widest number of groups. Seeking an explanation for these differences, Komarovsky, a sociologist, suggested an answer in 'personality variables,' a point on which she did not elaborate. She might just as easily have sought them in the organizational forms themselves and what they stood for, a point to which we shall return.

Reissman (1954), in a study of white males in Evanston, Illinois, concurred with Mather that the middle and upper classes could be said to 'dominate the organizational activity, the intellectual life, and the leadership of the community' (p. 77). It was not merely that middle-class groups could claim more numerous memberships than the working or lower classes, it was the fact that, within an organization, the former tended to hold office and were more active in promoting the activities and goals of the organization. In this respect, they could be said to control the 'agenda,' a dimension of the exercise of power not immediately visible to the outside world, or even the membership itself. (See Gaventa, 1980, for an important illustration of this point.)

One of the most often-cited studies of social participation is Axelrod (1956), who obtained interviews with a cross-section of city residents who were part of the Detroit Area Study back in the mid-1950s. He was testing the idea that urbanization is linked to low levels of social participation. Contrary to the general belief, then held as part of the so-called 'Chicago school,' that living in a city tended to produce alienated, disengaged individuals, Axelrod's results suggested that urban dwellers interacted a good deal with each other. As in Mather's study, almost two-thirds were members of formal groups. At the same time, activity levels were skewed: almost half of those who were members belonged to one organization only, while among members of groups in general only about one-quarter were active. It is to Axelrod's study, incidentally, that we owe one of the earliest and strongest endorsements of the correlation between social participation and social class, a point made repeatedly in Brunner *et al.* (1959):

> education is quite strikingly related to the extent of formal group participation. More than three quarters of all persons with some college experience have formal group membership, while only half of those with grade school have formal group membership. (pp. 40–1)

At the same time, almost everyone claimed *informal* association with others, that is relatives, friends, neighbors and co-workers, a tendency which was distributed equally between all significant divisions of the population: young, old, professional and blue-collar. From this Axelrod concluded that a majority of the sample had membership in formal groups and associations, though for a majority of those the degree of involvement was not intense. (This, incidentally, supports Wilensky's (1961) point that in self-reporting situations people will overestimate their levels of involvement.)

Thus, it may be that the US is a nation of joiners if only memberships are counted, but not if degree of involvement is being measured. Axelrod further noted that informal associations, such as visiting family, were 'near universal' among all segments of the population regardless of class or status level, and concluded that while 'formally organized associations have unquestionably an important role in the urban community' (p. 43), they are far less pervasive than the entire network of informal associations which, in their own idiosyncratic ways, serve many of the same functions as the more formal type of network, but mainly out of the public eye and indifferent to public scrutiny.

Findings, like those of Axelrod, Komarovsky and others, which had been based on samples from local populations, received a major boost when Wright and Hyman (1958) conducted a secondary analysis on over 5,000 men and women drawn from two combined national samples. They confirmed the general point that memberships in voluntary associations are confined to a minority (64 per cent reported no affiliations), while less than 10 per cent reported being involved in more than one organization. Whites tended to have more affiliations than Blacks; some religious groups, e.g. Jews and Protestants, were more active than others, e.g. Catholics. Again, economic factors were significant. Measuring such factors as income, education level and an individual's own estimate of his or her 'level of living,' Wright and Hyman noted, for example, that 92 per cent of those who rated the latter 'very low' belonged to no organization, while the figure was 18 per cent for those rating level of living 'very high.' Correspondingly, only 5 per cent of those in the 'very low' category belonged to more than one organization, compared with 36 per cent of those in the 'very high' category.

## The 'functions' of voluntary association

What was lacking in these early studies, however, as Shils (1948) and others have noted, was a sense of what functions voluntary associations appeared to serve and why people became involved in them. What was the significance in finding less participation where we expected more or in finding, as in cities, that urbanization did not seem to result in the dissolution of community ties? Second, how were differential, class-related rates to be explained? What exactly was the relationship between demographic factors and forms of community involvement? Third, to explain differences between occupational or social groups or variability in intra-group rates, was there nowhere else to turn but to personality and individual differences?

The literature of adult education has yielded at least one important, though now forgotten, attempt to provide a comprehensive answer to these questions. The year following his presentation of the distinction between motivation-to-learn and motivation-to-participate at the Chicago conference (Knox and Sjogren, 1962), Alan Knox joined Richard Videbeck in the publication of a study which more than any other single piece of research discussed here epitomizes the interdisciplinary character of PAE research up to the beginning of the 1960s. Theirs was the first real test of the connection between former schooling and later PAE, and was part of a research program whose goal was the construction of a 'general theory of participation' (Knox and Videbeck, 1963, p. 104).[4]

According to the outlines of this theory, social participation is the 'result of the interaction between an individual and his environment' (p. 104), a view similar to that of Boshier in his various depictions of PAE and its antecedents. (Boshier, 1979, acknowledges his debt to this study.) Participation is 'patterned,' which means that it is not so much a 'collection of discrete events' but rather a 'set of recurrent behavioral sequences' (pp. 104–5) which can be taken as a meaningful whole, for example a hobby, membership in a club, enrolling in a course. This brings their model very close to that of Love, Cross and Cookson.

A second major element of the model was the notion of a 'status configuration' (p. 106), which was akin to and was measured by common demographic variables, such as age, sex. The normal kind of correlation between demographic variables and PAE, according to the authors, concealed rather than revealed the real causal chain. In the case of age – the second most important determinant of PAE according to survey statistics reported in Chapter 2 – they argued that if status configurations were examined singly and contrasted with each other, the influence of age would fade or be diluted. Thus, they hypothesized that PAE is not really a function of age: 'rather, [it is] a function of the fact that many persons within some status configurations participate in adult education while few persons within other configurations do so' (p. 109).

This theory sought to bring together within a single conceptual scheme psychological orientations, social systems and environmental factors, making it a direct ancestor of the ISSTAL model. Furthermore, anticipating Aslanian and Brickell (1980), Knox and Videbeck also hypothesized that

PAE came in 'responses to critical changes in life circumstances' (p. 105), for instance starting a new job, getting married, having a child. Apart from one major study reported in the 1963 paper, there appears to have been no systematic attempt to develop, what on the face of it was, an extremely promising theory. A major text by Knox (1977), for example, which brings together this prominent figure's thoughts on adult learning and participation, contains no real follow-up to these early and very promising reflections.

The correlation of demographics with social participation phenomena yielded more or less the same results as in the case of demographics and PAE: they were revealing but far from conclusive. The stalemate was broken by a simple but exciting study carried out by Beal (1956), a rural sociologist like Brunner. Beal began by criticizing the tendency to see and measure participation in voluntary associations in the standard way: membership, attendance, contributions, membership on committees and holding office, as if the phenomenon had nothing to do with the type of organization being studied. On the contrary, Beal argued, participation could not be defined in an absolute manner, but had to be tied to a model of the organization (in his case the rural Cooperative Association).

What makes this argument more interesting, however, in the light of the research analyzed in Chapter 2, is Beal's decision to reject demographic factors altogether as an explanation of participation rates. These variables, like income, age, residence, and so on, he considered to be 'static,' because nothing could be done to change them. They formed the indelible identity of the would-be participant and were beyond the province of those interested in altering participation patterns. In a preliminary study, Beal found that only two of the 'static' variables were related significantly to involvement in cooperatives: overall social participation or sociability (London *et al.*'s general participation syndrome) and, not unexpectedly, socio-economic status.

Instead, he sought for 'dynamic' factors, those which reflected a person's understanding of the purpose and operation of the organization; his identification or satisfaction with it and his feelings of responsibility towards it. Using measures of these less visible, more rational and more psychological properties, Beal tested ten hypotheses, all of which proved significant in determining participation in the Cooperative, in contrast to the 'static' variables where all but two out of sixteen tested had turned up negative.[5]

Beal's insights influenced one of the foremost sociologists in the area of voluntary action, David Horton Smith. Smith (1966) tested the theory that 'most of the observed distal relationship between [participation in formal voluntary organizations] and environmental, physical and social variables may be explained in terms of [psychological] variables' (pp. 249–50). He examined three levels of psychological variable: personality traits, of the kind Boshier (1980) borrowed from Cattell; attitudes in general towards formal voluntary organizations, that is obligation to participate, preferring formal groups, and service orientation to leisure time; and, finally, specific attitudes towards organizations, that is feelings of support for a specific organization and commitment to it, these latter being Beal's dynamic factors.

In a survey conducted in Chile, which despite cultural differences is germane to the present study, Smith (1966) examined participation patterns in three areas: a center for mothers, religious auxiliaries and the Red Cross. He found that personality traits discriminated between active and less active members of the various groups but that, in a test using multiple regression, it was the attitudes, especially the organization-specific ones, which proved to be more powerful predictors of whether or not someone joined the group. In other words, attitudes to participation in general were better predictors of participation than features of the individual's personality. But attitudes tied to the specific workings of the organization were, as Beal had discovered, better predictors than the more general dispositions. This finding, incidentally, tends to give support to the Grotelueschen and Caulley (1977) model of PAE and its causes.

Approaching the explanation of organization-specific participation from another angle, Hodge and Treiman (1968) pointed to a neglect of the 'process of recruitment' into the organization. Analyzing the results of an empirical study done in the Washington DC area they noted that 'for both males and females, membership appears to be at least as strongly influenced by parents' level of participation in such organizations as by respondent's socioeconomic status' (p. 722). A similar relationship had been noted earlier by Anderson (1943), who judged social participation to be a 'family characteristic' (p. 424). These studies naturally raise questions about the function of voluntary associations in continuing the process of socialization, begun in early childhood, and extending into the adult years. A study by Hanks and Eckland (1978) makes this a suggestive issue for further analysis. In a study of 947 males and 1,130 females, originally part of a sample of high school students, they found that irrespective of social origins and ability and performance in school, being active in extracurricular activities has a direct effect on participation in 'adult secondary associations.' They concluded that

membership in adult voluntary associations [by adolescents] increases voting behavior and decreases political alienation, thus demonstrating the very broad and long-term effects of adolescent socialization in ultimately linking the individual to the political order. (p. 381)

What then is the significance of voluntary organizations as forces of social participation? And why do they appear to play such a major role in extending the process of socialization begun in the family and the school? Two basic hypotheses have been advanced to answer these questions. According to the first, the so-called 'integration hypothesis,' voluntary associations

> may represent the emergent interests of unspecified publics in the political domain, provide resources for useful contacts in the economic domain, allow the expression of altruistic impulses in charitable activity, and provide a variety of peripheral and ephemeral services. (McPherson and Smith-Lovin, 1986, p. 61.)

The integration hypothesis stresses the function of voluntary groups in bringing people together and thereby enhancing the feeling of community. By contrast, some see voluntary associations as playing a 'sorting' role in a society, according to which people classify themselves on the basis of their work and sex and join organizations which reflect these characteristics. According to this hypothesis, voluntary groups divide and stratify people according to status and are thus a mechanism for reducing the feeling of solidarity between disparate sectors of the community. In the McPherson and Smith-Lovin study, for example, nearly half of all organizations included in a ten-community study were exclusively female, while a further fifth were exclusively male. In these researchers' eyes, the sorting hypothesis was the more dominant, at least as far as sex was concerned.

One of the most detailed attempts to model social participation along integration lines is Edwards and Booth (1973) who brought together major research studies under the title, *Social Participation in Urban Society*. For these authors, social participation is a form of 'social exchange,' which involves (1) the act of sharing, common to all participants, (2) two or more persons mutually pursuing a specific, defined objective, and (3) undertaking activities which are separated from other social activities in time and space. For them all participatory behavior is goal-directed, a point made at the beginning of this chapter. The importance of this distinction lies more with the types of goals involved: whether they are instrumental or expressive. Instrumental goals characterize those activities directed outside of the group or organization and having consequences for the wider community or society. (These would be equivalent to the Social Goal factor in MO research.) Expressive goals, on the other hand, characterize those activities undertaken for their own sake; the attainment of objectives has no effect on participants: 'card-playing, for instance, is an outstanding example of the expressive activity' (p. 2). They also permit a third category which represents an equal mix of instrumental and expressive goals.

Whether formal or informal, expressive or instrumental, what functions do voluntary associations actually fulfill? First, according to Edwards and Booth, they serve to bring together people of like interest to pursue that interest through collective action; second, they serve to distribute power in a democratic society; third, they mediate between individuals and large social structures thus giving the isolated persons a sense of involvement with the larger collectivity; fourth, they 'facilitate the flow of information between separated social units' (p. 5). In this way they serve fundamental functions in society in general, by giving expression to interests not otherwise represented in the macro-structure. They permit a society to cope with unique or unusual demands not able to be handled within existing macro-structures. Finally, a point critical to our understanding of how adult education functions in the society it attempts to serve, social participation relationships extend earlier socialization. Here the authors cite the family, schools and industry which have similar and overlapping functions as transmitters of dominant values.

## Social participation and adult education

There are good reasons why the concept of PAE should be judged as an extension of the concept of social participation and why PAE research can benefit from a closer look at what social participation researchers have been doing for the last fifty years. First, it is clear that despite the new-found emphasis on informal adult learning and its pervasiveness throughout the community as a whole (Tough, 1971, 1978; Brookfield, 1986), adult education is as much a social as a 'personal' reality, and is easiest to understand when we can relate it to the organizations and institutions which provide it, those aspects of the polity where the most fundamental national goals are translated into concrete tasks and practices. In other words, PAE is essentially a 'social fact' in the sense used by Durkheim.[6]

Second, and related to the first point, we can learn much about PAE if we begin to compare the organizations which are responsible for adult education with other examples of voluntary associations, and to consider the attributes shared by each: that they often represent special interests; that they have policies of recruitment which implicitly if not officially attract some sectors of the community while rejecting those who traditionally do not share their ideology; and, finally, that through a collective they perform functions that individuals could not perform on their own.

Third, the concept of participation directs our attention beyond learning

NORTHERN COLL. LIBRARY OF ARTS & TECHNOLOGY

and into realms not normally associated with adult education. We see that just as PAE has certain demographic associations, such as age, education, residence, so too do other forms of participation. This suggests that those factors responsible for other forms of participation, particularly social and cultural, must also be responsible for voluntary educational participation. We find that a superficial, theoretical interrelatedness hides a deeper reality. For many of these participational forms 'cluster' together and appear to be the reflection of some larger dynamic. At the very least, this dynamic has to do with the way society is constructed, with the way power and wealth are distributed, and with the perceptions and feelings concerning power and influence, as much as with the reality of these more profound structural forms (Burman, 1959; Hymon, 1960; Boggs, 1974; Gaventa, 1980). Forms of participation, of which PAE is one, are, in other words, reflections of the type of society people live in and the access they feel they have to the various social, economic and political institutions and agencies which express the values and ideals of that society.

In this respect, too, we can begin to give greater meaning to London *et al.*'s concept of a 'general participation syndrome,' something which suggests the confidence a person of a certain social and educational background feels in exploring all forms of life around her, the welcome she feels as she moves through these social forms, and the overall sense she experiences – to generalize from the Beal hypothesis – that the institutions created to serve society's needs are really her institutions too, to do with what she would in furthering her interests and in enhancing her quality of life.

If PAE is a species of social participation and both are an expression of a larger concept of societal participation, then adult learning may need to be seen as something which occurs against a matrix of organizational forms and in conjunction with those forms and the interests they serve. This ultimately gives greater sense to the term 'schooling' as we shall see in Chapter 6, and to that function of schooling whose role is paramount even if its identity has all too often been ignored in discussions of PAE: the notion of socialization and, its corollary, social control.

Finally, the focus on the organization draws our attention to a simple but powerful fact: much of our lives are lived within organizations which are responsible for how we behave and how we think. Thus, we might begin to think of how organizations themselves, particularly work-related ones, construct or embody an attitude towards learning: what employers believe learning is really about, what they see as its final end, and what role they see it playing not only in their organization's day-to-day affairs but also in that of their employees.

## SOCIAL PARTICIPATION AND THE CONCEPT OF LEISURE

Just as PAE involves consideration of other forms of participation and the relationships between them, so too does adult learning defined as a form of discretionary, leisure-oriented behavior. For here also we are looking at a range of possible activities in which an adult might become involved during those periods of time which are not earmarked for work or the fulfillment of personal needs, for instance eating, sleeping. If then we define leisure as time not devoted to work, work-related activities, such as commuting, or essential personal activities, then, at the very least, adult learning becomes a phenomenon which occupies one's leisure hours and the reasons for it must be seen in the context of other competing leisure-activities. (Learning is also an activity which may occupy work-related activity as when a person tries to learn something while commuting to work, a point which will be discussed below.) We might expect then to find that the prominence given to learning over other forms of leisure consumption is as much a reflection of the evolution of leisure in the industrialized world as it is the evolution of educational institutions and the opportunities they have provided.

The idea of an industrial, technological revolution making the possibility of mass, sustained leisure a reality for many came to the fore at the end of the last century and intertwined with the earliest concerns of American sociology. Complementing the interest in community life mentioned earlier was an interest also in the different forms of leisure. Sociologists asked, 'How do people spend the time away from work? And what are the factors behind the appearance of leisure and the way people spend it?'

Probably the earliest and still classic statement on leisure patterns in American society is *The Theory of the Leisure Class*, Thorstein Veblen's irreverent attack on the new, professional, moneyed classes, first published in 1899. Veblen advanced the notion that leisure is not a random pursuit of activities permitted by time away from work. Leisure is indeed a commodity 'consumed' by different classes in different ways. Hence, Veblen's notion of 'conspicuous consumption,' a concept still very much alive today, and a depiction of how the better off economic classes spend their leisure hours. Though uncomfortably accurate in many ways, Veblen's was essentially a polemical work, a club with which to beat conceit and privilege, of an illustrious tradition stretching back to Aristotle (Noe, 1973). The first truly empirical work in this area, and still one of the classics of the field (Meyersohn, 1969), is *Leisure: A Suburban Study* (Lundberg, Komarovsky and McInerny, 1934).

Like Lorimer and McGrath, Lundberg *et al.*'s fieldwork was conducted in 1932 and 1933, significant years of the Great Depression, and their survey centered on the day-to-day, weekly leisure pursuits of the inhabitants of Westchester County, north of New York. They adopted a 'popular' definition of leisure as 'the time we are free from the more obvious and formal duties which a paid job or other obligatory occupation imposes upon us' (p. 2). Choosing the suburb as the site of the study, they quoted from contemporary writers who found it hard to understand why anyone would want to live so far from the city:

> A commuter is man whose life is divided into two principal parts: coming and going. He is a goat in antelope's clothing. He feeds on time-tables, asterisks and footnotes. He thrives on duplicated scenery. His life is one long series of two-hundred yard dashes. (p. 43)

Lundberg first tackled the question of where and how people spend their leisure. Outdoors and closer to nature, his list included the public forests, lakes and reservoirs, Tour and Trail Clubs, summer camps and the camps of organizations like the Boy Scouts and the YMCA/YWCA. Near the parks are the golf courses, tennis courts and other venues for organized sports. There was the interest in gardening, the toing and froing of 'thousands of motor cars . . . over the network of cement highways that cover the area' (p. 62), activities related to beaches and water, and a whole host of other mainly outdoor, active leisure pursuits. Still public but indoors the scene changes. Here are found voluntary organizations such as the Elks and the (Irish-inspired) Gaelic Athletic Association, hotels and inns, dance emporiums, 'moving picture theaters,' pool halls, bowling alleys, and the now no longer ubiquitous amusement park. Also indoors but now in the privacy of the home, we find such activities as visiting with friends and family, card-playing, reading, games, and so forth. Many are related to the family and to church involvement. Many more encompass the arts, such as singing, the theater and art exhibits. Among these were the more intellectual pursuits such as visiting the public library, poetry and scientific and historical societies.

Lundberg's study, then, gives us a sense of the type and range of potential leisure activities against which learning activity is to be evaluated. It is interesting to compare this list to the definition of adult education activity presented in Chapter 2. Clearly, for many adult educators today, PAE would include most of Lundberg's leisure pursuits, including sports and the theater, while for Lundberg, who devoted a chapter of his extensive study to adult education, the definition of the latter was restricted to more serious learning and 'passive' types of activities, such as reading. How did the Westchester population find time for all of these activities? How did it fill up its 'discretionary slots'? Lundberg *et al.* asked their sample to keep a diary of activities over periods ranging from a day to a week. In this way, they collected information on a total of 4,460 days from 2,460 different people. A year for most inhabitants of Westchester County, in the early 1930s, consisted of 280 working days, 52 Saturday afternoon holidays (most of the employed population worked Saturday mornings), 52 Sundays and 7 special holidays. 'Thus,' they concluded, '85 days (including the half holidays) per year constitute the standard time allowance for leisure in an industrial civilization' (pp. 90–1).

Social classes were compared with regard to their uses of leisure. Somewhat surprisingly, the range of non-leisure, that is work-related, hours was not as great as might have been expected between the 'labor' group with its eighteen hours of non-leisure in a day and nearly six hours of leisure and the professional class with its seventeen hours of non-leisure and nearly seven hours of leisure. Even the unemployed group judged that it had as many as fifteen hours of non-leisure. Here, however, the similarities end. White, who conducted a similar study in Ohio in the mid-1950s, summarized the differences between the classes as follows:

> Study of a random sample of families in Ohio shows that the uses of leisure are conditioned by social class and to the same extent by age and sex. The Upper Middle class selects libraries, home diversions and lecture and study groups more often than other classes . . . whereas the two lowest classes use parks and playgrounds, Community Chest agencies, churches, museums and commercial entertainment relatively more often. (White, 1955, p. 145)

A significant aspect of Lundberg *et al.* had to do with methodology, their attempt to attach numbers to the amount of time spent in the various forms of leisure activity. This introduced what, since the Second World War, has become one of the most important sub-disciplines within the leisure and social participation literature: time-budget analysis, the measurement and classification of how people use time in a daily or weekly timeframe. (See Kleemeier, 1961; DeGrazia, 1964; and Warwick and Bishop, 1972, for an extensive bibliography of the subject.)

One of the most significant of these studies, Szalai (1972), was conducted in the 1960s when researchers from twelve countries including the United States and the Soviet Union, Eastern and Western Europe, and Peru joined in an unprecedented international effort to research time usage among local populations. Among the myriad findings was the discovery of considerable homogeneity from country to country even where economic conditions and class structures differed dramatically.

Of particular relevance here was the classification of the normal day into thirty-seven primary activities within nine major headings: work, housework (for both males and females), household care, child care, personal needs, non-work travel, study-participation (which covered study, religious involvement and voluntary organizations), mass media, and leisure. It is worth seeing how these categories break out, in that it gives us some idea, and one which is usually totally absent from the PAE literature, as to where adult education might fit into a person's daily life. The following are lists of average times in minutes spent on each of a number of major activities during a single day, for a sample of men and women from forty-four cities in the US: main job – 225 minutes, housework – 142, household care (including shopping) – 45, child care – 32, sleeping – 470, non-work travel – 50, study (the only overtly educational category) – 12, mass media (TV, radio) – 134, leisure (entertainment, visiting, etc.) – 123. (Based on Szalai, 1972, Table 1, p. 114.)

According to Szalai, a typical day breaks down into three significant categories of activity, (1) those relating to physiological need, (2) those relating to work, and (3) those relating to free or leisure use. With respect to the first they noted that upwards of ten and a half hours or 44 per cent of the twenty-four-hour day was taken up in sleep (the most time-consuming), eating, and personal hygiene. With regard to the second category, work, the authors noted a tendency for an 'active strain toward constancy of time allocation' (p. 123), meaning that as people had more time away from work they filled it with other kinds of work rather than with significant additions of leisure or free time. Formal work (excluding housework) occupied between 7.0 and 9.0 hours for employed men, and 6.8 and 7.6 hours a day for employed women.

Finally, with respect to leisure or time at the discretion of the user, the researchers recorded an average of four and one-third hours per day for non-work, non-physiological activity. 'This means that on most days, employed people have only very limited amounts of free time. Indeed, on a typical workday, 10 per cent of women report no free time activities whatsoever, although virtually all men do report at least a little' (p. 131).

Within these rather cast-iron parameters of work and physiological need, how do researchers account for people's differential use of leisure, and how do their theories reflect on PAE as leisure use? It is fascinating to compare research in this area with PAE research, and to see, rather quickly, how much they resemble each other. Leisure researchers, like PAE researchers, have been concerned with rates of participation as well as their demographic and socioeconomic correlates. They have noted the cumulative effects of one lesiure activity on another (Allardt, Jartti, Jyrkila and Littunen, 1957; Wilensky, 1961); they have focused on the structure, including the 'factor analytic' structure, of motivation (Bishop, 1970; McKechnie, 1974; Crandall, 1980; Beard and Ragheb, 1983), 'situation' vs personality-based theories of action (Witt and Bishop, 1970; Kelly, 1977;

Stover and Garbin, 1982), leisure use as a 'theory of reasoned action' (Ray, 1981; Young and Kent, 1985), and most recently, echoing motivational orientation research, have turned to factor analysis to discover the patterns underlying people's expressions of reasons for participation (Bishop, 1970; McKechnie, 1974; Beard and Ragheb, 1983). Indeed, in some cases, PAE and leisure research clearly overlap as in Ray's (1981) test of Grotelueschen and Caulley's decision model, published in the *Journal of Leisure Research*.

## David Horton Smith and the concept of general activity

Nowhere has the urge to bring all of these myriad forms of social and cultural expression under some kind of overarching theoretical framework been strongest than in the work of David Horton Smith, spanning a couple of decades, and collected in his monumental *Participation in Social and Political Activities*. At the heart of Smith's reformulation is the ISSTAL model, summarized in Chapter 3. For the purposes of the present discussion, we shall look at what Smith calls a 'particular variant' of ISSTAL, his General Activity model, since it is this which appears to have the most relevance to various findings introduced earlier in this study.

The General Activity model, as does ISSTAL, rests on the premise, supported by time budget research, that a normal person's activities in everyday life and throughout the lifespan are 'nonrandom.' Some of this nonrandomness can be accounted for by 'biophysical' considerations such as the alternation of day and night; some by physiological considerations such as the need for sleep (the dominant use of an individual's daily time). Beyond that, according to Smith,

> one very important factor is a kind of mutual accommodation of the individual's sociocultural system and body, character and context. This accommodation, made primarily by the individual, in most cases, is fundamental to the operation of human society because it permits and indeed encourages the optimal accomplishment of activities (by individuals) that are considered good, useful, or proper in the framework of the sociocultural system involved. (p. 462)

Accommodation, of the individual to the system and of the system to the individual, is made necessary for the survival of both. Accommodation is made possible through the processes of socialization and culturation, according to which an individual learns the rules for living in society and accepting the various roles thrust upon him or her. (The essential conservativeness of the ideology underpinning this theory will be discussed in Chapter 6.)

A central thesis of Smith, and one which addresses this study directly, is that accommodation causes all 'discretionary social participation activities' to be 'cumulative' in nature. In other words, those who volunteer for some activities, attend classes, and so on, are more likely to be associated with other forms of community involvement. Smith's logic is far from clear on this point, however. What he appears to be saying is that those individuals who engage in a succession of 'socio-culturally encouraged' behaviors are doing so as part of their accommodation to the system. But it would also follow that the 'need' (whose need, Smith doesn't say) for accommodation makes the appearance of overlapping activities more likely. The first consideration makes 'general activity' a function of the individual, his psychology and personality. The second would make it (and accommodation) a natural outgrowth of the natural existence of society and thus a function of people's interactions and common group needs. In this respect, social participation, and by implication PAE, are natural aspects of group life and therefore much less reflections of individual, idiosyncratic motivation.

For Smith, a person's character has much to do with the varying levels of social participation in normal, everyday society and is the sum total of 'all . . . psychological states and processes, . . . [comprising] the unique pattern of motivation (personality traits and the full range of attitudinal variables), intellectual capacities, retained information, etc.' (p. 466), or, in other words, a significant division of the variables making up the ISSTAL model. While a full explication of this definition is somewhat beyond the scope of this study, one element of the definition holds promise for a better understanding of PAE. It is the idea that motivation (including expressed reasons and motives for PAE) is part of a person's character and must be judged in conjunction with other motivated actions rather than as a discrete entity in its own right. Or that, as Edwards and Booth (1973) put it, motivation to PAE must be interpreted as part of a 'vocabulary of motives' according to which individuals organize and attempt to give meaning to a range of disparate activities, bringing them under the same umbrella of rationalization.

## IMPLICATIONS OF SOCIAL PARTICIPATION RESEARCH FOR ADULT EDUCATION

Adult learning interpreted within a framework of social participation research is a 'social action' (Znaniecki, 1936/1967). This is not to say that learning is always and everywhere in the public eye, always visible as it were, only that the whole dimension of the public and the private, the formal and the informal, and how these are differentiated within a society are crucial to our understanding of why adults learn. Adults attend classes when they have the time, and little enough of it they appear to have, if Szalai and his associates are correct. They also go about their business and in that process undertake learning projects. (Tough, it appears, was correct.) What we have clearly lacked up until now, however, is a view of all adult learning activity as something which takes place within a definable social context, an organizational and societal nexus.

At the beginning, the question 'Why do adults learn?' was interpreted in two ways. The first had to do with the existence (or non-existence) of orientations towards learning (needs, motives, etc.). The second had to do with the conditions which facilitate or inhibit adult learning. In the typical model such factors become 'barriers' or provide 'opportunities' without being further analyzed as to their particular content. Rubenson, Cookson and others discuss social roles, status and related concepts, but it is not easy to see where they fit in or what makes these more potent variables, and thus better predictors, than the traditional indexes of socio-economic status as measured in the studies of Johnstone, London, and others. It seems from the discussion in this chapter that there are other more productive ways of talking about 'conditions' of learning, ways which take into account, first, the actions or perceived actions of others as they influence the self's actions and, second, the 'actions' (mission, patterns of recruitment, etc.) of institutions which also send signals to the would-be learner as to how he or she is expected to behave.

When we talk about the conditions – enabling or disabling – of learning, it would seem to be natural to talk about the whole idea of leisure or free-time and how it is used. Time-budget research promises a new and exciting perspective on some of the old problems. Take the notion of voluntariness, for example. Time-budget studies, as reported in Smith, Szalai, and others, distinguish between work- and non-work-related activity. What about on-the-job training or other learning activities undertaken within the context of work? Such activities are often not free in the sense of being at the discretion of the worker. Moreover, in many cases there is a strong, if silent, pressure in the direction of participation. It seems fair to reserve the term 'voluntary' only for those learning activities undertaken at the discretion of the individual and in his or her (defined) leisure hours. All others would be considered non-voluntary or mandatory.

Second, when discussed in the context of time usage, the decision to participate, to learn or not to learn (where learning is viewed as process rather than product), ought to be seen less as the result of a combination of factors such as personality, climate, and so on (as in all of the major decision models reported in Chapter 3) and more as a choice among competing activities. It is extraordinary how this aspect of the problem has been ignored over the years. McCloskey came closest to it with his Power-Load-Margin concept (Main, 1979), and the idea that people will engage in learning in the time and 'space' left over from other activities. London *et al.* (1963) disputed this rather appealing idea by showing that it was often those most active, that is engaged in a range of different 'active' behaviors, who were more inclined to participate in adult education, while the less active were more likely to engage in 'passive' behaviors like watching television. Nevertheless, anyone who has ever tried to persuade adults to undertake a sustained learning episode in their lives knows full well the competition between different roles, responsibilities, pleasures and proclivities. While over and above personal experience, research on time-use makes it abundantly clear that uses of free-time takes place against a background of different forms of leisure consumption while remaining a function of work and work-related activities. Boiled down to its essence, once we begin to view adult learning as a form of social action then we must start our analysis of the factors leading to it not with the individual and his or her motivation but with the environment of choice and constraint that is the normal adult's everyday experience.

If we look more closely at leisure research, however, two findings in particular appear to create problems for the normal manifestations of adult learning. It has been the accepted wisdom for many years (e.g. Johnstone and Rivera, 1965) that leisure has been increasing over the last few decades and certainly since the beginning of the century, and thus creating a 'space' for learning activities to flourish. Research by DeGrazia (1964), however, challenges this position. Certainly, the amount of actual time on the job, for some specific occupations, may have decreased relative to jobs a century ago. Nowadays, however, there are factors which are work-related, like commuting, which combined with time taken for other personal necessities may not have increased the overall amount of real, free-time available for leisure, and thus for learning, by a significant amount. Two observations can be made regarding this latter point. First, we should not assume greater absolute amounts of time available for undertaking formal learning. This carries implications for the traditional forms of educational provision. Second, there are many signs that men and women use work-related time such as commuting to undertake learning projects. This carries implications for new forms of educational 'provision,' that is self-directed learning.

The second finding with respect to time availability for learning has to do with what Szalai (1972) called 'constancy of time allocation,' a phenomenon which says that time freed up from work in the principal occupation is then spent in a second or third job. If this phenomenon is widespread, where is the real increase in leisure time that could be spent on learning activities?

Third, and related to the first point, we tend to count learners as units of individual men and women. Suppose instead we counted the family as the learning unit? Now if we compared a modern three-member family with that same unit a generation or two ago, we would find that there is a far greater likelihood that both husband and wife in the average middle-class family will be working than the same couple thirty or forty years earlier. Thus, as a learning unit the time available for the average family to learn, study and produce knowledge may have shrunk rather than expanded.

So time and the uses of leisure form a context within which individual men and women engage in learning activities over the lifespan. When those same men and women go to learn, however, they do so against a different backdrop, that of society organized along class and institutional lines. This world is composed of overlapping relationships between the world of work, personal and family life, as well as leisure. Some of these relationships are highly refined, ritualized and formal, and reflect the existence of concrete organizations or associations, while others are much more informal and spontaneous. PAE is a subset of such relationships, varying from the most to the least formal, and reflecting a social domain, such as the distinction between work and leisure.

Leisure activities, save a small portion that are quite out of the purview of society and its guardians, are like fashions in general. They involve men and women gathered into distinct groups or associations, each behaving in ways which conform to appropriate norms and rules of behavior. This seems like an obvious point, but it is rarely made in the PAE literature. And the point can be made by referring to the world of fashion. If we ask individual men and women why they dress the way they do they will give reasons which appear to reflect individual taste. Someone will say she would never wear black. Another will say he would never be seen in a turtle-neck. Despite these often idiosyncratic differences in taste, however, if we compare an office-full of people or a class of students, or children in a playground with similar groups of a generation or two ago we notice that they have a lot more in common with each other than anyone of them might have with a person of a previous age, regardless of how individually they think they behave. Put simply, people behave in groups, work and play together in groups and are moved to participate or not in various groups and associations according to group norms and pressures. It is essential that we see PAE as but another example of conformity, not of course at all times and in all contexts, but conformity, nevertheless, where individual motive may be much less important than the power of the group to persuade or dissuade one from taking a certain route or attempting to learn a particular skill.

This is what is essentially behind the findings of research on participation in voluntary associations. It reflects the various ways in which society is already divided up: along class lines, and those of gender, race and, in some cases, religion. Organizations which 'capture' people's leisure time are tied to where people live and work, their occupation and professional status. It seems then only logical to assume, since the point was already made over thirty years ago (Brunner *et al.*, 1959), that adult education really consists of many different kinds of often unrelated organizations or institutions and that each organization or organizational system will recruit those members who best reflect what its leaders and influential officers believe the organization stands for.

Organizations such as voluntary associations, as described by Booth and Edwards, Wilensky and others, are in many cases extensions of earlier systems designed to socialize the individual and acculturate him or her to the dominant social forms. This idea seems to hold the key to understanding much of the activity we call organized adult learning and its link to earlier, formal, educational activity or schooling. It is to this nexus we turn now in order to underscore the essential link between forms of adult learning and larger social structures and the importance of society, community, and the group to an understanding of why adults learn.

Concern for the social reality surrounding the act of PAE brings us *pari pasu* to the concept of education itself and the 'functions' it serves in modern society. We have examined PAE as a reflection of individual personality and motivation. We have also examined it in its social guise showing it in relationship to community and associational life in general. Now we need to turn to the concept of education itself, as distinct from the concept of learning and its historical connections with psychology. What function does adult education serve in modern American society? And how is this to be reflected in explanations of the central question of why do adults learn?

# 6  Adult learning and the social functions of education

> Middle class parents and children struggle more fiercely to hold onto what they have than do 'outsiders' to gain a foothold. This basic difference in motivation between the potentially mobile and the already arrived seems to us to explain far more of the variation in college entrance and graduation rates than theories that emphasize economic or cultural obstacles to mobility.
>
> (Jencks and Riesman, 1969)

One of the most enduring findings of the PAE literature is the strong relationship between levels of formal schooling and later involvement in postsecondary education: those who avail of opportunities for adult education tend to be those who have already achieved significant levels of earlier schooling. Newberry (1959), who surveyed many of the studies of organized participation up to the close of the 1950s, observed that 'effective formal participation' required facility in communications and human relations, skills that normally were learned in earlier phases of schooling. It also seemed that those with more education were more highly motivated. But beyond this he did not venture. Here is how he framed the question for future researchers: 'Whether the better educated participate more because their previous experience prompts them to seek solutions to needs through traditional and familiar patterns, while the less educated . . . do not perceive that pattern as the way to solve their needs' (p. 116).

For London *et al.* (1963) understanding the link between earlier schooling and later PAE had to begin with the fact that adult education continued rather than completed formal schooling: it was not a substitute for formal education. This meant that the reasons might be sought in the effects of schooling itself and in what happened to the individual later. According to the first speculation, schooling produced an appreciation for 'things educational' and for social participation in general. According to the second, the better educated were more likely to occupy the professions which placed strong emphasis on continuing learning. The second thesis was supported by London *et al.* in an interesting way. In most surveys of PAE, professional workers tend to participate more than those in managerial positions whose pattern of activity more often resembles clerical and kindred workers than it does professionals. In their study the PAE rate for professionals was 22 per cent, for managers 16 per cent. Breaking down the professional and managerial categories further, London disclosed a range of from 13 per cent to 38 per cent for five groups of professionals, and a range of from 17 per cent to 40 per cent for four groups of managers. In general the managers' rate of PAE was under 20 per cent and thus closer to that of the less skilled white-collar workers. The maverick manager category which showed a rate of 40 per cent was in fact 'professionals in management positions.' In other words, the category of workers titled 'manager' included those of high and of low educational attainment. The former were more likely to be professionals working in managerial positions and it was these who engaged more frequently in educational pursuits. Moreover, if there were enough of them, the level of PAE within the category as a whole would be raised.

When Cross (1978) implicitly updated Ozanne's (1934) survey of surveys she adduced three hypotheses to explain the connection between earlier schooling and later PAE. The first echoed London *et al.* as to the effects of schooling in producing a liking for education and learning in general. According to the second, however, 'those who have been successful in the fairly narrow demands of the educational system stay in it longer and also wish to return to the scene of their earlier success' (p. 12). According to her third hypothesis, all human beings are essentially curious and enjoy learning. The better off, however, are in a position to pursue this learning further, while the less well-off have obstacles placed in their way. Here Cross was content merely to raise the issues without saying which hypothesis she favored or what she had seen in the literature to support either one or the other. This was also her position in Cross (1979).

These hypotheses could be tested through longitudinal research which would correlate various aspects of the experience of high school with later postsecondary experience. Surprisingly enough, this approach to research has been almost totally absent from the annals of adult education.[1] That which exists is not recent nor does it cover an extended period of years. Carson (1965), for example, who studied a group of males who were high school sophomores during 1958–9, managed only a time lapse of six years. Nevertheless, he found a strong relationship between certain features of the earlier school experience and later PAE: vocational and educational aspiration, educational achievement and mental ability. Also significant were father's and mother's education, as well as father's occupation. In other words, and apart from the student's own aspirations and success while at school, the better the education of the parents and the higher the occupation the more likely was the subject to engage in later educational activity, a finding which is in line with research on the relationship between family background, schooling and later educational plans and experiences. Waldron (1968) who found similar correlations in his study of Wisconsin students, concluded that education perpetuated the desire for more education.

Boyle (1967) is particularly interesting in that he used the Houle typology to classify the motives of a sample of high school graduates from selected Wisconsin counties, as part of a longitudinal study begun in 1956. He noted that over half of the respondents expressed a goal-orientation, and that this combined with the high level of participation in vocational subjects indicated a high motivation among young male adults to improve their position in the world of work. He also noted that current occupation was more significantly related to reasons for PAE than were variables connected with earlier schooling, a finding which reflects conclusions by LeClair (1969), Devlin (1977) and Bergsten (1980) that PAE is more a function of contemporary concerns and attitudes than of earlier school and non-school experiences.

Survey research has thus established a strong link between social background and PAE. It has further demonstrated a link between the demands of the everyday world, especially that of work, and PAE. More importantly, it seems to show that while many people face similar problems and personal demands, not everyone interprets these problems educationally, and that those who do are already the beneficiaries of a more advantageous social and educational background. It is this kind of background which is more likely to produce white-collar and professional workers and it is in connection with this kind of employment that adult education seems most suited. At the same time, former schooling appears to create the kinds of attitudes, values and feelings about life which are translated into a more active and organized leisure. Adult education benefits from attitudes to life in general which in themselves have little to do with the explicit purpose for which a course or program is organized.

These are really questions about schooling and its influence on adult education, even about the function of adult education as itself a form of schooling. This kind of thinking takes us beyond the individual and his or her own particular learning experiences, his or her desire to learn, enjoyment of learning or goals for learning. Now we are really talking about learning in its 'official' guise, as 'education.' Our question now becomes, 'What is it about the function of education – schooling – in modern American society which contains an explanation of why individual men and women in later life engage in the common forms of learning we call adult education?'[2]

## EDUCATION AND SOCIETY

In notes to the introduction of his first volume on the history of American education, Cremin (1970) traced the etymology of the word 'education.' The earliest 'modern' use of the term appeared in the Act constituting the universities of Oxford and Cambridge, in the late 1500s. However, he noted, 'It was rather the term "institution" . . . that appeared again and again in Tudor discussions of the deliberate attempt to form human beings in accordance with certain cultural ideals' (pp. 595–6).

Two elements of this analysis stand out: the idea that education is historically synonymous with the existence of an institution and the idea that the institutions of schooling set out deliberately to mold and shape future citizens. The first element reflects in some ways the modern concern with education-as-schooling; the second the idea that schooling serves an important role as a socializing agent. Current criticism of the equation of learning with schooling, while patently justified in many cases, tends to ignore the broader implications of Cremin's analysis. His history, now an exhaustive three-volume work, concerned itself not only with schools, but also with all those other institutions – the home, church, the media, even published philosophical tracts – which separately and in concert educationally shaped the collective mind. What he was pointing out is that education is a function fulfilled by many institutions outside of the school, school being but one influence, and, in particular historical periods, a much less influential form of enculturation than any or all of the others. In this, Cremin was inspired by Bailyn's re-evaluation of the role of education in early colonial America, the central insight of which concerned the realization by the colonists that in the New World they could no longer expect the values they cherished to be transmitted unconsciously and automatically to each new generation:

> Where there had been ingrained habits, unquestioned tradition, automatic responses, security and confidence there was now awareness, doubt, formality, will and decision. The whole range of education had become an instrument of deliberate social purpose. (Bailyn, 1962, pp. 21–2)

Mainstream educators who doubt the validity of these observations have only to look at the current political situation in South Africa to realize the centrality of education not simply as discussions of how we should train our young people but as something which is at the very heart of the political struggle for power. The rise in importance of the movement among Blacks for a 'People's Education,' for example, reflects the irrelevance of most forms of official schooling for the deprived black population. The significance of the struggle over education in South Africa, as in other countries which have suffered the yoke of colonialism, points unerringly to the link between learning and real participation as a free person in the full range of a society's political, economic and social institutions.[3]

Education is at the heart of any society's attempts to create a civilization, preserve a world-order, socialize its citizens and, ideally, to provide one and all with the means for carving out an allotted place in the scheme of things. It is this essential range of ideological goals that is being referred to by the term 'schooling.' It is this set of goals which requires that we look beyond the individualism inherent in most modern theories of adult learning to the make-up of society and the role played by adult education in maintaining and occasionally changing the status quo.

Schooling is inextricably bound up with the existence of institutions. Indeed, schooling by its nature represents the institutionalization of learning. Thus, it makes little sense to talk about the identity or definition of adult education without considering the institutions which perform this function. And if we consider these institutions and in what ways they serve their superficially varying clientele, certain conclusions seem inevitable. Adult education – despite the ideology that it is everything and everywhere, from Sierra Club weekends in the mountains to Graduate Business programs in the cities, from English language classes for new immigrants to politics for senior citizens, from mixology to mineralogy, from How-To-Be-A-Swinging-Single to How-To-Be-A-Single-Parent, in other words, anything of an organized nature as long as it involves adults acquiring knowledge – most of these diverse activities and programs are essentially an extension of the normal system of schooling, and not basically different from it.

We can summarize this argument and the hypotheses it implies as follows. Adult education in the United States, through the transmission of ordered knowledge – mainly the sciences and technology, vocational education and industrial training – duplicates or otherwise augments the normal school system by fulfilling (sociological) functions similar to its major functions, that is placing people in particular roles with respect to the economic and political structure. Furthermore, as an environment for enjoying, using or otherwise consuming leisure-time, adult education in modern American society is a form of social practice which signals class identity and allegiance.

As an extension of schooling, the function of adult education becomes the transmission of culture and the diffusion of work skills. (See also Jarvis, 1983, on these points.) More importantly, however, schools and colleges –

which also form the major institutions of adult education – do not simply teach competence, knowledge and skills, rather they continue the socialization of young citizens within a climate of knowledge, competence and skills. That is to say, schooling, at the secondary and postsecondary level, provides a specific and important social context within which the activities that adult men and women engage in come to be approved and sanctioned as learning. The spirit of this interpretation is captured in the following remarks of Burton Clark:

> Institutes of adult work and pleasure find it to their self interest to encourage the emergence of an educational subsystem and thus to spread formal education through society. Thus, for an ever larger share of the population, formal education is the main means to cultural as well as occupational qualification. Knowledge is a prime ingredient of the society based on science, technology and expertise, and the primacy of knowledge is the primacy of education. In the face of large dangers and uncertainty, a learning society offers the opportunity that very large numbers of men may participate effectively in a complex culture and in the social and political affairs of a complex society. In this possibility lies the educational premise of modern man. (Clark, 1965)

In the following sections, arguments and evidence for this depiction of American adult education are adduced by treating the latter as a sociological phenomenon and considering the issue of motivation within a sociological framework. In doing so, I am mindful of the fact that 'no sociology of the education of adults exists in the same manner as there are sociological studies of initial education' (Jarvis, 1985, p. 3).

## EDUCATION AND MOBILITY: THEMES IN THE SOCIOLOGY OF EDUCATION

Mass higher education and the extension of educational opportunities to the widest margin of the adolescent and young adult population in the United States is a phenomenon of our time. A higher proportion of young people leave high school and attend an institute of higher learning in the United States than anywhere in the world. Only Canada comes close to this extraordinary number.[4] So ubiquitous is this phenomenon that it is sometimes easy to forget how recent it has been. Back in 1870, approximately one in fifty of those aged between 18 and 21 attended college. By 1935, the figure was one in five, by 1960, it had doubled to two in five (Jencks and Riesman, 1969).

    Much of this increase has occurred since the Second World War, a span of less than fifty years. At the same time, while the median number of years spent at school rose sharply to twelve during the 1920s and 1930s, in spite or indeed because of the Depression, the increase has been more modest in recent years. This is mirrored in the fact that while 67 per cent of the relevant age group graduated from high school in 1960, this figure had declined from an early 1970s peak to 73 per cent in 1980, and was projected to remain constant at this number until 1990. Thus, mass competitive higher education is a phenomenon whose precise shape is both historically new and sociologically stable (Trow, 1977).

With the rise in the level of educational attainment has gone a concomitant upgrading of the entire occupational spectrum, most evident in the growth of the category of employment described as 'professional.' In 1900, according to Jencks and Riesman (1969), some 42 per cent of all males worked on farms; by 1960, the figure had plummeted to 9 per cent. The figure for unskilled labor went from one in seven in 1900 to half of that by the later date. At the same time, white-collar 'professionals' increased in the workforce from one in thirty at the turn of the century to one in nine by 1960, with most of that increase coming after 1940. Again, as with educational attainment, the peak may already have been reached. Thus while the proportion of those in professional, technical and kindred occupations increased dramatically from 6 per cent in 1940 to 11 per cent in 1960 (the last year of the Jencks and Riesmann figures), between then and 1970 it rose to only 14 per cent, reaching 16 per cent by 1981. At the same time, while those in blue-collar employment continued to decline fairly considerably, the proportion of those in service occupations, a new hybrid which seems to fall between unskilled operative and white-collar employee, went from 6 per cent in 1940 to 13 per cent in 1981.

What was not generally true before the turn of the century has become the norm since the Second World War: educational attainment has been linked undeniably to social and occupational mobility. So sharply etched in the modern consciousness has the link between achievement in the world of school and success in the world of work become, that to many it must appear to have always been that way. It is in the perceived strength of this link and why it obtains that we may seek a comprehensive sociological account of PAE. To do so we draw on two schools of thought regarding the organization of society and the problem of order. One such school goes by the name of 'functionalism' or 'structural-functionalism,' the other, more recently emerging school and one whose evolution is not yet complete, goes by various names; here it will be called the 'conflict' school.[5] Both reflect the concern of sociologists with social structure and social control: how solidarity among members of a society is possible, especially given the existence of inequities and the tendency for individuals to pursue their own self-interest. Both also reflect an emphasis on the primacy of social structure over individual choice and decision-making. They differ, however, in their response to the question of change and whether society tends to be organized for the betterment of the many or the pleasure of the few.

## Functionalism and consensus

Education serves two principal functions, according to Burton Clark (who is known to adult education audiences for his work on the 'marginality' of the field as an institutional function) the transmission of culture and the provision of work skills. While appearing almost as a reverent restatement of the liberal ideal, the implications of his definition lie far from eulogy. Clark was writing at a time when the progressive education movement had fallen into disrepute, while a blanket of anxiety had spread over the country following Sputnik. Progressivism had become the holding pen of all that was molly-coddling and permissive in the treatment of children. Most importantly, it had focused almost exclusively on the individual to the exclusion of the group. Though the concern had been brewing since the Second World War, Sputnik sharpened the educational debate, with regard to technology, industrial competitiveness and ultimately the political supremacy of the United States as a world power. With these stirring words Clark heralded the 'real' educational tasks of the new era: 'Our age demands army upon army of skilled technicians and professional experts, and to the task of preparing these men the educational system is increasingly dedicated' (p. 3).

This statement epitomized the 'functionalist' perspective: the 'goodness-of-fit' between the type and level of individual skill in relation to the demand and future evolution of the economy. It owed much to contemporary economic thinking about the distribution of skills and rewards in a modern industrial society. More importantly, it was in keeping with a broadly based liberal ideology, which over the past hundred years has held to an almost impregnable belief in the power of education to offset the power of privilege to determine social position (Taylor, Rockhill and Fieldhouse, 1985).

The whole concept of a middle class in the United States as opposed to Britain, France and other countries is one which traditionally has contained workers as well as lawyers and skilled craftsmen as well as teachers, all of them positions of achievement rather than ascription (Turner, 1961). According to the functional-liberal perspective, education became the sole determinant of social and occupational mobility. It was another kind of investment, albeit a rather special form, with direct pay-offs in terms of occupational mobility and prestige. The link could almost be quantified: the greater the number of years spent at school the greater the status and financial rewards at the end. The apparent strength of the correlation between the highest level of schooling achieved and one's occupational rank compelled the conviction that the United States was characterized by rapid mobility, based on individual effort linked to education. Schools were the clearing house for talent. They mediated ambition.

Naturally, this relationship was not all one-way. Sociologists' and economists' understanding of how education benefited individuals was interpreted within a framework which saw first the benefits to society in general of an ever more highly trained workforce, and only then the fulfillment of individual aspirations. According to this *zeitgeist* and under the thrall of 'progressivism,' modern society was seen to be evolving in complexity, with technology continually transforming the world of work. This more than any other single idea has been the theme of American educational thought since the 1930s. (See Clark, 1962; Cotton, 1968.) Technology, social complexity and, by the late 1930s, totalitarianism, were direct threats to the survival of democracy. Of all of the major institutions a society has at its command, education was the chief weapon to combat social evil, ensure racial and class equality, and save democracy by providing, in a neutral manner, the knowledge and skills necessary to ensure personal survival and prosperity.

Functionalism took consensus as the basis of the social order. Education was the means of reinforcing that consensus. It was the simultaneous meeting ground of individual aspiration and societal demand. Individuals differed from each other only in terms of motivation and ability, and so the analysis of educational differences became a theory of psychology:

> The structuralist-functionalist is preoccupied with social integration based on shared values – consensus – and he conducts his analysis solely in terms of the motivated action of individuals. For him . . . education is a means of motivating individuals to behave in ways appropriate to maintaining the society in a state of equilibrium. (Karabel and Halsey, 1977, p. 3)

A number of observations may be made here as these relate to the problem of PAE. First, functionalism offers a theory of individual values and needs, particularly educational needs. These are imposed, by society, from without and are handed on from generation to generation without any real questioning. Second, though adult men and women may enter classes as a result of individual needs and motives, they are in a sense merely expressing the kinds of needs which the society wants them to express and, more importantly, are taking the kinds of actions to fulfill those needs, such as participating in formal education, which the society prefers. Finally, educational participation is itself a crucial motivator of individual human action rather than the simple beneficiary of it. It is the means by which a society proffers a rationale for individual action and ensures that it continues in predictable and law-abiding ways.

## Class and conflict

This perspective did not remain unchallenged for long. Studies by Jencks and Riesman (1969) and Collins (1977) sounded early warnings by pointing to the lack of mobility among certain ethnic groups and classes and the undeniable fact that, despite ability and intelligence, young men and women from the 'lower' social classes had less chance of going to college, and thus tended to forfeit the opportunity for mobility granted their educationally equal but more well-off student counterparts. Jencks (1972) questioned the school's capacity to deliver equality of opportunity. Karabel (1977) revealed the latent tracking developing in the community college system as it began to be increasingly linked to the demands of business and industry. This system, Karabel found, tended to steer working-class students away from the opportunity of the four-year college. Berg (1970), Collins (1977), Rodriguez (1978) and Pincus (1980), by challenging the conventional wisdom that educational credentialing came as a response to increased job complexity, queried the whole basis of the functionalist premise which saw education as the great regulator of talent and ambition.

Some of this reaction is captured in Jencks and Riesman (1969), for whom an analysis of the impact of higher education on American society since the late 1800s was impossible 'without talking about social stratification and class' (p. 67). Within a strong statistical analysis, they demonstrated that if 'social class' was defined in terms of income and occupation (which in turn reflected the amount of power each group has or the amount of goods and services each consumes), then there had been little or no change in the size of the various social classes over a twenty-year period, from 1940 to 1960, and no real change in the distribution of income or concomitant power and prestige.

The importance of this conclusion cannot be overemphasized, for it shapes our over-all analysis of the relationship between social class and higher education. If, for example, the size of the various classes is taken as fixed, social mobility must be treated as a two-way street. Upward mobility will be possible only if vacancies occur in higher strata for some reason (p. 72).

At the same time, the education level of the general population has risen dramatically, especially since the Depression. If this is taken as a measure of 'cultural class,' it should be assumed that the upper cultural classes had expanded considerably since the Second World War. Again Jencks and

Riesman found relative stability where they had expected dramatic change. They also found that despite the enormous progress in the spread of education to ever larger numbers of the general population, the 'absolute gap between the best and worst educated third ... widened from 5.8 to 7.0 years between the 1910–1914 generation and the 1930–34 generation, even though the distribution of schooling had grown more equitable' (p. 83).

Thus, it seemed, paradoxically, that the spread of mass higher education in the United States had been accompanied by the concentration of both economic and cultural status within certain groups, leading to the situation where 'subcultures are more hierarchical than they used to be, and the "lower" tend to defer increasingly to the "higher"' (p. 75). Despite the rise in the levels of income and education, and the more equitable distribution of both, the authors concluded cautiously, it seemed that the best paid men occupying the most prestigious jobs were also the best educated. 'This suggests a considerable overlap in America's economic, occupational and cultural elites' (p. 86). Here we have a persuasive account which, if true, would explain the reason for overlapping populations with respect to the various forms of social participation analyzed in Chapter 5.

Collins (1977) launched a more spirited attack on what he called the 'technical-functionalist' perspective whose major premises he identified as follows. First, growth in technology changes the skill requirements for jobs. In other words,

> the mix of skills in the labor force is set by the economy's industrial structure. People's decisions about how much education to acquire lead to a given distribution of educational attainments in the labor force, but this process is merely the result of market forces set in motion by the economy. (Rodriguez, 1978, p. 56)

As a society grows more industrially complex so does the specificity of its functions and roles. The number of skilled jobs increases, while the number of unskilled positions correspondingly decreases. According to the second premise identified by Collins, the same jobs are upgraded in skill demands. Hence the need for more and more education. Formal education provides the necessary training and general knowledge to keep pace with these changes. Third, the educational requirements for jobs constantly increase making more and more people spend a longer time at school.

On the first point, Collins argued that through much of the period 1940–60, over which there had been a sharp decline in the number of unskilled jobs, 85 per cent of the rise in educational credentialling could be attributed to educational upgrading *within* and not *between* jobs. (Rodriquez, 1978, who carried out a similar analysis for the period 1950–70 came to similar conclusions.) Furthermore, Collins found evidence of over-education: a rise in the level of educational attainment had far outstripped the demands of actual jobs. He agreed with Berg, who in an earlier powerful indictment of the world of job training, had concluded that 'Americans of diverse educational achievement perform productive functions adequately and perhaps well in all but a few professional occupations' (Berg, 1970, p. 41). This sentiment was further echoed in Pincus (1980): 'Even the Carnegie Commission . . . agrees that high school graduates have the qualifications for at least 80 per cent of the jobs that now exist' (p. 345).

Turning now to the argument, apparently unassailable, that formal education provided the necessary skills and background knowledge to meet the technological challenge, Collins posed two questions: 'Do people with higher levels of education perform better in work?' and 'Does formal education provide vocational skills?' Evidence from a variety of sources cited by the author supported a negative answer to the first question. Berg had earlier concluded that quite often those with higher levels of schooling performed poorer in certain jobs, especially when they felt that these did not demand a level of responsiblitiy commensurate with their educational preparation. In answer to the second question, while the evidence was more difficult to marshall, it appeared that the link between specific types of vocational education and later employability was weak.

All of this set the scene for Collins's own 'conflict theory of stratification.' This argued that jobs are sources of competition between social and ethnic classes, and that educational or other requirements are often posed as barriers to prevent encroachment by 'new' groups and to keep jobs and power in 'old hands.' Societies, according to Collins, are composed of 'status groups' sharing common cultures within which they achieve their individual identity. Status groups are constantly vying with each other for 'goods,' that is power, wealth and prestige. Within this nexus, the primary purpose of schools is to teach status culture, both inside and outside of the classroom:

> In this light, any failure of schools to impart technical knowledge . . . is not important: schools primarily teach vocabulary and inflection, styles of dress, aesthetic tastes, values and manners. (Karabel and Halsey, 1977, p. 126)

Most importantly, in so far as particular status groups control the educational system, they may use credentialing to augment their control of the work situation. This means that educational requirements, far from being necessary for successful performance on the job, are really used 'to select new members for elite positions who share the elite culture,' while, at the lower level, to hire those who have respect for those values and manners.

## EDUCATION, POWER AND CULTURE: THEMES OF THE NEW SOCIOLOGY OF EDUCATION

Jencks and Riesman raise a critical problem at the heart of liberal ideology: equality of educational opportunity, where it exists, does not in and of itself lead to greater social and economic equality. The traditional, dominant pattern of power, wealth and prestige, stirred up by educational reform, shifts a little but hardly moves, and after a little while seems to settle back into its old form. Functionalist thinking sees continued inequality as 'error' in the selection system of an otherwise consensus-based society. Writers like Collins see problems of selection too, but where others see abstract laws of consensus at work, they see only live combat and conflict over limited resources. Education is but one more resource in a limited pool, and many groups and classes – not individuals – compete. Moreover, schooling takes on a symbolic function of signaling class identity. Rather than serving the instrumental function of providing necessary job skills, it serves an equally important – some would argue more important – function of placing people in social categories with respect to each other.

The issues raised by these writers take on the shape of fullblown theories of society in the writings of Bowles and Gintis. The major thesis of Bowles and Gintis (1976) is that the educational system reproduces the consciousness needed to fit in with a hierarchically based economic system. By consciousness they mean thought-patterns and values which espouse discipline, sociability, obedience and a willingness to accept, unquestioningly, the authority of others. Theirs is a so-called 'reproduction theory' in that it emphasizes, albeit in a fairly deterministic manner, the school's function in replicating the economic system within the school and in socializing children into the modes of personality considered by business and industry to be most appropriate to its own needs. In this context, they argue, education has never really been a force for equality in American society: 'Despite the vast increase in college enrollments [since the Second World War], the probability of a high school graduate attending college is just as dependent on parental socio-economic status as it was thirty years ago' (Bowles and Gintis, 1976, p. 8).

For them the key issue is not the question of mental ability and how it is measured, tracked or developed. All analyses of schooling, they believe, must begin with the central fact that *schools (and colleges) produce workers*. The statistical and empirical analysis at the core of their study compares the kinds of evaluation students receive in class – those considered the 'better' students and those the 'worse' – with the kinds of traits employers find desirable in new employees.

There have been many criticisms of this approach, some of it coming from sympathizers like Giroux, who agree that the 'main functions of the schools are the reproduction of the dominant ideology, its forms of knowledge and the distribution of skills needed to reproduce the social division of labor' (Giroux, 1983, p. 257), but who do not follow Bowles and Gintis down the path of reproductive determinism.[6] Instead, Giroux argues, the theory must allow for human agency and the recognition that schools are not mere passive sifters of the dominant forms but battlegrounds in which imposition meets resistance, and individual actors – students – struggle against the usurpation of their own and their community's identity by societal norms and unchallenged definitions of good behavior: 'Schools represent contest terrains marked not only by structural and ideological contradictions but also by collectively informed student resistance' (Giroux, 1983, p. 260).[7]

While in many respects similar, Bourdieu differs from Bowles and Gintis in giving greater autonomy to the school as an independent disseminator of values, and in emphasizing its 'cultural' function in relation to knowledge, rather than its economic function in relation to work. Bourdieu's task has focused on the 'hidden forms of domination that are consciously and unconsciously reproduced in everyday life' (Sulkunen, 1982, p. 105). For him, the educational system is 'the very institution *par excellence* symbolizing the ideology of equality, [when it] is in fact a cultural instrument of class domination' (p. 105). Everyday life, according to Bourdieu, an anthropologist by training, is characterized by different forms of participation and consumption in relation to the family, leisure and work. All of them require two major forms of 'asset': money and cultural competence. Just as the first can be characterized as economic capital, the latter may be termed 'cultural capital.' Forms of participation like attendance at museums and concerts, the reading of books and magazines, musical tastes and other leisure patterns require not only money but also an appropriate level of culture. The acquisition of cultural competence is the function of the school. In a telling quote which puts much of the American literature on social participation and PAE into a more revealing perspective, Bourdieu writes:

> The statistics of theatre, concert and, above all, museum attendance (since, in the last case, the effect of economic obstacles is more or less nil) are sufficient reminder that the inheritance of cultural wealth which

has been accumulated and bequeathed by previous generations only really belongs (although it is theoretically offered to everyone) to those endowed with the means of appropriating it for themselves. (Bourdieu, 1977, p. 488)

The schools accomplish this, Bourdieu believes, through the transmission of a culture that 'tacitly affirms what it means to be educated' (Giroux, 1983, p. 267). So when Clark says that cultural transmission is one of education's two major functions he neatly sidesteps the issue of 'Whose culture is it that is involved?' He overlooks the fact that what constitutes the knowledge and skills to be transmitted is not defined in the same way by all social classes in society:

> The culture transmitted by the school is related to the various cultures that make up the wider society in that it confirms the culture of the ruling class while simultaneously disconfirming the cultures of other groups. (Giroux, 1983, p. 268)

Culture becomes the visible means by which the dominant group engenders the acquiescence, if not outright collaboration, of the subordinate groups. Students of adult education need only dip into the pages of their history to see in Americanization, for example, one of the great episodes of cultures in conflict, and how the educational system was harnessed in a great experiment of cultural domination masquerading as the neutral-sounding transmission of culture. (See especially Carlson, 1987, who makes this point forcefully.)

Finally, according to Bourdieu, reminders of this cultural hegemony are reproduced daily in people's homes – surely an extraordinary feat by any standard – by the form television commercials take, with their images of who is successful and who is not and of who is socially visible and who is not. Forms of knowledge taught by schools are not simply theoretical or practical ways of solving problems or understanding the world; they, like 'qualities of style, modes of thinking and types of disposition' (Giroux, 1983, p. 268), are culturally determined ways of behaving: the reliance on theoretical knowledge with its emphasis on moderation and seeing both sides of the argument implies a political stance and a perspective on how society is organized and ought to be organized. In this respect, Giroux notes: 'High-status knowledge often corresponds to bodies of knowledge that provide a stepping stone to professional careers via higher education' (p. 269).

## THEMES IN THE CULTURE OF TRANSMISSION: TOWARDS A SOCIOLOGY OF PARTICIPATION IN ADULT EDUCATION

Researchers have been slow to trace the connection between participation in the educational system in general and PAE in particular, and more importantly have been slow to consider the interplay between PAE and the economy. Where they have examined this connection, looking at the effects rather than the causes of PAE, they have typically taken a 'functionalist' line, seeing in PAE for vocational reasons a rational response to job reskilling or job dissatisfaction and seeing in adult education a practical way of handling both problems.

London *et al.* (1963), for example, distinguished between the motives for vocational as opposed to other forms of education. Involvement with the former was, following the economist line of Schultz (see Halsey *et al.*, 1961), an 'investment' of time, money and self-esteem, and was expected to pay off in those terms. According to this analysis,

> men will take courses to help them on their jobs if, and only if, the nature of the job requires formal training. A high skill level . . . is a necessary and sufficient condition for [their] taking courses to aid [their] job performance; [secondly] men will take courses to assist in getting a better job only if their present jobs are of low status and they wish to leave them. Being discontent with a low status job is a necessary but not a sufficient condition for taking courses to obtain a better job. (p. 120)

Devlin (1977) is one of the few PAE studies to take the relationship of adult education and occupational mobility as its central theme. Echoing London (1970) and anticipating Bergsten (1980), he found that reasons for PAE had more to do with an individual's work milieu than with either demographic background or previous educational experiences. Like LeClair (1969), he found that work milieu included the perceived opportunity for advancement and belief in education as a means to mobility. Second, it seemed that both PAE and mobility were related to an 'antecedent motivational state' – an orientation in the language of Boshier – which he called 'level of occupational aspiration' (p. 195).

Devlin took a distinctly 'functionalist' perspective on the relationship between PAE and later job mobility, when he wrote that 'in an industrial society whose economic organization is based on the rational distribution of resources to production tasks, there must be social mechanisms by which human talent is allocated to jobs of requisite difficulty' (p. 200). The educational system is the major social mechanism for ensuring equality and compatibility between talent and job demand. However, there are 'imperfections' in the system resulting from a mismatch between what a person can do and what he or she is required to do. Hence, the necessity of adult education which can help mitigate these imperfections in a number of ways. First, PAE could be taken as a sign – even in the absence of formal educational credentials – that a person could perform at a higher job level. Second, in those cases where educational credentialing is required for job mobility but the individual has not completed school – something which is particularly true of certain minority groups, he observed – adult education could step in by providing an alternative to school completion, such as the GED test. Devlin concluded:

> Adult education plays an important role in relation to the occupational structure beyond that popularly recognized. While the manifest function of individual participation in adult education may be the enhancement of occupational mobility, the latent function of such participation in the aggregate is to contribute to the allocation of talent on the basis of ability. This function thus supports the rational organization of economic life. (p. 201)

In other words, adult education serves an important societal function in relation to the distribution of material rewards with respect to real talent and real effort. It becomes the means for improving on the basic function of schooling, which traditionally faces a problem when it attempts to 'regulate' personal ambition in the context of societal need. It is thus, *par excellence*, the means by which earlier deficiencies can be made up and where talent not previously used now finds a new basis of opportunity, at the same time that the continuing needs of an evolving economy are being met.

This analysis, however, takes the functionalist argument for granted. It assumes that the economy grows more complex and thus demands a more educated and highly trained workforce, while formal education – adult education in this case – is the means of enhancing or otherwise creating work skills. Apart from being overtaken by much recent work on the relationship between education and role allocation (Meyer, 1977), it has no place for conflict between groups who command the resources and those who don't, and no place for the insight, developed by Bourdieu and others, that schooling is less concerned with actual transmission of job skills than of job attitudes, less concerned with the rational allocation of talent than with reproducing a social order intact. Nevertheless, Devlin was not unmindful of these other non-functionalist contenders, when he observed that the pursuit of adult education is evidence of a 'normative and ideological structure,' characterized by the learning of a 'pattern of behaviors and values whose effects may be ultimately more important than the mastery of specific subject matter' (p. 204).

Devlin's argument should make the most sense for those near the bottom of the labor market who continue to lack the technical skills made necessary by the constant upgrading of jobs. On the basis of rational allocation, those most in need are precisely those – steelworkers and others employed in heavy manufacturing – who have seen their skills become obsolete and who are in supreme danger of dropping out from the job market entirely. But this runs counter to the reality that adult education is not really peopled by those who may appear to need it most; nor have retraining programs for older workers been successful in general. Likewise, it ignores the fact that adult education is not used by those who do not already have appropriate educational credentials, and in this basic respect is certainly not a way for such people to show that apart from a formal *rite de passage* they are otherwise able to meet the challenge of radical change. Finally, it ignores the small but significant minority of men and women who seem banished forever beyond society's 'pale,' for whom organized learning is perceived as a kind of dreamworld which promises a way out of their misery but which is also forever beyond their grasp (Burman, 1959; Hymon, 1960).

Concern for those functions – how the school manages to meet personal needs while responding to societal demand – was the starting-point for Hopper and Osborn (1975). Deriving their framework from Weber and Durkheim, they began with a fundamental question, 'How is society possible?' That is to say, 'How is consensus maintained among disparate and unequal groups such that society can both proceed and reproduce itself?' Modern society, they pointed out, makes minimal use of force to bring about the desired degree of 'law and order.' This means in effect that people have internalized 'the order of things,' the reigning system of inequalities and social contradictions, as natural. People become their own policemen. In a society like the United States the order of things can be maintained by locating within the educational system the chief duty of allotting social roles and status purely on the basis of merit, native ability and achievement – 'contest mobility' (Turner, 1961). Education is not just the means to mobility but the very symbol of how open a society can be to its most able members. For Hopper and Osborn the basic question became:

> How does an education contribute to a society's attempts to solve simultaneously the fundamental problems of social selection, which involve training, selection proper, recruitment or allocation to jobs and the regulation of ambition. (Hopper and Osborn, 1975, p. 12)

They answered provisionally by arguing that the principal function of an educational system in modern industrial countries is 'effective social control' rather than the attainment of what we normally think of as educational and instructional goals:

In no industrial society are the aims of formal education primarily the development of intellectual and emotional potentials and the fostering of curiosity and creativity . . . In each society the central aims of education are, first, to continue the process of socialization, and, then, to try to solve the fundamental problems of social selection of their populations. (p. 19)

The elementary and secondary systems of schooling are given not merely the function of socialization but also that of role allocation. They develop within the person a concept of self-worth, a sense not only of potential but also of limitations. With this goes an appropriate level of 'normative expectation,' or what individuals will come to feel is or is not rightfully theirs, depending where they 'stand' in society, and which Hopper defines as 'an internalized source of self-evaluation, a censorious imperative from within, a standard by which a person evaluates himself as a success or failure' (p. 34). Meyer (1977) speaks of the school's 'chartering' role whereby 'adult success is assigned on the basis of duration and type of education, holding constant what they may have learned' (p. 59), while 'students tend to adopt personal and social qualities appropriate to the positions to which their schools are chartered to assign them' (p. 60).

But the system is not perfect. Tensions and conflicts abound and it is within the realm of the system's 'mistakes' – Devlin's 'imperfections' – that Hopper and Osborn located the logic of adult education. Looking at the British educational system, on which their study was based, they asked: 'Why has there been a fairly dramatic increase in the demand for adult education of late?' They examine in turn the major factors in the conventional wisdom, namely, that both the need and reason for increasing involvement by the adult population in post-school forms of education and training have to do with retraining in the face of new technology, obsolescence of skills and preparation for increased leisure. Each is rejected on the grounds that they account for only a small portion of the total volume of courses and programs which institutions – educational and non-educational – provide.

The authors turn instead to consider what lay behind the fact that the bulk of those participating in education throughout the middle and late 1960s were individuals who had benefited from the British Education Act of 1944 and the tremendous expansion in educational provision which took place at the end of the Second World War. Was their return to education in the 1960s, then, an unanticipated consequence of their experience in the secondary school system during the 1940s and early 1950s?

Their central thesis rests on the notion of selection 'errors.' As a result of the 1944 Act, two major 'tracks' were created within the secondary system: the grammar school, which effectively prepared young men and women for university or teacher training, that is the professions; and the secondary 'modern' school, which pushed students into technical and 'vocational' areas, or those most directly related to specific jobs. According to Hopper and Osborn, individuals who later become adult students (and here it is important to note that they are talking about those who enter university or colleges of further education for teacher training) have experienced 'initial rejection' followed by 'selection' or 'initial selection' followed by 'rejection.' That is to say, they were students who went through the better stream and later found themselves in jobs which did not match either their status expectations or their perceived abilities. Alternatively, they were channeled into the less prestigious system when they were capable of more, and later found themselves in higher-status jobs requiring skills and expertise they felt they did not have. Both routes provide quite different reasons for wishing to become involved with adult education, though it is implied by Hopper and Osborn that those who experienced initial selection followed by later rejection fill educational courses in far greater numbers. And they conclude: 'According to this argument each adult who returns to further or higher education is an indication that the education system made an error' (p. 28).

## Adult learning and the functions of schooling

In line with the Hopper and Osborn thesis, and the analyses of Bourdieu, Collins and others cited here, adult education in the United States is hypothesized as a set of institutions serving fairly clear-cut and significant functions which duplicate or parallel the functions of schooling with regard to the world of work and leisure, as well as the social order in general. Collins and others have pointed to the overall rise in the level of educational attainment in the country generally, and the constant trend towards educational upgrading within occupations, which they attribute to competition between classes and status cultures for society's limited resources rather than to real industrial need. Adult education, as a result, has become the 'new' force by which the fierce competition for jobs may be continued. McGrath's (1938) point is well taken. His finding that PAE among the most well-educated rose dramatically during the Depression highlights the likely result that in the absence of other means of enhancing competitiveness or gaining necessary work experience, adult education becomes the ideal substitute.

Even where no formal credentials are awarded – the norm as Johnstone and Rivera (1965) noted – adult education has become a form of implicit credentialing, a conclusion in line with Devlin's findings. (These conclusions are, of course, major starting-points for the far more in-depth analyses by Illich and Freire and the interested reader is referred to them.) If these writers are correct, the complexity of modern life, the transformation of jobs through technology, newer demands in the home and family pale next to the need to compete for jobs and cultural status. Adult education joins higher education and the high school in becoming a new battleground for the struggle between classes. Indeed, when we consider who performs much of the adult education function and who avails themselves of the opportunity for it, for all practical purposes higher education and adult education are one; high schools and adult schools are one.

Moreover, this approach to explaining why adults learn accounts for many of the more important statistics uncovered by survey research. The institutions and organizations which provide adult education consist mainly of those aged 17 to 24 (a classification category of the NCES) who are not in 'higher education,' that is four-year college or university. They may be either attending two-year junior or community colleges, or in 'non-collegiate' institutions: technical institutes, business and commercial schools, trade, art and design schools, and so on. They have been attending educational institutions continuously, with at the most a year's break between high school and postsecondary experience. Such students will be counted in PAE reports as 'adult learners' especially if the individuals in question attend the institution on a part-time basis.

However, in terms of motives and orientations to life and education, these 'adults' really belong with students of a similar age who are attending higher and non-collegiate institutions on a full-time basis, since all of them together represent the 'first wave' of participants in postsecondary education. This includes not only those who pick educational alternatives to higher education, but also all those who enter the job market for a short number of years before returning to higher or further education to 'finish' their schooling. According to this line of argument, high school leavers would prefer to enter the job market directly and to pick up specific job skills while being paid by an employer. When the job market is particularly tight – as it was during the early 1980s – they enter non-collegiate institutions to earn an educational qualification in place of job experience. Proprietary schools, for example, are really substitutes for employment training which employers are increasingly reluctant to provide (Pincus, 1980). London *et al.* (1963) have captured the function of adult education with regard to this group of young adults by calling it a kind of 'halfway house' between adolescence and maturity: 'Adult education is a practical service-oriented institution which adds a few final adjustments to a young adult's preparation for full maturity' (London *et al.*, 1963, p. 143).

The need to stay on at school to acquire the right credentials or simply in lieu of work experience reflects two other significant trends in recent American history: the tendency for job training to move out of the work setting and into the college classroom, and the creation of new semi-professions defined less by skill content than by educational credentials. Since the Second World War a generation of men and women has grown up which can boast the highest levels of education achieved by any generation in the country's history. This is also the 'baby boom' generation of the war years. At the same time, the older professions – those in the medical field, law and engineering – are not growing; thus new semi-professions are being created – in the health field, for example – which require a 'lower' level of qualifications but do not command the kind of status traditionally associated with established professions. Moreover, the jobs themselves have become increasingly fragmented and elementary in terms of the skills and knowledge base required to perform them. Professional-type occupations which are perceived to carry high social status have multiplied even as the jobs themselves carry less and less responsibility.

Along with this tendency to break down professions into quasi-professions has gone a concomitant tendency to upgrade occupations and demand qualifications for entry not formerly required. Apart from his argument that most of the jobs in the market could be adequately performed by high school graduates, Berg has further shown that raising the educational requirements for a position that did not formerly require it may in fact be counterproductive, since the position is occupied by someone who is prepared for something better and therefore less inclined to carry out his or her functions in an appropriate manner. Moreover, 'credentialing isolates a significant population group' (Meyer, 1977, p. 53), making those with less education less capable of getting into the job market:

> The more binding the allocation rules, the earlier and more convincingly are nonstudents committed to passive roles in society; this means that society relying on credentials could well lower even further the modern competence of people of low education. (p. 62)

Pincus, for example, cites a study which examined the work being performed by two occupations for which training took place at the community college level. These 'highly skilled industrial technicians' performed mostly specific manual skills requiring little in the way of theoretical scientific or technical knowledge. They included automobile mechanics, draftsmen and repairers of home appliances and industrial machinery: 'In other words industrial technicians are relatively skilled manual workers, many of whom did not have to attend college to qualify for those jobs in the past' (Pincus, 1980, p. 342).

Second, the school system – particularly the community college – is taking on the training functions which industry traditionally performed. This is seen by Pincus to have more to do with saving business money than with making sure that their client-students are being genuinely prepared for jobs with appropriate levels of responsibility. The reality, however, is that the vocational, as well as the more academic, preparations create aspirations and expectations which the realities of the job market cannot meet.

What all of this suggests to the student of PAE is that adult education, as a form of institutionalized learning, will be used by men and women who are equally qualified for a dwindling number of appropriate positions and who can see that increased credentials provide a competitive advantage. This tendency is exacerbated by the parallel tendency by which prospective employers increasingly rely both on external certification to demonstrate qualifications for entry-level positions and on the schools and colleges to carry out basic forms of job training, more appropriately the function of industry itself.

Moreover, educational upgrading is not simply a reflection of individuals in free and equal competition for jobs. Adult education is performed by institutions, and institutions are controlled by groups and classes. Groups and classes compete, not individuals. Consider the example cited in Chapter 1 where a survey of the California community college system revealed that it was no longer serving, if it had ever served, the function of providing cheap education and training for minorities. PAE, like the other forms of social participation discussed in Chapter 3, reflects a class-based society. Participation is a means for those of similar status culture to signal solidarity with their group. Havighurst spoke of education as a means of maintaining engagement with society. Of whose society was he speaking? Might it not be more appropriate to speak of people seeking, through education, to belong to the dominant group, and to feel that they are part of the right group, culturally as well as economically?

Adult educators have asked why adults do not take advantage of what is being provided, pointing out with apparent dismay that only those who need it least participate the most while those who need it most are nowhere in sight, an 'irony,' according to Niemi and Nagle (1979). But is it really such an irony? Might it not be more accurate to say that those who need it most participate most; that adult education is the domain of the middle class because it is they who have already benefited from the educational system in relation to jobs and wish to do so again? If this is really the case, researchers should not continue to look for an answer to nonparticipation and drop-out in the motivation and underlying personality characteristics of 'disadvantaged' adults – as do Burman (1959), Hymon (1960), Boggs

(1974) and many others. Instead they ought to ask whether the institutions are really designed for those who appear to need education most, and whether the so-called demands of modern society are best met by continued educational upgrading, rather than a shift in economic and political power – as is implied in Hagstrom (1964), Chertow (1974), Gaventa (1980), Thompson (1980) and others.

If we accept the views of Hopper, Collins, and others, then mainstream education – and by implication adult education – is not a mere passive sifter of talent and drive. Through it the social order is maintained, culture is transmitted, and society, such as it is, survives. Education in modern society, however, is less a transmitter of culture and diffuser of work skills than it is a *culture of transmission*, both of knowledge and of skills. That is to say, the way knowledge is transmitted in a particular society may be more important than what that knowledge is all about. It is not neutral, objective knowledge which is transmitted so much as an attitude towards knowledge, a belief in objectivity, and an obedience to neutrality.[8] Schools also socialize by introducing students to the values of order, discipline, canons of taste, articulation, association and the constructive use of leisure (Kelly, 1977). Schools, in other words, teach culture. Indeed, schools are culture 'clubs.' They are organizations where people become members, pay dues and obtain benefits. Adult education is a series of such clubs, where membership is occasioned by the desire to associate with others of like mind, interest and taste.

Adult education is also 'continuing' in the sense that it *continues* the culture of transmission. As an extension of schooling – and to the degree that it does not renounce schooling – it becomes the paramount means whereby people who have been enculturated to see the world in certain ways are reinforced in their beliefs and perceptions. People do not come back to school to learn skills necessary for work so much as they come back to a certain 'order of reality,' one in which knowledge is organized along rational lines, scientific and technical truth are the only sources of true knowledge, the power of chance and fate are minimized, and the abilities of individuals to succeed by dint of an adherence to the rules of good conduct are given their rightful place in the scheme of things. Adult education is a true culture for those who feel they are most successful with this environment. Adult education continues the job of status allotment and socialization by confirming or enhancing status position or preparing for new positions. This is how vocational motives for PAE ought to be interpreted.

In these ways, echoing Havighurst's instrumental function, adult education becomes an avenue to higher-status cultures. This is the real meaning behind Houle's goal orientation. At the same time, high-status cultures are no longer demarcated simply by economic power and prestige but more importantly by the possession and *consumption* of knowledge – scientific, technical and aesthetic. Adult education becomes itself an expression of this higher-status culture, and is for this reason sought as an end in itself, surely another angle on Houle's learning orientation. Here, unlike Havighurst's *expressive* function which emphasizes that the internal content of education is enjoyed for its own sake, it is the symbolic function of education as a mark or sign of class belonging that is emphasized. This is Houle's activity-orientation *par excellence*. Indeed, it begins to look like these orientations as well as Havighurst's dichotomy are dialectically linked. It may be more accurate to say, for example, that in performing an expressive function, education also simultaneously performs an instrumental one. It is not instrumental because people use it that way. On the contrary, it is precisely because education serves an instrumental function, and is intended to serve such a function with regard to society in general and the economy in particular, that adults come to it with instrumental motives.

From within this perspective, that of the 'new' sociology of education, the real question is not 'How are adults motivated to learn?' (a question which implies that the motives for learning are not bound up with the nature of the educational enterprise itself). The real question, and one which I believe is at the heart of a general theory of PAE, is to understand how education (as the independent variable in statistical terms) itself motivates people to perform their various roles in society, to participate, to adjust to society's demands and to contribute in whatever way they can to the grand scheme of maintaining a society's fragile equilibrium, by not commiting crime or inciting others to sedition, by being patriotic and community-minded and, in the most general of ways, by acting like a good neighbor.

# 7   Beyond the current paradigm

> The greatest reason for adult education is that it offers an escape from boredom.
>
> (Jarret, 1960)

The concept of participation appears in the literature of adult education in connection with two categories of concern. It denotes an 'active' agenda, which is at once pragmatic as well as moral, to increase the numbers of men and women, in general, who are willing to commit themselves to organized forms of learning and, in particular, to create educational opportunities for those sections of the population normally unrepresented in the classes of the sponsoring institutions. It denotes a 'reflective' agenda designed to help the community understand the causes of adults' involvement in educational activities.

The active concern predominates among those who identify themselves as adult educators. For many it is their bread and butter. For some at least it has the makings of a moral crusade against ignorance and on behalf of the ideal of a truly democratic society. For most, however, it is a job or career like any other, and perhaps more fun than being a lawyer or doctor. The reflective concern is the domain of the few committed to research.

The problem of PAE from the point of view of those with the active agenda divides essentially into two issues. One is the problem of achieving a better understanding of educational motives and choices, to better anticipate and fulfill the needs of those who are willing and able to participate. It is also the problem of understanding the motives and choices of those who are neither. Basically then, what may be termed the 'practical' problem of PAE – the problem from the point of view of practitioners – comes down to twin issues of marketing and of social service: orchestrating a product for the generically 'advantaged' and creating a necessary opportunity for the generically 'disadvantaged.' If practitioners have any expectations of researchers, and it is not certain that they have many, it is that research will contribute solutions to these problems.

Over the years researchers have attempted to demonstrate their awareness of an obligation to practice. Scholarly papers often begin with remarks to the effect that as society becomes more complicated and the speed of change accelerates, adults are compelled to keep learning to keep up. Adult educators need to meet these demands for learning, researchers will argue. To meet these needs they need to know something about the nature of the adult as learner and what it is that motivates him or her. That is where research comes in: helping to identify the person most likely to participate and the kinds of educational choices he or she is likely to make.

Similarly, researchers will argue, despite enormous strides in social progress there are still millions who cannot read or write. How can those for whom formal education is most desirable be persuaded to participate in programs designed for their own good? Again, it will be implied, only through systematic, scientific inquiry can we hope to answer this question. It is often through this kind of transparent lip-service, that research stakes its claim to the disinterested pursuit of knowledge. Even if individual researchers have little time for 'active' concerns or individual practitioners for 'reflective' ones, there is an underlying momentum which is characteristic of the phenomenon of adult education in general to the effect that research on PAE ought somehow to illuminate or otherwise change practice.[1]

Despite this bias to practice, however, it is probably fair to say that few practitioners are aware of the advances made in the study of PAE and its causes over the past few decades. This study was intended to fill that gap, and to begin again to encourage discussion in an area of practice that has been central to its evolution but which now threatens to wither away from lack of interest before it has been expertly and sincerely exploited.

## THEORIES OF PARTICIPATION AND THEIR IMPLICATIONS FOR PRACTICE

In what remains, I would like to focus on a number of related questions. First, what relevance do theories of PAE have for the ongoing practice of adult education? Second, what aspects of the problem should we be investigating, from the perspective of practice? Finally, where ought we to look for future trends in the shaping and determining of this important subject? The remainder of this chapter will be devoted to exploring possible answers to this question, in the context of current practice.

Theories of PAE might be relevant to the practice of the field in at least one of three ways. First, when we use the term we often mean the immediate, the concrete, the kind of 'hands-on' method or technique that we are likely to encounter or expect to encounter when we attend workshops and the like. To the best of my knowledge, nothing that has been discussed in this study has yet 'outputted' as a practical set of suggestions or techniques to help improve practice. It is possible to tell an audience about Houle's typology and to show them Boshier's Educational Participation Scale (EPS) in action. If the audience consisted of teachers of adults, for example, the idea would be to suggest to them that the students/learners in their class had one of three major orientations to learning and that this scale could be administered the first day of class to see which students fell into which categories, and so on.

However, even if dominant orientations emerged it is not certain what implications this piece of 'knowledge' might have for the conduct of a class. In the case of learning-oriented students, for example, it might be assumed that simply letting them know that there is much to read on the subject in question would be sufficient. Their natural curiosity for the subject and delight in reading would be the main motivator; they would not need more structure than that. With the goal-oriented, on the other hand, much more structure would be required since they will read only what is directly relevant to the course and mastery of the subject. As for the activity-oriented, it is hard to say: maybe they need structure, maybe they don't.

Notice, however, that in order to make the Houle typology (and by implication the theory of motivational orientations) relevant to practice and to answer potential questions from teachers we were led naturally to make certain extrapolations from what we think we know about three types of learners: namely, that the orientation in question has implications for the kind of structure the learner wants in a classroom situation. Here, then, is a situation where a concern for more effective practice drives research questions rather than the other way around. Here are hypotheses, and obviously many more could be generated, which have yet to be put to the test.

In general, PAE research appeals to this first or concrete level of practice by furnishing it with scales and measures which are easy to administer and relatively uncomplicated to interpret. Besides the EPS of Boshier, which is incidentally commercially available, there are the two other orientation scales, one by Burgess, the other by Sheffield. Of these, Sheffield's scale is the least useful. As I have shown elsewhere (Courtney, 1984), the statements which comprise it are strikingly awkward in composition and thus open to ambiguous interpretation and there are questions about the appropriateness of the methodology. More interestingly, perhaps, Houle, who was closest in time to Sheffield's work and who supervised his dissertation, does not discuss his student's instrument or conception of orientations in later publications (Houle, 1974, 1983) or in the new postscript to Houle (1961). Though the Burgess scale has rarely been used in the 1980s, it has had a recent, significant application in a major survey of PAE undertaken by British researchers (Woodley and associates, 1987). Apart from these instruments, there are others like Litchfield's *Leisure Activity Scale* which are important because they give us some sense of a person's overall level of involvement with adult education on a regular basis. Though rare in the adult education literature, within the leisure research literature such scales are much more common. Finally, though problematic in major ways, it is clear that the Aslanian and Brickell (1980) study might yield the kind of easy, informal questionnaire which would enable administrators, teachers or program planners to tap the 'triggers' or 'transitions' – the motives – which have led people to their agency, program or class.

## Motivation-to-learn and the principles of practice

According to the second meaning of the term 'practice,' PAE research might be important to the principles according to which administrators, teachers and program planners are trained. By principles I mean the kind of statement we find in the opening chapter of Brookfield (1986), where he talks about 'principles of good practice' or in the popular publication by Zemke and Zemke.[2] Here, in these cases as in others where the 'principles' of adult education are at stake, the issue is less one of veracity (Are these really the principles of effective practice? Do we really know these things for sure?) than of a more than convincing commonsense which is used to inspire practitioners and guide aspects of their professional, everyday conduct.

Consideration of how PAE research might influence this second level of practice needs to take place in the context of the third meaning of the term used here: the kind of knowledge, theory and research, which is passed on to students in graduate programs of adult education. For in general, when we teach a subject like PAE or adult motivation-to-learn in graduate courses in adult education, we are presenting knowledge of the field, the kind of basic knowledge which may ultimately earn for adult education its place as a university discipline. And we are saying that in order to function effectively as a professional in adult education, your practice must be informed more than by principles or theories of good practice; it must also be influenced by scientific or abstract theory, the kind of knowledge which traditionally has been the domain of universities and the kind of knowledge that has been the subject of the present study. This chapter closes then with what we appear to know about the phenomenon of adult learning and motivation-to-learn as we might teach it to graduate students or attempt to convey to client groups of administrators, program planners and teachers of adults in workshop or conference settings.

I have tried to show that, as a problem for research, the study of PAE goes back a long way, back indeed to the very first attempts to coordinate the field of Adult and Continuing Education in the United States, and clearly also born of that effort. From the very beginning, surveys were launched to find out who was involved in educational activities in the local community and why they were prepared to make the effort. At the same time, it was not sufficient to tally aggregates. Neither knowledge nor policy-making could be advanced without explanation and theory. Essentially, then, though it often does not appear that way from some reviews of the literature, the question of why adults learn is an enduring one, which has received many answers over the years, not all of which deserve to be carelessly forgotten in the rush to the new.

For the purpose of this study, three main strands of thought, three main forms of research, were isolated. One strand, the survey, interpretable as policy-oriented in the broadest meaning of that term, focused on the identities of adult learners and measured their motives for learning by means of interview schedules and questionnaires. Survey research has been responsible for providing the field with some of its most enduring findings. The correlation of age with PAE, of formal education with PAE, the strength of the vocational or practical motive for most forms of organized, deliberate learning projects, and the existence of a general participation syndrome, are among some of the more important legacies of this research design.

Survey research has failed, however, to provide a convincing explanation of PAE based on demographic factors alone. It is unable to show how motivation-to-learn (which is never defined) translates into actual participation (because of the general failure to compare participants with nonparticipants, or even to say exactly what might constitute a nonparticipant). It has not shown why formal schooling leads almost unerringly to PAE. Finally, it does not account for significant amounts of nonparticipation among the most 'prone' groups (Douglah and Moss, 1968), nor for the opposite phenomenon among those least likely to become involved.

At the same time, there are other issues of significance which the survey strand has revealed that still await an explanation. The finding, for example, that American adults have pragmatic motives for learning need not necessarily mean an interest which is primarily vocational or even work-related, though that species of goal does loom large. In many cases this expression of motive is highly ambiguous, as we saw in Chapters 2 and 3, particularly within the work on motivational orientations. While often linked to work, it also has to do with the individual's need for knowledge and skills which can be applied in family or community environments, for example home-repair or learning how to organize. The tendency to dismiss the practical motive for learning arises, in part, from a curious elitism which sometimes reaches almost to the level of the absurd.³ The United States has a strong history, going back to Franklin, of adult education as the 'diffusion of useful knowledge' (Cremin, 1970; Grattan, 1955); it is an 'impulse' which finds strong echo even today (Stubblefield, 1987). While occasionally bordering on the anti-intellectual, having a practical motive for adult education need only mean that adults come to the realm of knowledge in the hope that information and technology can help solve day-to-day problems or help them acquire wealth. In the final analysis, it is testament to the progress of a civilized country that men and women can and do turn to education to solve problems rather than resort to violence or sink into the reflex pit of bigotry and 'no-nothingness.'

Finally, motives for learning as expressed to survey researchers may confound both motives and conditions which facilitate action. The common survey tends to assume that there is nothing else going on in the environment of the learner which makes active learning a real possibility. It also tends to assume that PAE is a rational act which comes about when someone, for whatever reason, decides that he or she would like to learn something and, with minimal interference, acts on that idea. Implied in this model of action is a belief that all acts of learning are essentially rational movements from means to ends, rather than justifications – after the fact – which actors provide once they have made decisions (which are only half understood) and acted in particular ways.

The tendency to view PAE as a rational means–end relationship obscures the important point, rarely observed, that people may undertake formal programs of learning due to a lack of clear goals, and not because of them, or a desire to obtain goals within the new environment and not because they already have them. This was precisely the point made by Karabel and Halsey (1977) in Chapter 6 when they talked of the power (or function) of education as a motivator of future action, thus turning the problem of PAE more or less on its head. Nor should this surprise us. Young men and women join the Army, just as they once joined the priesthood or ministry, not because of a 'vocation' for either but because they could not think of anything more worthwhile, more motivating, to do with their lives. The United States is a culture which abhors lack of ambition much as nature abhors a vacuum. It ought not to surprise us if people arrive at stages of their lives when former goals can no longer sustain them. In their search for new goals, new dreams, they may encounter education, and that too becomes part, but only part, of the grand search.

## The current status of knowledge on adult motivation-to-learn

Currently, there is no general theory of PAE which holds widespread allegiance, and for this reason. A comprehensive theory of PAE would have to do more than deal with reasons for learning as a function of position in the life cycle or motivational orientation. It would have to be more than a decision model. It would have to take account of sociological factors; it would have to recognize learning as a discretionary activity singled out or in competition with other customary and non-customary activities; and it would have to deal with the place of adult education in a capitalist economy, one in which roles and rewards are 'meted out' in accordance with a liberal-conservative ideology of opportunity and individualism.

I cannot see any theory on the horizon being at once sufficiently broad and yet remaining real and detailed enough to accomplish all of these tasks. I am aware that the Smith-Cookson model and the limited studies it has spawned constitute an attempt at the grand theory but am not convinced that it can succeed. Nor ought this to disturb us. It has already been argued that adult education is not driven by theory and research, so that the absence of an overarching concept does not detract from the ongoing program of improving what we do by whatever means at our disposal, of which research-and-theory is but a single set of tools. Nevertheless, some new direction is possible, and this I believe can be accomplished by putting the problem of PAE within a much broader framework than has hitherto been attempted. The elements of that framework are discussed briefly here.

Unintentionally, this book is indebted to the memory of Jack London, who died in the spring of 1988. Why London? Because from him comes the idea of PAE as an expression of a 'general participation syndrome.' From him comes the vital idea of adult education as a kind of 'half-way' house between high school and the 'real' world of work, an idea which integrates adult education into the larger milieu of higher and postsecondary education. From him, too, comes the idea of the adult learner as someone more active in his or her lifestyle than the nonparticipant, suggesting that the learner is someone who is more involved with life, more likely to try something new, more open to life's possibilities and challenges. The adult learner is more the 'life-spacer' than the 'life-chancer' to paraphrase Boshier (1977). There is also, however, a more indirect and, for that reason perhaps, more profound influence. I was delighted to come across his writing and thoughts on the subject of PAE at a time when much of what I was reading seemed unduly narrow in range and unexciting in a basic way.

London's work contains implications for a radical change in our ways of conceiving PAE, its causes and effects. Such a change would begin with a shift away from the notion of learning as an internal, invisible, cognitive, knowledge- or skill-oriented activity, a conception which is the legacy of twentieth-century American psychology, because it seems little related to the idea of participation in its fullest sense, a sense which inevitably contains the concept of community and social involvement. While undoubtedly still the essence of the issue for many writers, the emphasis on knowledge and skill acquisition tends to focus our minds on learning as accomplishment and product rather than as effort and process. More importantly, the older conception tends to ignore one of the essential ingredients of even the most cognitivist definitions of learning: change.

All learning appears to involve change. Following the logic of this definition it would also be correct to say that the more significant the learning the greater the change. But here, are we talking about a mere change in understanding, knowledge or skill? Potentially, are we not talking about a change in personality, in the organization of the ego, in the individual's way of construing of him- or herself, and especially are we not talking about changes in the social and political environment within which the learner as actor endeavors to effect the lives of others. Call it 'perspective transformation' if that seems more agreeable, but we are talking of changes of such a magnitude that they promise salvation to those who most desire transcendence over their ordinary, everyday lives, while being just as stoutly resisted by those who suspect the possibility of such change and oppose it.

Nor should this surprise us. A society, like that of the United States, is constructed on an ideology which espouses change. If we ignore the contradictions which sometimes accompany the 'application' of this ideology to real life, change permeates the American psyche. Paradoxically, it is the one constant of which we can be confident that it will still be with us tomorrow. Change is a mighty variable for the field of adult education because a profound and unshakable rhetoric tells us that when all around us is in flux, adult education is the only sure means of keeping your sanity and getting ahead. Adult education thrives in a world which knows only change.

At the same time, real change cannot be 'managed' unless we assume that men and women are themselves capable of real and profound changes. In other words, we cannot deal with the 'objective' change which is all about us unless we can see in humankind's essence a potential for change. It is this potential for change which drives our philosophy of adult learning.

If adults are not in essence learning beings then they cannot really embrace change and transform it to their bidding. No assumption within the philosophy of adult learning is more vital to adult education and yet is more unexamined. For even if we accept that people are in essence beings capable of profound transformation, mental and spiritual as well as physical and material, it ought not to be assumed that they welcome such transformation or would not be satisfied with a little less of it than is being foisted on them everyday by the media, the economy and their political mentors.

Boiled down into a form that responds to the present inquiry, it seems not too unlikely a hypothesis to say that a driving force behind much PAE is the encounter with change. This is not to say that either all adult learners are driven by the need or desire for change, or even that a majority of a sample in some study or other would agree with a statement citing change as a vital reason for participation. All that is required of this hypothesis is that we recognize the importance of change as a major factor behind orientations to learning, and that as a corollary of this, that we begin to treat acts of participation in terms of the desire or lack of desire for change.

## CONCLUDING REMARKS

In closing I offer the following remarks about the future of this problem. This study did not address issues of PAE theory as it affects specific programs or populations, the kinds of issues traditionally addressed in the various American handbooks of adult education. Nor did it focus as such on Adult Basic Education, literacy, training, or on older adults, minorities and so forth. Nevertheless, implied in the discussion of social participation (Chapter 5) and the focus on the concept of organization is the idea that different groups are not merely served by different organizations, but that organization itself, its nature and structure, is at the very center of the act of learning. And I say all of this knowing that there is a current move to eschew the organizational component in adult learning and to focus almost exclusively on self-directedness.

Coolie Verner (Jensen *et al.*, 1964) uses a much misunderstood concept called 'method' when referring to the processes of adult education. It is confusing because, in the same passage, he talks about 'technique' which he contrasts with the term method. The choice of term is, I believe, deliberate. By method, Verner really meant organization. And organization was at the heart of his definition of adult education and how it is facilitated. Researchers like Marsick and Watkins (1990) are talking more and more about the notion of the organization as a 'learning environment.' I would like to see more research focused in this area.

This study, as I noted at the beginning, does not address dropout or persistence though, as Boshier (1973 and elsewhere) theorized – correctly I believe – drop-out and nonparticipation may be connected. At present, research on nonparticipation and drop-out appears to have reached new levels of activity though I am not sure that this research is moving in the right direction.

Missing almost totally from the current research picture is a concern for the *effects* rather than the *causes* of PAE, something which Anderson and Darkenwald (1979) called for over a decade ago and which is still not being addressed. Reasons for lack of research in this area would probably include a lack of sophistication about conducting evaluation studies, which is what research on effects might entail. However, an impetus for conducting such research might come from an interest in the *economics* of adult learning, a dimension which is surely lacking in our field as a whole.

Again, I did not address foreign research on the problem of PAE though I am aware of recent important work in this area, mostly English-language and wholly European in origin (Rubenson and Hoghielm, 1980; Woodley *et al.* 1987; Parjanen, 1989). Clearly we need to look abroad to see what has been done and, more importantly, to look into the possibilities of truly comparative or cross-cultural research, as has happened successfully in areas like communication and management.

Similarly, though this study is preoccupied with research and theory I have said little here about methodology. Some researchers have argued (Rockhill, 1982; Matkin, 1979) that this ought to be a concern and that we ought to be using other ways of researching this phenomenon, some of which might surely result in a redefinition of the problem. I am aware of, and, for a time in the early 1970s, worked a little with, some of what are broadly termed qualitative or hermeneutic methods. I have no doubt that a study which was philosophically as well as methodologically qualitative in nature would begin with a different set of premises than the more common hypothetico-deductive form practiced by Boshier and others (e.g. Scanlan, Darkenwald, Valentine, Dimmock, etc.), and would undoubtedly come to some very different conclusions than I have reached here. But this is an issue not merely for PAE researchers but also for the field of adult education as a whole, particularly since it touches on its very existence as a distinct university discipline.

PAE is not a problem that belongs to a small group of researchers anxious to stake vague claims to posterity. Nor is it merely a problem of practice in the here and now. It is in the final analysis a problem of our history and how we interpret that history. To date, current theories of PAE have had almost no application to history nor have historical precedents been adduced to test a theory. And yet, examples abound in the historical literature of adult educators' concerns with adult motivation to learn. Indeed, it would not be unrealistic to argue that the whole history of *adult education in this country is in reality the history of efforts to create, improve or even prevent participation in adult education.* Viewed from the widest possible meaning, it is possible to see participation as an issue from the very beginnings of organized adult education in this country. It appears to be part-and-parcel of white colonization of this continent, as for example, in Carlson's (1987) unsparing account of Americanization. Subsequent attempts to convert native Americans to Christianity, thinly disguised as efforts to make them literate, was interpreted by Carlson as a failed attempt to convert – Americanize – the Indians to the ways of the white man. This surely is adult education too, and it is education serving a very different sort of end.

Similarly, when we examine and marvel at the success of the Lyceum and Chautauqua movements are we not marveling at the notion of mass, voluntary participation in organized forms of adult learning? Thus, to ask 'Why do adults learn?' is really to ask a series of historical questions. What accounted for the success – measured by PAE rates among other things – of the Lyceum and Chautauqua, or Cooperative Extension movements? Why did the Mechanics Institutes fail? And in this century, how do we explain the extraordinary successes respectively of the GI Bill and the community college movement?

Thus, what this study has attempted to accomplish, through the various links made between diverse bodies of literature, is hopefully the redefinition of the question of PAE and its expansion into realms not normally associated with it. If the link with history is valid, then it makes the study of history that much more vital. For it allows us to consider the phenomenon of PAE and non-PAE in modern times and the forces facilitating or inhibiting it by being able to peer over our shoulders and look backwards in time, at particular historical periods, asking questions of these periods which may throw light on significant movements in our own time.

From the perspective of close on ten years observing American adult education, both as a researcher and practitioner, and from the perspective of a European it is clear to me that the field in general does not take its own research very seriously nor, in some respects as a result of this, is it taken seriously by other related disciplines. These disciplines accept the well-worked axiom that a profession rests, at the very least, on established bodies of knowledge, while the claim to being a scientific discipline, however applied, rests on the existence of well-thought-out, defensible, testable and interesting theories. What I have tried to show here is that adult education can be taken seriously as a discipline because, while it may not wish to own it, it does indeed have a body of knowledge that it can respond to and wrestle with.

Adult education in the United States contains an amazingly rich body of ideas, folk-knowledge, bona fide theory and impeccable philosophy. The writing about PAE is a good case in point. The legacy which earlier adult educators have left the current generation is ill-served if we continue to trade in defensive postures and do not submit our ideas and theories to the good light of our colleagues' opinions. The benefits to be derived from a dialogue among researchers and between researchers and practitioners can do much to strengthen our beliefs and commitment to intervention on behalf of human inadequacy and injustice. Ultimately, this dialogue is necessary to insure that we survive as a recognizable entity into the twenty-first century.

# Notes

## 1 Explaining participation in American adult education

1 The standard sources of statistics on Participation in Adult Education in the United States are government surveys which have been appearing triennially under that title since 1969. The reports for 1969, 1972, 1975 and 1978, which are now out-of-print, are available on microfiche through the services of the Educational Resources Information Center or ERIC. Researchers should note that the published reports after 1975 are quite limited in number of cross-tabulations. Complete data files are available, however, on computer disc. These along with the 1981 report and, most recently, *Trends in adult education 1969–1984* are available from the Center for Education Statistics, Office of Educational Research and Improvement of the US Dept of Education, 555 New Jersey Ave NW, Washington, DC 20208-1404. For a critical comparison of adult education trends over the last two decades see O'Keefe (1977) and Chimeme (1984).

2 This phrase appears commonly in American educational discourse, though its value as currency is undoubtedly spreading. See R. Boshier. (1980). *Towards a learning society* (Learningpress Ltd, Vancouver), a book about the state of adult education in New Zealand, and various European studies of 'lifelong education' as a 'master concept,' published by Pergamon Press in the 1970s. While the term's vogue among adult educators suggests that it began with them, it may have come into general use with educational writings of the middle and late 1960s: see R. Hutchins. (1968). *The learning society* (Mentor, New York), and the extended quote from Burton Clark in Chapter 6 of this volume.

3 Conceptually, the project to shake off the classroom-biased perspective and see education in a great many other institutional and non-institutional spheres may have begun with Bailyn (1962), was taken up by Cremin (1970), and 'officially' entered the adult education literature in Darkenwald and Merriam (1982). Other reflections of this changed perspective can be seen in the flourishing of the movement to grant degree-credit recognition to the many forms of 'experiential' learning, which continues to flourish to this day, even gaining popular ground abroad (Evans, 1985).

4 The rhetoric itself, however, has come under increasing attack. See, for example, Taylor, Rockhill, and Fieldhouse (1985); K. Rockhill. (1983). *Academic excellence and public service: A history of University extension in California.* Transaction Books, New Brunswick, NJ; and Welton (1986).

5 Anderson and Darkenwald (1979) conducted their secondary analysis using multiple regression. A defect of earlier surveys, they argued, was their reliance on simple cross-tabulation, which would not reveal whether the correlation between a demographic variable and educational activity was due to the effects of that variable or to another. Multiple regression would clarify such relationships by holding the effects of particular variables constant and allowing others to play their true part in the variance equation. This approach to statistical analysis reflects the thinking of researchers such as Boshier for whom theories of participation are multi-variate phenomena reflecting both social and psychological influences. See Dickinson (1971) also for a similar use of multiple regression. Even the effectiveness of multiple regression in this context has, however, been challenged. In an untitled paper by Robert Prater, forwarded to the author by Alan Rogers, from the British Isles, the 10 per cent variance finding of the Anderson and Darkenwald study was criticized. Citing Shipp and McKenzie (1981), Prater noted that their use of discriminant analysis had helped explain 33 per cent of the variance between participants and nonparticipants. This increase in statistical power was helped by the 'inclusion of variables associated with attitudes, barriers to participation, leisure pursuits, and participation by neighbours, friends, and family' (Prater, no date, pp. 4–5), variables which were not included by Anderson and Darkenwald but which are clearly relevant to the PAE phenomenon and anticipate the perspective developed later in this book.

6 G. Dickinson and D. Rusnell. (1971). A content analysis of adult education, *Adult Education, 21*, 177–85; H. Long and S. Agyekum. (1974). Adult education 1964–1973: Reflections of a changing discipline, *Adult Education, 24*, 99–120; Matkin (1979); and I. Pipke. (1984) The gatekeepers: A multivariate study of accepted and rejected adult education research conference abstracts (1978–1980), *Adult Education, 34*, 71–84.

7 The 'official' version of what this mission was intended to accomplish can be found in Knowles (1977) and Grattan (1955), the two standard histories of American adult education. Challenges to the validity and simplicity of this interpretation can be found in Stubblefield (1987) and Rose (1989), to cite but a few examples of the 'new' history being written.

8 Information on the Marsh study is taken from Ozanne (1934) and McGrath (1938).

9 Given the popularity of environmental issues nowadays, it is interesting to note how early the focus on 'human ecology,' may have begun. It is evident in other works of Lindeman and Brunner. Within the field of psychology, it may have begun with Lewin, continued in the pioneering research of Barker and Wright in the 1950s, and is evident today in the focus on 'community psychology.'

10 *Current Biography*, 1958, pp. 66–8. A native of Pennsylvania, Brunner taught at Columbia University for most of his academic life. He was President of the Rural Sociological Society, 1945, and Member of the prestigious Sociological Research Association, 1950. Interestingly enough, the Lynds' *Middletown* came to sociology through a series of social and religious surveys directed by Brunner and Luther Fry. It was at Columbia, incidentally, that the first graduate program in adult education came into being, and where the first dissertations on PAE were produced: Smith (1936) and Dunstan (1939).

11 This important book has now at last been reissued, along with a short postscript by the author, by the University of Oklahoma and may be obtained by writing

to the Oklahoma Research Center for Continuing Professional and Higher Education, University of Oklahoma, Norman, OK 73019.

12  Professor John Niemi of Northern Illinois has argued, in discussions with the author, that the 'psychologizing' of adult education had begun long before the 1960s, and was evident in the speed with which the research on mental testing by the noted psychologist, Edward Thorndike, entered the annals of adult education.

13  The quote in full reads, 'Particular learning sites are embedded within a general cultural framework or logic which sustains the reproduction of society, its division of labor and social hierarchy.'

14  Indeed, in a recent book, *Developing critical thinkers* (Jossey-Bass, San Francisco, 1987), Brookfield has even moved away from the general practice of attaching 'adult' to everything normally claimed as turf by a turf-conscious discipline. Among other things this shift in linguistic custom carries implications for the evolution of the field, implications which have yet to receive serious attention.

15  For an example of the anthropologist's perspective on schooling, learning and education and the interchangeability of terms see the chapter on learning in Hall's (1977). *Beyond culture* (Anchor/Doubleday, New York).

16  Newberry treated all previous research as examples of surveys and his classification scheme reflected degrees of sophistication and scope among them. The schemes of Douglah, Burgess and Flinck were developed with theories of PAE in mind, and studies were classified according to the kind of explanation being proffered by a particular theory, e.g. one based on Maslow's hierarchy of needs.

17  The most-often cited study used to be Johnstone and Rivera (1965), followed by references to work by Roger Boshier, according to R. Boshier and L. Pickard. (1979) Citation patterns of articles published in adult education, *Adult Education, 30*, 1, 34–52.

18  Unlike the situation in the British Isles, where unpublished dissertations and theses are usually made available through interlibrary loan free of charge, most universities in the US require that doctoral candidates submit copies of their manuscripts to University Microfilms Inc., in Ann Arbor, who will charge around $20.00 for the privilege of examining another scholar's work. Naturally, unless one is in receipt of a grant, most students would not be in a position to buy more than a very small number of these dissertations, thus reducing their overall usefulness for research and scholarship. This rather scandalous monopoly has not, to my knowledge, ever been seriously challenged.

19  A great deal of work has been done in this area. After going through a period of disinterest, the focus appears again to have shifted back to the issues of persistence and nonparticipation. Some of the more recent publications include Scanlan and Darkenwald (1984), Darkenwald and Valentine (1985), Darkenwald and Gavin (1987), and Garrison (1987) who has conducted at least one test of Boshier's (1973) model of 'congruency.' Indeed, much of the recent research on persistence and nonparticipation seems influenced by this concept.

20  The *Handbook of Adult and Continuing Education* (Sharan Merriam and Phyllis Cunningham (eds) 1989, San Francisco, Jossey-Bass) shows the extent to which the professionalization of the field has advanced, as will the planned up-dating of the old 'black book' (to be edited by Peter Jarvis and John Peters) edited in the mid-1960s by Gale Jensen and his colleagues. Many arguments, most

notably by John Ohliger, were made against 'mandatory continuing education' in the late 1970s and early 1980s. At one point, a Task Force on the subject reported to the annual conference of the Adult Education Association. Nevertheless, events may have overtaken the movement. Recent statistics published by the Center for Education Statistics (see Chapter 2) show that the highest jump in PAE rates over the last fifteen years can be attributed to the demand by individual states for mandatory continuing education in order to ensure relicensure for stipulated professions.

21 The strongest statement to this effect was made by R. Boyd and J. Apps. (1980). *Redefining the discipline of adult education* (Jossey-Bass, San Francisco), a gallant but ill-fated attempt to argue that adult education could develop its own questions, concerns, theories and methodologies from within, rather than continue the borrowing from other disciplines as had been the case in the past (most notably in the 'black book'). This attempt continues. See for example D. Plecas and T. Sork. (1986). Adult education: Curing the ills of an undisciplined discipline, *Adult Education Quarterly, 37,* 48–62.

## 2 'Who are these people and why do they come to us?'

1 The title is a quote from Ozanne (1934, p. 19).
2 For a critique of early national estimates, their methodologies and limitations on the PAE 'question,' see Courtney (1985).
3 The definition adopted by the government in 1969 equates adult education with organized instruction 'including correspondence courses and private tutoring, usually at a set time and place; ordinarily under the auspices of a school, college, church, neighborhood center, community organization or other recognized authority; and generally with a predetermined end result which may or may not be a certificate, diploma, or degree' (NCES, 1969, p. 2).
4 These problems, which have mainly to do with methodologies of sampling and data collection, are discussed at length in Courtney (1985). Copies of this paper may be obtained directly from the author.
5 Marsh (1926) was probably the first researcher this century to survey PAE in the United States. However, there are doubts about the systematic and representative nature of his sampling techniques (McGrath, 1938).
6 This figure undoubtedly reflects the impact of Americanization programs begun in earnest in the 1900s. See R. Carlson. (1970). Americanization as an early twentieth-century adult education movement, *History of Education Quarterly, 10,* 440–64; M. Seller. (1978). Success and failure in adult education: The immigrant experience 1914–1924, *Adult Education, 28,* 83–99.
7 These figures compare interestingly with the findings of Penland (1979) who found that only 40 per cent of the American population reported using the public library on a regular or occasional basis during the year prior to November 1976; some 60 per cent reported not using it at all.
8 London's study analyzed the findings of two surveys. The first, called the Community Survey, randomly sampled the Oakland male population aged 20 to 59. Of the 2,708 persons in the sample, 337 reported participation in adult education, a rate of 12 per cent, not unlike the more conservative national estimates discussed in Chapter 1. The second, called a Matched Sample, compared the participants of the general survey with 599 nonparticipants,

matched according to age and occupation. This was to enable the researchers to get closer to the reasons for participation by different groups.

9   Of those counted by the survey as being involved with adult education, Holden noted that around 1 per cent were classified as 'functionally illiterate,' 13 per cent had elementary or high school education, while as many as 46 per cent had been to college.

10  The NCES report of 1975 remains by far the most comprehensive and detailed of the reports so far published by the government on involvement with adult education. Reports appearing since that time have been consistently meagre in the amount of published statistics; it may thus be time to exert pressure on federal authorities to produce more comprehensive and useful aggregate data. (For additional information on this point see note 1, Chapter 1.)

11  At the same time, Lorimer found that more liberal motives for education – here labeled as 'general education,' 'culture,' and 'intellectual stimulation' – received significant votes from both men and women, 14 per cent and 24 per cent respectively, while proving equal in strength to the principal vocational motive in the responses of the women: 24 per cent against 23 per cent.

12  Knox (1958), in a survey of adult students attending the adult education division of Syracuse University, found that about three-quarters chose a vocational reason for attending, while a quarter chose a cultural reason. In a study of adult students at the University of Alabama Resident Center in Huntsville, Franklin (1960) found that while over 90 per cent were employed, almost a quarter of these wanted to change their line of work. In a survey of 130 extension credit students representing an eighteen-county area in northwestern Michigan, Hagelberg (1960) found that of four reasons for PAE, three of which were degree-related, the most prominent was 'to be more effective in present job,' affirmed by almost half of the sample.

13  Dowling (1963), for example, surveyed a number of agencies providing adult education for the Brown County Council of Adult Education in Wisconsin. Of the four 'reasons' available to respondents (education, economic, social and recreational), few gave 'economic' as a response. Dowling was surprised, noting that 'very few persons believe or wish to state that their main reason for acquiring education as an adult is "economic"' (p. 88). The correlation of motive and institutional mission is not, clearly, that straightforward.

14  In 1940 Mortimer Adler introduced his 'Great Books' concept to the general public (Stubblefield, 1987, p. 87). The concept, which was really the brainchild of both Adler and Robert Hutchins, both of the University of Chicago, requires adults to engage in an extensive reading program of the 'Great Books' of Western Culture from literature to psychology, from science to politics. It reached its peak audiences in the 1940s and 1950s. Today, it is represented by the Great Books Foundation based in Chicago (Davis, 1957).

15  It is important to note, however, that both samples, if not actually the same sample, overrepresent those with some educational background and those in employment. We can assume, therefore, that they may not represent what we nowadays refer to as the 'permanent underclass.'

16  Contrary to previous findings, course-taking for job preparation was given more often as a reason for PAE in the Johnstone and Rivera study than was enrollment for job advancement reasons. Since they did not discuss other similar studies, they appear not to have considered this anomalous. It is interesting to compare them with London *et al.* on the same point, justifying opposite findings with

similar arguments. The former, who found job advancement to be a more potent reason than job preparation, explained it *ex post facto* by emphasizing the need to maintain job competency once a career path had been chosen. Johnstone and Rivera, on the other hand, tended to see adult education as a form of academic training, and since the latter meant, for them, preparation for a job, they may not have felt a need to explain their findings.

17 Houle reviewed Johnstone and Rivera, McGrath, Burgess (1971a) and Carp *et al.* and concluded that, though it was usually possible to tell from the subject studied the most likely reason for participation, nevertheless there were problems with this approach. First, while the 'dominant' motive and subject matter choice were usually in alignment, other important 'supplementary' motives appeared which seemed to have little to do with the subject matter. Why, Houle asked of Johnstone's sample, 'do 13 per cent of those taking salesmanship do so in order to perform home-centered tasks, 12 per cent of those studying office machines hope to escape the daily routine, and 21 per cent of those learning to be nurses wish to meet new people?' (p. 16). Houle concluded that

> A much more complicated relationship exists between motives and the content of educational activities than has customarily been thought to be true ... Participation in any type of educational activity is undertaken for a number of different motives which operate collectively, [and which] reinforce and supplement one another. (p. 32)

18 In Lorimer's study, for example, almost no one mentioned the demands or influence of other people or the desire for social contact as reasons for PAE. Yet Lorimer speculated that they 'frequently operated as subsidiary or unrecognized factors' (p. 53). By contrast, he noted that while the desire for social status was not included in the checklist of reasons because he believed people would not respond to it truthfully, it was frequently mentioned by participants as a reason for participation. A more recent corroboration of the influence of reference group and status considerations can be found in Parjanen (1989).

## 3 Adult learning and the psychology of motive

1 The latter is a version of a question put by Gordon Darkenwald and quoted in a summary of proceedings of the Commission of Professors of Adult Education, which was part of the annual conference of the then Adult Education Association (USA), held in St Louis in 1980.

2 These models are not part of nor should they be mistaken for that body of research which grew up around the Theory of Games in the 1950s and which made much use of the notion of decision processes linked to the concept of probability, as in, for example, the work of Patrick Suppes and John Von Neumann.

3 Based on remarks in J. Blumler. (1962). The effects of long-term residential adult education in post-war Britain (Oxford University, unpublished dissertation), the most likely source of Nedzel's British data would have been questionnaire material used in E. Williams and A. E. Heath. (1936) *Learn and live* (Methuen, London), which was later deposited with the National Institute

of Adult Education in London for use in a follow-up study, but which the Second World War intervened to prevent.

4 The G.I. Bill of Rights, known officially as the Servicemen's Readjustment Act of 1944, made it possible for returning soldiers to avail themselves of opportunities for vocational and higher education through the use of federal subsidies as employment benefits.

5 Where PAE is explained in terms of current aspects of an individual's situation, according to London, it is the most successful. 'When explanation is attempted in terms of an individual's past, or in terms of presumably stable values and psychological configurations' (London, Wenkert and Hagstrom, 1963, p. 86), current involvement is much more difficult to predict.

6 Cookson remarks that few, if any, studies of PAE have incorporated such variables into explanations of participation. See, however, Boshier's (1980) interpretation of Haag (1976), Snyder (1951), Carson (1965), Boyle (1967) and Waldron (1968), where personality, intelligence and educational attainment factors are examined in their relationship to PAE.

7 This dichotomy has proved to be a particularly fruitful one and is at the heart of a number of theories of participation, including Edwards and Booth (1973) and Ordos (1980).

8 Naturally, there is some confusion over these terms. Some writers (e.g. Clausen, 1986) discuss 'stage' theories of adulthood, which Lasker and Moore would refer to as 'phase'; others (e.g. Schlossberg, 1984) divide the field up into categories of theory which overlap and do injury to the Lasker and Moore typology.

9 While Dow (1965) found only two factors and Boshier (1971) found fourteen, most 'solutions' have ranged between five and eight factors, with six factors being the mode. This is the Morstain and Smart solution which has been favoured by Boshier (1977, 1980), Haag (1976), Bova (1979), King (1980), Hawes (1981) Governanti (1981) and Boshier and Collins (1985).

10 Motivational orientations are probed using one of three psychometrically tested instruments: the Continuing Learning Orientation Index (CLOI) (Sheffield, 1962); the Reasons for Educational Participation Scale (REP) (Burgess, 1971a), and the Education Participation Scale (EPS) (Boshier, 1971, and elsewhere). During the late 1960s and up to the mid-1970s more studies had used CLOI than either of the others. Currently, the EPS is the most widely used of the three.

## 4 Adult learning as motivation and action

1 The idea that motives appear as they do, both informally in everyday interaction and formally in responses to surveys, because of the language or 'discourse' available to the interlocutor is treated in C. Wright Mills. (1967). Situated actions and vocabularies of motive. In I. L. Horwitz, *Power, politics and people: The collected essays of C. Wright Mills* (Oxford University Press, New York), and H. Gerth and C. Wright Mills. (1970). *Character and social structure* (Harcourt, Brace and World, New York). I have not been able to pursue the implications of this line of analysis, which appears to be a kind of marriage between sociological theory and the Whorf-Sapir hypothesis. Interested readers are referred to the above and to a chapter by Maria Slowey in M. Cullen. (1987). *Girls don't do honours: Irish women in education in the 19th and 20th centuries*

(Women's Education Bureau, Dublin), which applies Mills' perspective to an analysis of motives for adult education.

2   The concept of action has had a venerable place in the literature of American sociology, and in fact forms a decisive thread which has influenced much contemporary thought on the nature of social processes. For examples of this paradigm, see Znaniecki (1936/1967), Parsons (1949) and Parsons and Shils (1951).

3   From *Essay on Criticism*, Volume 1, Twickenham Edition, Yale University Press, lines 335–6.

## 5 Adult learning and the concept of social participation

1   Despite this early interest, less than 20 per cent of published work on the subject of social participation appeared in sociology journals up to the 1950s (Edwards and Booth, 1973). It was after 1950 that research in this area grew dramatically, with over half of all research publications in this area occurring between 1950 and 1959. The cumulative index of the *American Journal of Sociology* alone lists over fifty different studies of participation between 1895 and 1965, and ten titles between 1965 and 1970.

2   Queen went on to investigate the wide variation in the extent of social participation (SP) among the American adult population: there are real joiners who are involved with a variety of organizations and activities, others for whom informal friendship networks, but not formal organizations are a significant aspect of their lives, and a minority who are veritable recluses. For Queen the 'social problem' dimension to social participation had to do not merely with the lack of involvement in community life by those who were otherwise able for it, but actual impediments to participation by those who otherwise were interested, e.g. the physically impaired.

3   'Voluntary associations,' according to Booth and Edwards, 'are formal groups embodying continuity, rules governing eligibility, goals and prescribed rights and obligations of members. Such groups are *integrative systems for the individual and the community*; they play a vital role in society' (p. 77; emphasis added).

4   The introduction to this paper contains an interesting error. The authors were quarreling with previous research for 'two trends which thwart a fuller understanding' of PAE: first, it was descriptive rather than 'analytical'; second, there was the tendency to treat 'participation in the diverse spheres or domains of social life as being highly interrelated' (p. 102). The second quotation appears to find fault with research which puts different forms of social participation, including PAE, under the same heading. At the same time, they go on to demand that 'a conceptual framework' which, among other things, should be 'adequate to deal with the broader question of social participation generally' (p. 102). In other words, a theory of PAE should also be a theory of social participation, thus contradicting the thrust of their opening remarks.

5   The Beal study is a good example of the interdisciplinary climate which affected PAE research from the 1940s to the 1960s, having been referenced in Brunner (1959), Knox and Videbeck (1963), Verner and Newberry (1965) and Boshier (1979).

6   See S. Luke. (1973). *E. Durkheim: His life and work* (Penguin, Harmondsworth).

# 6 Adult learning and the social functions of education

1   The recent *National Longitudinal Study* (NLS), conducted by the Center for Educational Statistics in Washington, which has been following a national sample of high school seniors from their graduation in 1972 into adult life, promises a rich source of information for adult education researchers. As yet, however, no studies of PAE based on NLS data have been published.

2   Major figures including Grattan, Bryson, Hallenbeck, as well as London, have written about the 'functions' of adult education. With the exception of the latter, however, these treatments have tended to equate the term with institutional purpose and individual goals. London, by contrast, has interpreted it to mean the everyday and historically evolved roles which adult education plays *vis-à-vis* society at large. This approach, though 'functionalist' in tone, permits integration with the newer sociologies of education, thus creating the basis for a full-blown sociology of adult education.

3   Various black educational and political organizations within South Africa have been discussing and producing documents on the subject of 'people's education' since the Soweto rising in 1976. A recent issue of *Historical Foundations of Adult Education* contains a representative sample of this mostly unpublished material. The establishment of a link between adult education and political emancipation – empowerment – as well as repression, not always so obvious in the past, belongs of course to Paulo Freire. Many adult educators would acknowledge a debt to his work, even if they disagree with his philosophy or methods.

4   National Center for Education Statistics. (1989). *Digest of Education Statistics 1989* (25th edn). US Dept of Education (NCES89-643). The 'enrollment ratio' for the US is 59.3; for Canada it is 54.6. 'Data are the total enrollment of all ages in the school level divided by the population of the specific age groups which correspond to the school level' (Table 34.1). The closest other countries are Argentina (38.7) and the Phillipines (38.0).

5   There are, according to Jarvis (1985), four major schools of sociological thought, which differ, *inter alia*, on the degree to which power is associated with human agency.

6   Despite its apparent counterpoint to functionalism, the criticism has been made that the determinism inherent in Bowles and Gintis is implicitly functional. See the report of a symposium convened at Harvard to discuss the 1976 publication (Burke, 1977). In the fifteen years since then, many analyses have appeared either expanding on or refuting central theses of their position. As a result, 'no longer does a theory of correspondence figure prominently, and no longer does a base/superstructure model provide the basic conceptual apparatus that lies behind their arguments. . . Thus, the economy is not always predominant, nor are class relations. Social movements based on gender and race, not only class, are placed center stage' (Apple, 1988, p. 241).

7   A poignant example of this statement in practice is the analysis of working-class experiences in the British school system by P. Willis. (1981). *Learning to labor* (New York). Willis's work is in a singular tradition of British sociology whose

contemporary 'father' may be Basil Bernstein (see Halsey, Floud and Anderson, 1961, and elsewhere).

8    For further treatments of this issue see Fieldhouse's chapter in Taylor *et al.* (1985) and Blumler (1963).

## 7 Beyond the current paradigm

1    The apparent 'split' between theory and practice and how to reconcile the two is a recurring theme in the literature of adult education, even to the extent of becoming the title for an annual conference held in the Midwest since the early 1980s. Although this is not the context in which to discuss a matter of some complexity, it is my belief that much of this debate is ill-conceived. Historically, we already know from the writings of Durkheim and Dewey that education is an applied something-or-other. Pedagogy, according to Durkheim, is a 'practical theory . . . neither the educational activity itself, nor the speculative science of education,' but rather the 'systematic reaction of the second on the first, the product of thought which seeks in . . . psychology and social psychology principles for the practice or for the reform of education' (Luke, 1973, p. 111). Adult education research never deals with matters of pure theory (Courtney, 1986), another reason why the Boyd, Apps position is untenable; it is always somehow tied to practice, however tenuously.

2    R. Zemke and S. Zemke. (1981). 30 things we know for sure about adult learning. *Training, 18*(6), 45–50.

3    The strongest position on this issue, so far as I am aware, is Patterson, who equates 'education' with 'liberal education' and so finds the phrase 'liberal education' redundant. Naturally, then, there is no need for a phrase like 'liberal adult education' since the homage to the liberal ideal is already enshrined in the phrase 'adult education.' But there is a precedent for this view in the British literature of adult education; see Williams and Heath (1936). (See Note 3 Chapter 3 above.)

# Bibliography

Allardt, E., Jartti, P., Jyrkila, F., and Littunen, Y. (1957). On the cumulative nature of leisure activities. *Acta Sociologica, 3*, 165–72

Anderson, W. A. (1943). The family and individual social participation. *American Sociological Review, 8*, 402–24

Anderson, R. and Darkenwald, G. (1979). *Participation and persistence in American adult education*. College Entrance Examination Board, New York

Apple, M. (1988). Standing on the shoulders of Bowles and Gintis:Class formation and capitalist schools. *History of Education Quarterly, 28*, 231–41

Arbeiter, S. (1977). Profile of the adult learner. *Journal of Adult Education, 6*(1), 1–12

Aslanian, C. and Brickell, H. (1980). *Americans in transition: Lifechanges as reasons for adult learning*. College Entrance Examination Board, New York

Atkinson, J. and Birch, D. (1970). *The dynamics of action*. Wiley, New York

Axelrod, M. (1956). Urban structure and social participation. *American Sociological Review, 21*, 13–19

Bailyn, B. (1962). *Education in the forming of American society*. Norton, New York

Baltes, P. B. and Lipsitt, L. P. (1980). Life-span developmental psychology. *Annual Review of Psychology, 31*, 65–110

Barnes, H. E. (1948). *An introduction to the history of sociology*. University of Chicago Press, Chicago

Barron, H. H. (1953). A study of adult educational interests and programs in Salt Lake County. Unpublished doctoral dissertation, University of Utah

Beal, G. (1956). Additional hypotheses in participation research. *Rural Sociology, 21*, 249–56

Beals, R. and Brody, L. (1941). *The literature of adult education*. American Association for Adult Education, New York

Beard, J. and Ragheb, M. (1983). Measuring leisure motivation. *Journal of Leisure Research, 15*, 219–28

Bell, W. and Force, M. (1956). Urban neighborhood types and participation in formal associations. *American Sociological Review, 21*, 25–34

Bennet, L. (1968). Air Force nurses' participation in programs of continuing education as related to selected criteria. (Doctoral dissertation, Boston University). *Dissertation Abstracts International, 30*, 2316–17A

Berg, I. (1970). *Education and jobs: The great training robbery*. Praeger, New York

Bergsten, U. (1980). Interest in education among adults with short previous formal schooling. *Adult Education, 30*, 131–51

Bernard, L. L. (1928). Some historical and recent trends of sociology in the United States. *Southwestern Political and Social Science Quarterly, 9*, December, 264–93

—— and Bernard, J. (1943). *Origins of American Sociology: The social science movement in the United States.* Thomas Y. Crowell, New York

Bischoff, L. J. (1976). *Adult psychology* (2nd edn). Harper & Row, New York

Bishop, D. (1970). Stability of factor structure of leisure behavior: Analyses of four communities. *Journal of Leisure Research, 2*, 160–9

Boggs, D. (1974). An interpretative review of social science research on behaving-valuing patterns of low status people. *Adult Education, 24*, 293–312

Booth, A. (1961). A demographic consideration of non-participation. *Adult Education*, 1961, *11*, 223–9

Boshier, R. (1971). Motivational orientations of adult education participants: A factor analytic exploration of Houle's typology. *Adult Education, 21*, 3–26

—— (1973). Educational participation and dropout: A theoretical model. *Adult Education, 20*, 255–82

—— (1976). Factor analysts at large: A critical review of the motivational orientation literature. *Adult Education, 27*, 24–47

—— (1977). Motivational orientations revisited: Life-space motivation and the educational participation scale. *Adult Education, 27*, 89–115

—— (1979). A conceptual and methodological perspective concerning research on participation in adult education. In J. Niemi (ed.), *Viewpoints on adult education research.* Columbus, Ohio: ERIC Clearinghouse on Adult, Career and Vocational Education

—— (1980). Socio-psychological correlates of motivational orientations: A multivariate analysis. *Proceeding of the Twenty-First Adult Education Research Conference* (pp. 34–40). Vancouver, British Columbia, Canada

—— and Clarke, G. (1981). Relationships between motivational orientations and participant satisfaction with institutional environments: Multivariate perspectives. *Proceedings of the Twenty-Second Adult Educational Conference* (pp. 31–6). DeKalb, Ill.

—— and Collins, J. (1982). Educational participation scale factor structure and correlates for 12,000 Learners. *Proceedings of the Twenty-Third Adult Education Research Conference* (pp. 26–36). Lincoln, Nebr.

—— (1985). The Houle typology after twenty-two years: A large scale empirical test. *Adult Education Quarterly, 35*, 113–30

Bourdieu, P. (1977). Cultural reproduction and social reproduction. In J. Karabel and A. H. Halsey (eds), *Power and ideology in education.* Oxford University Press, New York

—— and Passeron, J. C. (1977). *Reproduction in education, society and culture.* Sage, London

Bova, B. (1979). Motivation orientations of adults in technical vocational and post-secondary institutions. Unpublished doctoral dissertation, University of New Mexico. (ERIC Document Reproduction Service no. ED 189–291)

Bowles, S. and Gintis, S. (1976). *Schooling in capitalist America.* Basic Books, New York

Boyd, R. (1960). Basic motivations of adults in non-credit programs. *Adult Education (USA)*, 11, 92–8

—— (1965). A model for the analysis of motivation. *Adult Education, 16*, 24–33

Boyle, W. (1967). Adult participation in educational activities (Doctoral dissertation, University of Wisconsin). *Dissertation Abstracts International, 28*, 2972–3A

Brody, N. (1980). Social motivation. *Annual Review of Psychology, 31*, 143–68

Brookfield, S. (1983). *Adult learners, adult education and the community.* Teachers College Press, New York

—— (1986). *Understanding and facilitiating adult learning.* Jossey-Bass, San Francisco

Brunner, E. DeS., Wilder, D., Kirchner, C. and Newberry, J. (1959) *An overview of adult education research.* Adult Education Association, Chicago

Burgess, P. (1971a). Educational orientations of adult participants in group educational activities. Unpublished doctoral dissertation, University of Chicago

—— (1971b). Reasons for adult participation in group educational activities. *Adult Education, 22*, 3–29

Burke, J. (1977). Symposium on *Schooling in Capitalist America. History of Education Quarterly, 17*

Burman, A. (1959). Aspirational fulfillment among adults on lower socio-economic levels with implications for adult education (Doctoral dissertation, Indiana University). *Dissertation Abstracts International, 20*, 1252

Burnett, I. E. (1976). A study of selected motivational factors influencing regular adult General Educational Development (GED) student enrollment in a large public school system (Doctoral dissertation, University of Mississippi). *Dissertations Abstracts International, 37*, 1897A

Canning, W. (1955). A psycho-educational study of a group of adult, non-high school graduates matriculated in a college degree program (Doctoral dissertation, Northwestern University, 1955). *Dissertation Abstracts International, 15*, 2095

Carlson, R. (1987). *The Americanization Syndrome: A quest for conformity.* St. Martin's Press, New York

Carp, A., Peterson, R. and Roelfs, P. (1974). Adult learning interests and experiences. In K. P. Cross and J. R. Valley (eds), *Planning Non- Traditional Programs.* Jossey-Bass, San Francisco

Carson, R. (1965). Factors related to the participation of selected young adult males in continuing education (Doctoral dissertation, Florida State University). *Dissertations Abstracts International, 27*, 96A

Carter, G., Kerr, W., and York, S. (1962) Characteristics of extra-mural students. *Adult Education, 12*, 223–30

Cartwright, M. (1935). *Ten years of adult education.* Macmillan, New York

Chapin, S. (1939). Social participation and social intelligence. *American Sociological Review, 4*, 157–66

Chapman, C. E. (1959). Some characteristics of adult part-time students. *Adult Education, 10*, 27–41

Chertow, D. (1974). Literature review: Participation of the poor in the war on poverty. *Adult Education, 24*, 184–207

Chimene, D. (1984). Beyond 1984: Future participants in adult education. *Proceedings of the Twenty-Fourth Annual Adult Education Research Conference* (pp. 51–6), Montreal, Canada

Clark, B. (1962). *Educating the expert society.* Chandler, San Francisco

—— (1965). In *International Encyclopedia of the Social Sciences* (Volume 4).

Macmillan and the Free Press, New York

Clausen, J.A. (1986). *The Life Course: A sociological perspective.* Prentice-Hall, New York

Clayton, D. E. and Smith, M. M. (1987). Motivational typology of re-entry women. *Adult Education Quarterly, 37,* 90–104

Cofer, C. N. and Appley, M. H. (1964). *Motivation: Theory and research.* Wiley, New York

Collingwood, R. G. (1940). *An essay on metaphysics.* Clarendon Press, Oxford

Collins, R. (1977). Functional and conflict theories of educational stratification. In J. Karabel and A. H. Halsey (eds), *Power and ideology in education.* Oxford University Press, New York

Conrad, R. (1974). Educational values of adult rural disadvantaged students: An affective evaluation report. In J. Niemi *et al. Research Investigations in Adult Education – 1976 Annual Register.* Educational Resources Information Centre (ERIC), Adult Education Association (USA)

Cookson, P. (1983). Determinants of adult educational participation. *Proceedings of the Twenty-Fourth Annual Adult Education Research Conference* (pp. 69–74), Montreal, Canada

—— (1986). A framework for theory and research on adult education participation. *Adult Education Quarterly, 36,* 130–42

Cotton, W. (1968). *On behalf of adult education: A historical examination of the supporting literature.* Center for the study of Liberal Education for Adults, no. 56, Chicago

Courtney, S. (1981a). The factors affecting participation in adult education: An analysis of some literature. *Studies in Adult Education, 13,* 98–111

—— (1981b). *The Magee experiment: An analysis of adults in education.* Institute of Continuing Education, University of Ulster, Northern Ireland

—— (1984). Visible learning: Adult education and the question of particpation (Doctoral dissertation, Northern Illinois University). *Dissertation Abstracts International, 45,* 3512

—— (1985). The politics of number: National estimates and the definition of adult education, 1924–1985. Unpublished manuscript, National College of Education

—— (1986). On derivation of the research question. *Adult Education Quarterly, 36,* 160–5

—— (1989). Defining adult and continuing education. In P. Cunningham and S. Merriam (eds), *Handbook of Adult and Continuing Education,* Jossey-Bass, San Francisco

—— (1990). Social science and the making of adult education theory: Influences on the study of participation, 1930 to 1960. In R. Rohfeld (ed.), *Breaking New Ground: the Development of Adult and Worker Education in North America, Kellogg Project, Syracuse University*

Crandall, R. (1980). Motivations for leisure. *Journal of Leisure Research, 12,* 45–54

Cremin, L. (1970). *American education: The colonial experience, 1607–1783.* Harper & Row, New York

Cross, K. P. (1978). A critical review of state and national studies of the needs and interests of adult learners. In C. Stalford (ed.), *Adult learning needs and the demand for lifelong learning,* National Institute of Education, Washington, DC

—— (1979). Adult learners: Characteristics, needs, and interests. In R. E. Peterson and associates (eds), *Lifelong learning in America,* Jossey-Bass, San Francisco

—— (1981). *Adults as learners*. Jossey-Bass, San Francisco

—— and Valentine, T. (1985). Factor structure of deterrents to public participation in adult education. *Adult Education Quarterly, 35*, 177–93

—— and Gavin, W. J. (1987). Dropout as a function of discrepancies between expectations and actual experiences of the classroom social environment. *Adult Education Quarterly, 37*, 152–63

Cunningham, P. (1973). *The effects of self-esteem and perceived program utility on persistence and cognitive achievement in an Adult Basic Education program.* Unpublished doctoral dissertation, University of Chicago

Darkenwald, G. and Merriam, S. (1982). *Adult education: Foundations of practice.* Harper & Row, New York

Davies, J. (1950). A study of participant interest and ability in adult general education programs in Iowa. Unpublished doctoral dissertation, University of Iowa

Davis, J. (1957). *A study of participants in the Great Books Program.* National Opinion Research Center, Chicago

Davis, P. B. (1960). Selected factors associated with attendance at adult farmer classes in Michigan (Doctoral dissertation, Michigan State University). *Dissertation Abstracts International, 20*, 3609

Deane, S. (1950). Who seeks adult education and why? *Adult Education, 1*, 18–25

DeCharms, R. and Muir, M. (1978). Motivation: Social approaches. *Annual Review of Psychology, 29*, 91–113

Defee, J., Schultz, J. and Pasewark, R. (1974). Organizational level and organizational membership. *Journal of Leisure Research, 6*, 20–6

DeGrazia, S. (1964). *Of time, work, and leisure.* Doubleday (Anchor), New York

Devlin, L. (1977). Participation in adult education and occupational mobility. Unpublished doctoral dissertation, University of Chicago

—— (1977). Participation in adult education and occupational mobility. Unpublished doctoral dissertation, University of Chicago

Dickinson, G. (1971). Educational variables and participation in adult education: An exploratory study. *Adult Education, 22*, 36–47

—— and Clark, K. M. (1975). Learning orientations and participation in self-education and continuing education. *Adult Education, 26*, 3–15

*Digest of education statistics 1985–1986.* Office of Educational Research and Improvement, US Dept of Education

Dimmock, K. (1985). Models of adult participation in informal science education (Doctoral dissertation, Northern Illinois University). *Dissertation Abstracts International, 46*, 2519

Disman, M. (1979). Cultural participation and social exchange theory. *Sociological Abstracts, 63–82* 5, S08206 (Abstract #)

Divita, C. (1969). Adult Basic Education: A study of the backgrounds, characteristics, aspirations and attitudes of undergraduate adults in W. Virginia. W. Virginia Research Coordinating Unit for Vocational Education, Huntington

Dolphin, P. and Schrage, B. (1989). Cross's chain-of-response as a predictor for registered nurses' participation in continuing education. *Proceedings of the Thirtieth Annual Adult Education Research Conference*, Madison, Wisconsin

Dotson, F. (1951). Patterns of voluntary association among urban, working-class families. *American Sociological Review, 16*, 687–93

Douglah, M. (1970). Some perspectives on the phenomenon of participation. *Adult Education, 20*, 88–98

—— and Moss, G. (1968). Differential participation patterns of adults of low and high educational attainment. *Adult Education, 18*, 247–59

Dow, J. (1965). Characteristics of noncredit university extension students (Doctoral dissertation, University of California). *Dissertation Abstracts International, 26*, 3734

Dowling, W. (1963). A study of adult education participants in Green Bay, Wisconsin. *Journal of Experimental Education, 32*, 85–93

Dugger, J. (1965). Motivation and factors characterizing adult learners enrolled at evening courses at Drake University (Doctoral dissertation, Iowa State University). *Dissertation Abstracts International, 26*, 5195

Dunstan, J. (1939). A study of some factors making for the continued participation of individuals in the program of a city church, with particular attention to the adolescent–adult transition. Unpublished doctoral dissertation, Columbia University

Edwards, J. and Booth, A. (1973). *Social participation in urban society.* Schenkman, Cambridge, Mass.

Essert, P. (1950). *Creative leadership in adult education.* Prentice-Hall, New York

Evans, N. (1985). *Post education society: Recognizing adults as learners.* Croom-Helm, London

Fingeret, A. (1983). Social network: A new perspective on independence and illiterate adults. *Adult Education Quarterly, 33*, 133–46

Flaherty, J. (1968). The prediction of college level academic achievement in adult education students (Doctoral dissertation, University of Toronto). *Dissertation Abstracts International, 31*, 997A

Flinck, R. (1977). *Why adults participate in education.* University of Lund, Department of Education, Sweden

Forsythe, D. (1983). *An introduction to group dynamics.* Brooks/Cole, Pacific Grove, Calif.

Foskett, J. (1955). Social structure and social participation. *American Sociological Review, 20*, 431–8

Franklin, E. (1960). Characteristics of the student population, University of Alabama Resident Center, Huntsville, Alabama (Doctoral dissertation, George Peabody College for Teachers). *Dissertation Abstracts International, 21*, 534

Garrison, D. R. (1987). Dropout prediction within a broad psychosocial context: An analysis of Boshier's congruence model. *Adult Education Quarterly, 37*, 212–22

Gaventa, J. (1980). *Power and Powerlessness: Quiescence and rebellion in an Appalachian Valley.* University of Illinois Press, Urbana, Illinois.

Giffis, B. (1982). Adult women students: The relationship of their life characteristics to enrollment in a Bachelor's Degree program. Unpublished doctoral dissertation, Michigan State University

Giroux, H. A. (1983). Theories of reproduction and resistance in the new sociology of education: A critical analysis. *Harvard Educational Review, 53*, 257–93

Goodnow, B. (1982). Increasing enrollment through benefit segmentation. *Adult Education, 32*, 89–103

Gould, R. L. (1978). *Transformations: Growth and change in adult life.* Simon & Schuster, New York

Governanti, M. (1981). A study of the motivational orientations of adults attending a comprehensive community college (Doctoral dissertation, Virginia Polytechnic Institute and State University). *Dissertation Abstracts International, 41*, 4949A

Grabowski, S. (1972). Motivational factors of adult learners in a directed self-study Bachelor's degree program (Doctoral dissertation, Syracuse University). *Dissertation Abstracts International, 34*, 1052A

Grattan, C. H. (1955). *In quest of knowledge: A historical perspective on adult education* (reissued, 1971). Association Press, New York

Griffith, W. (1970). Adult education institutions. In R. M. Smith, G. F. Aker and J. R. Smith (eds), *The handbook of adult education*. Macmillan, New York

Grigsby, M. (1980). Motivation of adults in noncredit college courses (Doctoral dissertation, University of Southern California). *Dissertation Abstracts International, 41*, 1426A

Grotelueschen, A. and Caulley, D. (1977). A model for studying determinants of intention to participate in continuing professional education. *Adult Education, 28*, 22–37

Haag, U. (1976). Psychological foundations of motive for participation in adult education. Unpublished master's thesis, University of British Columbia

Hagelberg, M. (1960). A study of the goals and characteristics of extension credit students in northwestern Michigan (Doctoral dissertation, Michigan State University). *Dissertation Abstracts International, 21*, 115

Hagstrom, W. (1964). Poverty and adult education. *Adult Education, 16*, 145–60

Hall, C. (1965). Why Illinois women participate in home economics extension. Unpublished doctoral dissertation, University of Chicago

Halsey, A. H., Floud, J., and Anderson, C. A. (1961). *Education, economy, and society*. Free Press, New York

Hanks, M. and Eckland, B. (1978). Adult voluntary associations and adolescent socialization. *Sociological Quarterly, 19*, 481–90

Hartig, M.E. (1962). An analysis of selected factors of interruption or persistence in attendance in the Community College at Evansville College. Unpublished doctoral dissertation, Indiana University

Hausknecht, M. (1962). *The Joiners*. Bedminster Press, Totowa, New Jersey

Havighurst, R. (1963). Changing status and roles during the adult life cycle: Significance for adult education. In H. W. Burns (ed.), *Sociological backgrounds of adult education*. Center for the Study of Liberal Education for Adults, no. 41, Chicago

—— (1973). *Developmental tasks and education* (3rd edn). David McKay, New York

—— and Orr, B. (1956). *Adult education and adult needs*. Center for the Study of Liberal Education for Adults, Chicago

—— and Neugarten, B. (1957). *Society and education*. Allyn & Bacon, Boston

Hawes, J. (1981). A study of the relationship between the motivational typologies of adult learners and the institutions and educational courses in which they are enrolled. (Doctoral dissertation, Duke University). *Dissertation Abstracts International, 42*, 960

Hodge, R. and Treiman, D. (1968). Social participation and social status. *American Sociological Review, 33*, 722–40

Holden, J. B. (1958). A survey of participation in adult education classes. *Adult Leadership, 6*, 258–60, 271

Hopper, E. and Osborn, M. (1975). *Adult students: Education, selection, and social control*. Frances Pinter, London

Houle, C. (1961). *The inquiring mind*. University of Wisconsin Press, Madison. (Reissued 1984, University of Oklahoma, Norman).

—— (1974). *The provision of post-compulsory education: The relationship between motivation and participation, with special reference to non-traditional forms of study.* Prepared for the Organization for Economic Cooperation and Development, Paris

—— (1983). *Structural features and policies promoting (or inhibiting) adult learning.* Prepared for the European Conference on Motivation for Adult Education, Hamburg, Germany

Hymon, M. (1960). The awareness and perception of adult education as factors in the motivation of adults on the lower socio-economic levels (Doctoral dissertation, Indiana University). *Dissertation Abstracts International, 21,* 934–5

Jack, R. (1969). A survey analysis of the clientele of an ABE program for welfare recipients. Unpublished doctoral dissertation, Indiana University

Jarret, J. (1960). Adult education and freedom. *Adult Education, 10,* 67–73

Jarvis, P. (1983). *Adult and continuing education: theory and practice.* Croom-Helm, London

—— (1985). *The sociology of adult and continuing education.* Croom-Helm, London

—— (1987). *Adult learning in the social context.* Croom-Helm, London

Jeffres, L. and Robinson, J. (1980). Participation in mass media consumption. In D. H. Smith, J. Macaulay and associates (eds), *Participation in social and political activities,* Jossey-Bass, San Francisco

Jencks, C. (1972). *Inequality: A reassessment of the effects of family and schooling in America.* Basic Books, New York

—— and Riesman, D. (1969). *The academic revolution.* Anchor, New York

Jensen, G. E., Liveright, A. A. and Hallenback, W. (eds) (1964). *Adult education: Outlines of an emerging field of university study.* Adult Education Assocation, Washington, DC

Johnstone, J. and Rivera, R. (1965). *Volunteers for learning: A study of the educational pursuits of American adults.* Aldine, Chicago

Kaplan, A. (1945). *Socio-economic circumstances and adult participation (in certain cultural and educational activities).* Teachers' College, New York

Kaplan, M. (1960). *Leisure in America: A social inquiry.* John Wiley, New York

Karabel, J. (1977). Community colleges and social stratification: Submerged class conflict in American higher education. In J. Karabel and A. H. Halsey (eds), *Power and ideology in education.* Oxford University Press, New York

Kelly, J. (1977). Leisure socialization: Replication and extension. *Journal of Leisure Research, 9,* 121–32

Keogh, L. (1980). An exploration of factors motivating adult students to return to college (Doctoral dissertation, University of Michigan). *Dissertation Abstracts International, 41,* 1896A

Kindell, C. R. (1959). Factors associated with the participation of farmers in organized instruction in vocational agriculture. Unpublished doctoral dissertation, Oklahoma State University

King, G. A. (1980). The participation patterns and motivational orientations of an adult, part-time, graduate student population within an urban academic institution (Doctoral dissertation, Boston University). *Dissertation Abstracts International, 41,* 1896A

Klandermans, B. and Oegema, D. (1987). Potentials, networks, motivations and barriers. *American Sociological Review, 52,* 519–31

Kleemeier, R. W. (ed.) (1961). *Aging and leisure: A research perspective into the meaningful use of time.* Oxford University Press, New York

Knowles, M. (1955). Adult education in the U.S. *Adult Education, 5,* 67–77

—— (1977). *The adult education movement in the U.S.* (revised). Robert Krieger, Malabar, Fla

—— (1980). *The modern practice of adult education* (revised). Follett, New York

Knox, A. (1958). Adult college students: An analysis of certain factors related to the characteristics of students attending a university adult college (Doctoral dissertation, Syracuse University). *Dissertation Abstracts International, 19,* 1984

—— (1965). Clientele analysis. *Review of Educational Research, 35,* 231–9

—— (1977). *Adult Development and Learning.* Jossey-Bass, San Francisco

—— and Sjogren, D. (1962). Motivation to participate and learn in adult education. *Adult Education, 12,* 238–42

—— and Videbeck, R. (1963). Adult education and adult life cycle. *Adult Education, 13,* 102–21

Komarovsky, M. (1946). The voluntary associations of urban dwellers. *American Sociological Review, 11,* 686–98

Larsen, C. L. (1953). Participation in adult groups: The relationship between participation and valence in two Air Force reserve squadrons. Unpublished doctoral dissertation, University of Michigan

Lasker, H. and Moore, J. (1980). Current studies of adult development: Implications for education. In H. Lasker, J. Moore and E. Simpson (eds), *Adult development and approaches to learning,* National Institute for Community Development, Washington, DC (ERIC no. ED 195 854)

LeClair, V. (1969). A study of the relationship of three factors – perceived need deficiency, importance of need fulfillment, perception of education – to participation in education (Doctoral dissertation, Michigan State University). *Dissertation Abstracts International, 30,* 4756A

LeVine, J. and Dole, A. A. (1963). Salient enrollment determinants in adult classes. *Adult Education, 13,* 133–48

Levinson, D. (1978). *The seasons of a man's life.* Ballantine Books, New York

Lewis, R. B. (1969). A study of selected factors associated with participation orientation toward education and job training among adults residing in low socioeconomic communities of North Carolina. (Doctoral dissertation, North Carolina State University at Raleigh). *Dissertation Abstracts International, 30,* 4757-A

Litchfield, A. (1965). The nature and pattern of participation in Adult Education activities. Unpublished doctoral dissertation, University of Chicago

London, J. (1970). The influence of social class behavior upon adult education participation. *Adult Education, 20,* 140–53

—— Wenkert, R. and Hagstrom, W. (1963). *Adult education and social class.* (Cooperative research project no. 1017). Survey Research Center, University of California at Berkeley

—— and Wenkert, R. (1974). Adult education: Definition, description, and analysis. In D. W. Swift (ed.), *American education: A sociological perspective,* Houghton Mifflin, Boston

—— and Ewing, J. B. (1982). Adult education and the phenomena of social change. *Adult Education, 31,* 229–47

Lorimer, F. (1931). *The making of adult minds in a metropolitan area*. Macmillan, New York

Love, R. (1953). The use of motivation research to determine interest in adult college-level training. *Educational Record, 34*, 210–18

Lowe, S. D. (1987). Expanding the structure of adult learning orientations (Doctoral dissertation, Michigan State University). *Dissertations Abstract International, 48*, 3033

Luke, S. (1973). *E. Durkheim: His life and work*. Penguin, Harmondswoth

Lundberg, G., Komarovsky, M. and McInerny, M. (1934). *Leisure: A suburban study*. Columbia University Press, New York

Macaulay, J. and Berkowitz, L. (eds) (1970). *Altruistic and Helping Behavior*. Academic Press, New York

McGrath, E. (1938). *The adult student in Buffalo*. Buffalo Foundation, Buffalo

McKechnie, G. (1974). The psychological structure of leisure: Past behavior. *Journal of Leisure Research, 6*, 27–45

McLaughlin, L. K. (1951). Population in the Univeristy of California extension classes. Unpublished doctoral dissertation, University of California

McPherson, J. and Smith-Lovin, L. (1986). Sex segregation in voluntary associations. *American Sociological Review, 51*, 61–79

Main, K. (1979). The Power-Load-Margin formula of Howard Y. McClusky as the basis for a model of teaching. *Adult Education, 30*, 19–33

Marple, D. (1969). Motivational tendencies of women participants in continuing education (Doctoral dissertation, Columbia University). *Dissertation Abstracts International, 30*, 1824–5A

Marsh, D. (1926). *Adult education in a community*. American Association for Adult Education, Buffalo

Marsick, V. (1987). *Learning in the workplace*. Routledge, London/New York

—— (1990). Altering the paradigm for theory building and research in human resource development. *Human Resource Development Quarterly, 1* (1), 5–24

—— (1990). *Informal and incidental learning in the workplace*. Routledge, London/New York

Mather, W. G. (1941). Income and participation. *American Sociological Review, 6*, 380–3

Matkin, G. (1979). Theory, method, and appropriateness in adult education research. Unpublished manuscript, University of California, Berkeley, School of Education

Mezirow, J. (1978). Perspective transformation. *Adult Education, 28*, 100–10

Meyer, J. (1977). The effects of education as an institution. *American Journal of Sociology, 83*, 55–77

Meyersohn, R. (1969). The sociology of leisure in the United States: Introduction and bibliography, 1945–1965. *Journal of Leisure Research, 6*, 53–67

Milbraith, L. W. and Goel, M. L. (1965). *Political participation*. Rand McNally, Chicago

—— (1977). Participation in adult education and occupational mobility. Unpublished doctoral dissertation, University of Chicago

Miller, H. (1967). *Participation of adults in education: A forcefield analysis*. Center for the Study of Liberal Education for Adults, Chicago

Morrill, J. G. (1960). A study of factors related to non-participation in extension education programs in the three O.A.H.U. extension districts (Doctoral dissertation, Cornell University). *Dissertation Abstracts International, 21,* 3339

Morstain, B. and Smart, J. (1974). Reasons for participation in adult education courses: A multivariate analysis of group differences. *Adult Education, 24,* 83–98

Mortimer, J. and Simmons, R. (1978). Adult socialization. *Annual Review of Sociology, 4,* 421–54

Moses, S. (1971). *The learning force: A more comprehensive framework for educational policy* (Occasional paper, no. 25). Publications in Continuing Education, Syracuse University

NCES (National Center for Education Statistics). (1969). *Participation in adult education, final report 1969.* US Dept of Education, Washington, DC

—— *Participation in adult education, final report 1972.* US Dept of Education, Washington, DC

—— *Participation in adult education, final report 1975.* US Dept of Education, Washington, DC

—— *Participation in adult education, 1981.* US Dept of Education, Washington, DC

—— *Trends in adult education 1969–1984.* Office of Educational Research and Improvement, US Dept of Education, Washington, DC

Nedzel, L. (1952). The motivation and education of the general public through museum experiences. Unpublished doctoral dissertation, University of Chicago

Newberry, J. (1958). A descriptive study of certain aspects of the ecology of formal organizations in a Southern town. Unpublished doctoral dissertation, Florida State University

—— (1959). Participants and participation in adult education (with E. Brunner). In E. Brunner *et al., An overview of adult education research.* Adult Education Association, Washington, DC

Nicholson, D. (1955). Why adults attend school: An analysis of motivating factors. *University of Missouri Bulletin, 56.*

Niemi, J. and Nagle, J. (1979). Learners, agencies, and program development in adult and continuing education. In P. D. Langermann and D. H. Smith (eds), *Managing adult continuing education programs and staff.* National Association for Public Continuing Adult Education, Washington, DC

Noe, F. (1973). The political and social ideology of the leisure class. *Journal of Leisure Research, 5,* 49–59

Odum, H. W. (1951). *American sociology: The story of sociology in the United States through 1950.* Greenwood Press, New York

O'Keefe, M. (1977). *The adult, education, and public policy.* Aspen Institute for Humanistic Studies, Cambridge, Mass.

Ordos, D. (1980). Models of motivation for participation in adult education. *Proceedings of the Twenty-First Adult Education Research Conference,* Vancouver, British Columbia, Canada

Ozanne, J. (1934). *Regional surveys of adult education.* American Association for Adult Education, New York

Parjanen, M. (1989). Adult studies: Seeking for status? In R. Makinen and P. Maatta (eds), *Students and studying in higher education in Finland.* Institute for Educational Research, Jyvaskla

Parsons, T. (1949). *The structure of social action* (2nd edn). McGraw-Hill, New York

—— and Shils, E. (eds) (1951). *Toward a general theory of action*. Harper & Bros, New York

Patterson, R. W. K. (1979). *Values, education, and the adult*. Routledge & Kegan Paul, London

Pattyson, J. W. (1961). The influence of certain factors on attendance in public school adult education programs (Doctoral dissertation, Florida State University). *Dissertation Abstracts International, 22*, 1078

Penland, P. (1977). *Self-planned learning in America*. University of Pittsburgh, Book Center

—— (1979). Self-initiated learning. *Adult Education, 29*, 170–9

Peters, R. S. (1958). *The concept of motivation*. Routledge & Kegan Paul, London

Phifer, B. (1964). Change of interest between young adulthood and early middle age among participants in adult education programs. Unpublished doctoral dissertation, University of Chicago

Philips, A. (1958). An analysis of relationships between enrollments and fees in public school adult education classes in the state of Washington (Doctoral dissertation, State College of Washington). *Dissertation Abstracts International, 19*, 1278

Pincus, F. (1980). The false promises of community colleges: Class conflict and vocational education. *Harvard Educational Review, 50*, 332–52

Pritchard, D. (1979). Motivational orientations of older adult participants in adult education (Doctoral dissertation, University of Southern California). *Dissertation Abstracts International, 39*, 5264–5A

Pryor, B. (1990). Predicting and explaining intentions to participate in continuing education: An application of the Theory of Reasoned Action. *Adult Education Quarterly, 40*, 3, 146–57

Queen, S. A. and Gruener, J. R. (1941). *Social pathology (obstacles to social participation)*. Thomas Y. Crowell, New York

Ray, R. (1981). Examining motivation to participate in continuing education: An investigation of recreation professionals. *Journal of Leisure Research, 13*, 66–75

Reissman, L. (1954). Class, leisure, and social participation. *American Sociological Review, 19*, 76–84

Rockhill, K. (1982). Researching participation in adult education: the potential of the qualitative perspective. *Adult Education, 33*, 3–19

Rodriguez, O. (1978). Occupational shifts and educational upgrading in the American labor force between 1950 and 1970. *Sociology of Education, 51*, 55–67

Rose, A. (1989). Beyond classroom walls: The Carnegie Corporation and the founding of the American Association for Adult Education. *Adult Education Quarterly, 39*, 140–51

Ross, N. (1978). Variables influencing the decision to enter adult education graduate programs (Doctoral dissertation, Kansas State University). *Dissertation Abstracts International, 39*, 2692A

Rubenson, K. (1978). Participation in recurrent education: Problems relating to the undereducated and underprivileged. In C. Stalford (ed.), *Adult learning needs and the demand for lifelong learning*. National Institute for Education, Washington, DC

—— and Hoghielm, R. (eds) (1980). *Adult education for social change: Research on the Swedish allocation policy*. CWK Gleerup, Stockholm

Savides, H.A. (1960). *An identification of some characteristics of students who complete and students who drop out of an evening technological curriculum.* Unpublished doctoral dissertation, The University of Wisconsin

Scanlan, C. and Darkenwald, G. (1984). Identifying deterrents to participation in continuing education. *Adult Education Quarterly, 34*, 155–66

Scharles, H.G. (1966). *The relationship of selected personality needs to the participation, drop-out and achievements among adult learners.* Unpublished doctoral dissertation, The Florida State University

Schlossberg, N. (1984). *Counseling adults in transition: Linking practice with theory.* Springer, New York

Schroeder, W. (1970). Adult education defined and described. In R. M. Smith, G. F. Aker and J. R. Smith (eds), *The handbook of adult education.* Macmillan, New York

Scott, J. (1957). Membership and particiation in voluntary assocations. *American Sociological Review, 22*, 315–25

Sheffield, S. (1962). The orientations of adult continuing learners. Unpublished doctoral dissertation, University of Chicago

Shils, E. (1948). *The present state of American sociology.* Free Press, New York

Shipp, T. and McKenzie, L. R. (1981). Adult learners and non-learners: Demographic characteristics as an indicator of psychographic characteristics. *Adult Education, 31*, 187–98

Sitts, M. R. (1960). A study of the personality differences between a group of women who had participated in sewing classes in an adult education program and a group of their friends and neighbors who had not participated in any adult education activities (Doctoral dissertation, Michigan State University). *Dissertation Abstracts International, 21*, 1120

Sjogren, D., Knox, A. and Grotelueschen, G. (1968). Adult learning in relation to prior adult education participation. *Adult Education, 19*, 3–10

Smith, A. E. (1962). Profile of the evening college student: The background, life roles, and academic performance of evening division students in an urban university (Doctoral dissertation, St Louis University). *Dissertation Abstracts International, 21*, 4075

Smith, D. H. (1966). A psychological model of individual participation in formal voluntary organizations: Applications to some Chilean data. *American Journal of Sociology, 72*, 249–66

—— (1975). Voluntary action and voluntary groups. *Annual Review of Sociology, 1*, 247–70

—— Macaulay, J. and associates (1980). *Participation in social and political activities.* Jossey-Bass, San Francisco

Smith, G. B. (1936). Purposes and conditions affecting the nature and extent of participation of adults in courses in the home study department of Columbia University, 1925–1932. Unpublished doctoral dissertation, Columbia University

Snyder, F. F. (1951). A follow-up study of adults who in the public school of Lincoln, Nebraska, were rated superior in intelligence. Unpublished doctoral dissertation, University of Nebraska

Solomon, D. (ed.) (1964). *The continuing learner.* Center for the Study of Liberal Education for Adults, Chicago

Sovie, M. (1972). The relationship of learning orientations, nursing activities, and continuing education (Doctoral dissertation, Syracuse University). *Dissertation Abstracts International, 33*, 4781A

Stover, R. and Garbin, A. (1982). Explanations of leisure behavior: An analysis. *Journal of Leisure Research, 14,* 91–9

Strange, C. (1979). Intellectual development, motive for education and learning styles during the college years: A comparison of adult and traditional-age college students (Doctoral dissertation, University of Iowa). *Dissertation Abstracts International, 39,* 4768A

Stubblefield, H. (1987). *Towards a history of adult education in America.* Croom-Helm/Methuen, New York

Sulkunen, P. (1982). Society made visible: On the cultural sociology of Pierre Bourdieu. *Acta Sociologica, 25,* 103–15

Sworen, S. (1960). A study to determine the motivations of adults attending evening sessions at the Wyoming Valley Technical Institute. Unpublished doctoral dissertation, Penn State University

Szalai, A. (ed.) (with P. Converse, P. Feldheim, E. Scheuch and P. Stone) (1972). *The use of time* (Daily activities of urban and suburban populations in twelve countries). Mouton, Netherlands

Taylor, R., Rockhill, K. and Fieldhouse, R. (1985). *University adult education in England and the U.S.* Croom-Helm, London

Thompson, J. (ed.) (1980). *Adult education for a change.* Hutchinson, London

Tough, A. (1968). *Why adults learn: A study of the reasons for beginning and continuing a learning project.* Ontario Institute for Studies in Education, Toronto (ERIC no. ED 025 688)

—— (1971). *The adult learning projects: A fresh approach to theory and practice in adult learning.* Ontario Institute for Studies in Education, Toronto

—— (1978). Major learning efforts: Recent research and future directions. *Adult Education, 28,* 250–63

Trow, M. (1977). The second transformation of American secondary education. In J. Karabel and A. H. Halsey (eds), *Power and ideology in education.* Oxford University Press, New York

Turner, R. (1961). Modes of social ascent through education: Sponsored and contest mobility. In A. H. Halsey, J. Floud and C. A. Anderson, (eds). *Education, economy, and society.* Free Press, New York

Verba, S. and Nie, N. (1972). *Participation in America: Political democracy and social equality.* Harper & Row, New York

Verner, C. and Booth, A. (1964). *Adult education.* Center for Applied Research in Education, Washington, DC

Verner, C. and Newberry, J. (1965). The nature of adult participation. In C. Verner and T. White (eds), *Participants in adult education.* Adult Education Association, Washington, DC

Waldron, M. (1968). A study of selected background factors and their relationship to participation in and aptitudes toward participation in adult educational activities of young adults from rural areas (Doctoral dissertation, University of Wisconsin). *Dissertation Abstracts International, 29,* 113A

Wanderer, J. (1961). *Great Decisions Survey 1961.* A study report for the Bureau of Class Instruction, Extension Division of the University of Colorado

Warwick, P. and Bishop, D. (1972). A bibliography of literature dealing with the general concept of time, time-related data analysis, and time-budget studies-with an emphasis on leisure. *Journal of Leisure Research, 4,* 232–44

Welton, M. (1986). 'Vivisecting the nightingale': Reflections on adult education as an object of study. *Studies in the Education of Adults, 19* (1) 46–68

—— (no date). 'On the eve of a great mass movement': Reflections on the origins of the CAAE. Unpublished paper, Dalhousie University

White, R. C. (1955). Social class differences in the uses of leisure. *American Journal of Sociology, 61*, 145–50

Wilensky, H. (1961). Life cycle, work situation, and participation in formal associations. In R. W. Kleemeier (ed.), *Aging and leisure: A research perspective into the meaningful use of time.* Oxford University Press, New York

—— (1973). Orderly careers and social participation: The impact of work history on social integration in the middle mass. In J. Edwards and A. Booth (eds), *Social participation and urban society*. Schenkman, Cambridge, Mass.

Williams, E. and Heath, A. E. (1936). *Learn and Live*. Methuen, London

Witt, P. and Bishop, D. (1970). Situational antecedents to leisure behavior, *Journal of Leisure Research, 2*, 64–77

Woodley, A., Wagner, L., Slowey, M., Hamilton, M., and Fulton, O. (1987). Choosing to learn: Adults in education. Open University Press, Milton Keynes

Wright, C. and Hyman, H. (1958). Voluntary association memberships of American adults: Evidence from national sample surveys. *American Sociological Review, 23*, 284–94

Young, R. and Kent, A. (1985). Using the Theory of Reasoned Action to improve the understanding of recreation behavior. *Journal of Leisure Research, 17*, 90–106

Zeman, S. J. (1960). A study of University of Buffalo evening college students receiving the Bachelor's degree, 1952–1958 (Doctoral dissertation, University of Buffalo). *Dissertation Abstracts International, 20*, 4327

Znaniecki, F. (1967). *Social actions*. Russell & Russell, New York

# Index